B
MATE

M

The

After thousands of years of human existence, the mystery of sexual attraction and the struggle and delight of sustaining intimate, satisfying partnerships still baffle men and women. Attempts to solve the mystery frequently offer cliches such as "like marries like" or "opposites attract." *Beneath Mate Selection and Marriage* shows surprisingly that the social experts and neighborhood sages are both right. Years of close observation of couples and families have revealed the patterns of human desire and interaction which Dr. Klimek painstakingly unfolds here. He describes the ways in which human beings require and demand satisfaction from one another. His fascinating study encompasses the universal social, emotional, and psychological forces which propel men and women into pairing.

Dr. Klimek explains how the first significant family relationship affects each person's capacity to relate intimately to others. He shows how the positive experiences of trust, closeness, openness, and interdependence in this early intercourse act later as necessary components of a healthy intimate adult relationship.

Both successful and unsuccessful relationships are described in detail, with examples of each stage of maturation and deterioration. Dr. Klimek's discussion of opposite character traits—restrained vs. impulsive, internalized vs. externalized, organized vs. disorganized—investigates the positive and negative interactions which can exist between two different people. From his experience in counseling couples and families, the author describes 25 different types of intimate relationship. His comprehensive study examines the stages of sincerity, trust, and autonomy which a maturing couple reach, as well as therapeutic separations which can help a couple evaluate their partnership.

From the origins of trust and dependency in early family relationships to the sometimes unhappy experiences later in life, Dr. Klimek explains how early patterns and expectations of closeness and love recur and later affect adult capacities for sustaining intimacy. This honest and earthy book offers a clear framework for understanding the psychological give-and-take of intimate relationships and possibilities for change.

BENEATH MATE SELECTION AND MARRIAGE

The Unconscious Motives in Human Pairing

David Klimek, Ph.D.

VNR **VAN NOSTRAND REINHOLD COMPANY**
NEW YORK   CINCINNATI   ATLANTA   DALLAS   SAN FRANCISCO
LONDON   TORONTO   MELBOURNE

Van Nostrand Reinhold Company Regional Offices:
New York Cincinnati Atlanta Dallas San Francisco

Van Nostrand Reinhold Company International Offices:
London Toronto Melbourne

Copyright © 1979 by Litton Educational Publishing, Inc.

Library of Congress Catalog Card Number: 78-16595
ISBN: 0-442-23074-5

Manufactured in the United States of America

Published by Van Nostrand Reinhold Company
135 West 50th Street, New York, N.Y. 10020

Published simultaneously in Canada by Van Nostrand Reinhold Ltd.

15 14 13 12 11 10 9 8 7 6 5 4 3 2 1

Library of Congress Cataloging in Publication Data

Klimek, David.
  Beneath mate selection and marriage.

  Includes index.
  1. Interpersonal attraction. 2. Mate selection.
3. Marriage. I. Title.
HM132.K48   301.41′43   78-16595
ISBN 0-442-23074-5

This book is dedicated to the memory of my father, August F. Klimek, who died on July 9, 1973. It is also dedicated to my best friend, my lover, and my partner, Ginny Larson Klimek, and to our two very special children, Christopher and Jennifer.

Preface

This book is a culmination of over 15 years of persistent observation of the motives involved in human pairing, intimacy, marriage, divorce, and family life. To my knowledge, it is the first sustained, clinical investigation into the motives and process of successful human relationships. Despite the longitudinal duration of this study, it was only about six years ago that my casual, random, and often fragmented observations acquired a scientific methodology. Quite by accident, while on my doctoral internship, several clinical skills and experiences fell into place which provided me with the beneath-the-surface tools required to more effectively examine the psychological motives of human pairing.

My first endeavor was the mastery of the Rorschach test, and I will always be indebted to Dr. Bob Atkison of the Sedgwick County Mental Health Center in Wichita, Kansas, for his time and patience in my individual tutelage. I am also indebted to Dr. Margaret Cheatham of the Wichita Psychiatric Center for her help in guiding me through my own psychotherapy and for her supervision of my work in directing classical psychodrama. It was through regressive psychodrama that I experienced the full impact and importance of an individual's first relationship and its influence upon emotional and psychological development and upon subsequent relationships. I am also indebted to Dr. Joseph Brewer, Director of the Wichita Guidance Center, for his personhood, personal supervision, and his direction of my clinical experience. In addition to these professionals, I wish to extend a special appreciation to all the couples participating in the initial sample, and to all subsequent couples contributing to the theory and illustrations presented in this volume.

The initial experimental sample was comprised of couples

wishing to foster or adopt children through the Sedgwick County Social Service network in Wichita. As a psychologist, it was my job to conduct a complete diagnostic battery on these couples in order to determine their suitability for effective parenting. After many months of interviewing and testing couples and subsequently studying their individual psychodynamics, predictable patterns of partner selection began to emerge. After I had acquired the necessary skills and the fine edge of microsensitivity to human feelings, I began to see attraction, pairing, intimacy, and marriage as reasonably consistent and predictable phenomena. Once some of the patterns were detected, I could see that partner selection and marriage were not mysterious or blind events at all, but an intricate network of human needs attempting to be mutually satisfied by the unconscious needs and conscious desires of each partner. At the time a couple decide to commit themselves to each other, there is no doubt that each needs what the other has to offer. Discovering exactly what it is one needs from the other in order to feel complete, and the inherent problems of those needs, is what this book is all about.

The in-depth material of this book does not begin until Chapter 2. The first chapter is a brief overview of the "outside" influences on pairing, while the remainder covers the emotional and psychological operations. Because the real determinants of pairing are unconscious, the reader is encouraged to take special notice of the ideas or illustrations that stimulate an emotional reaction, particularly a negative, angry, or nervous reaction. It is in these resistant feelings that the deeply buried, blind parts of one's personality might be striving for protection.

Sometime after this book has been finished, it might be beneficial for the reader to study those ideas that aroused anger or anxiety. Most often, when anxious or angry feelings surface over a statement or idea, an unresolved conflict or denied truth about the self has been stimulated in the unconscious. Highly sensitive, insight-oriented individuals will be brutally honest with themselves and will want to explore the real origin of their anger or anxiety. It is the personal introspection into the varied feelings stimulated by this volume, and the conclusions drawn about the real self, that will be helpful to the reader. Some people, however, will be unable to be honest with themselves about their contribution to the problems in their central relationship, and so they may be offended by this book. Still others will easily detect the message beneath the printed words, and may wonder if I haven't been "snooping" inside their homes. Whatever the individual response to this book, truly knowing oneself is a difficult process because all of us tend to resist knowledge that might be contrary to our beliefs, especially beliefs about ourselves.

I would like to think this book is more than just another treatise on what people are calling love and intimacy—and I believe it is. Because it is written about real people and real relationships, most readers will be able to identify with the material herein. Several of the typists working on the rough draft of the manuscript, and as many colleagues reviewing it, reported feeling anxious and a little naked as they read. One reviewer said, "This book has a way of creeping up on you," while another reported feeling tense about the shoulders and neck. Another reviewer promised, "The book will never become popular because it is too honest." She went on to say, "People need hope, and because of that they like to be deceived." Another believed the book might be too complicated for the general reading public. This was difficult for me to believe because its subject is the human relationships of ordinary people. Because of my desire to share this knowledge with as many people as might be interested, I have attempted to gear the writing so that it appeals to the general reading public. Even so, I hope that it will also be useful to my professional colleagues.

Some authors conclude a preface by sharing the enjoyment they experienced in the creation of their work. I cannot make such a claim, however, because this volume was by far the most grueling project I have ever completed. Through the years, as the "truth" behind pairing began to unfold, I was frequently saddened, depressed, elated, and amazed. The sadness came from noting the heartache and suffering inherent in unsatisfactory relationships; the depression from the awareness that helpless children are invariably damaged and bruised by their parents' misery; the elation from the fact that beneath-the-surface patterns and processes became evident, which may someday help people know what they are experiencing, thus allowing a true sense of choice in their pairing. Feelings of amazement and sometimes bewilderment surfaced when I realized the strength, tenacity, and endurance that couples exhibit in their attempts to make their relationships work, sometimes against hopeless odds. I want the reader to know that some of the material in this book also makes me a little nervous. Being as human as anyone, there are too many pages that hit uncomfortably close to home.

David Klimek, Ph.D.
Ann Arbor, Michigan

Contents

BENEATH MATE SELECTION AND MARRIAGE

The Unconscious Motives in Human Pairing

1 / *Introduction*

. . . the purpose of science is neither to alarm or assure but to discover what is and make it known.

While conducting seminars, lectures, and workshops on partner selection and marriage, I have often heard members of the audience exclaim with some degree of frustration and anger, "I wish I knew all this stuff when I got married!" My response, governed partially by clinical experience and partially by skepticism toward simplistic answers, has been, "Do you believe you would have done anything differently?" Some couples indicate that knowing what they do about themselves, they would probably choose the same partner again. Such a response usually comes from people committed to their relationship. That is, over a certain period of time, their marriage is more satisfying than dissatisfying, and fulfills more needs than could be fulfilled outside the relationship. Others believe that they "made their bed and must forever sleep in it." Occasionally, those most vindictive toward their spouse for not living up to marital expectations are unable to contain years of hurt and unhappiness and vocalize a "You're damn right I'd do something different." These people are often surprised by their outburst and quickly retreat following the social catharsis. Delayed nervous laughter dissipates anxiety for the many who feel the same way, but don't say so.

The silent couples sit apprehensively during the seminar, trying not to be noticed by me or the others. They exchange unrestful and furtive glances with each other and with their peers, and hope no one asks about their relationship. Dulled by years of painful living and unmet needs, their emotions tend to be guarded, defensive, and void of genuine spontaneity. They no longer acknowledge feelings of concern and gentleness and have usually given up

1

dealing with each other because, they have learned, "it was more trouble than it was worth." Talking to each other about anything personal results in arguments, misunderstanding, and more hurt. Any feelings vocalized about their relationship are imbued with a condescending self-righteousness, which makes it clear that "they haven't had an argument in years."

The silent partners return home after the seminar and say nothing. Each knows something is wrong and is sure the misery is caused by the other. Each has devised maneuvers to disparage, frustrate, and destroy the partner. Implementation of such destructive tactics, however, is always "accidental" or "unintentional." Even so, the undercurrent of hurt, depression, and hostility is sensed in full force by the couple's children, who respond to it by displaying a variety of symptoms. For reasons beyond their awareness, members of the family are frequently sick and in need of a physician's care. If the wife is not ill, the husband is; if he isn't, the children are. In fact, the family's most time-consuming activity seems to be responding to crisis. It is much less painful and more convenient to pay the doctor's bills than it is to build a healthy relationship.

Often, it is only after a relationship has become stagnant, cumbersome, and destructive that one wishes to know "why" and "how" such a mess developed. Most couples can cite cogent reasons for selecting a new car, house, item of clothing, or household furniture, but can give few, if any, for selecting each other. Furthermore, most people have not given serious thought to why they chose one another; those who have are often dissatisfied with the reasons and conclusions they've drawn. Some of the more intellectually oriented couples become embarrassed when they realize that they made the most important decision in their lives with insufficient knowledge.

Contemplation of reasons for partner selection is always a delicate proposition. While courting, couples are virtually unable to objectively examine their interactions for there is an insidious blindness in all impassioned relationships. The blindness is especially limiting when attempting to evaluate oneself, one's partner, or reality. If parents or friends should offer an accurate but contrary appraisal, not only are the facts ignored, but the myopia worsens. After marriage, objective evaluation of reasons for partner selection is likely to be tainted by the intrusion of reality and accrued unresolved conflict.

When the needs of the human organism become aroused, they demand fulfillment. The higher the intensity of the needs and the longer the deprivation, the greater is the magnitude of focus toward the object promising gratification. Thus, the blindness associated with mate selection is in part a manifestation of the encompassing sense of urgency experienced while attempting to meet basic and primitive psychological needs. Anyone interfering with a relationship that promises so much is sure to be met with resistance.

The forces, motives, and energy generated by the deepest of human needs are referred to as *psychodynamics*. *Psyche*, which means "soul" or "heart," and *dynamics*, which means "energy" or "forces," have their origins in the developing personality. An explanation of exactly how childhood development influences subsequent preferences, needs, desires, and interests would take volumes. Suffice it to say that psychodynamics is the bottom layer of feelings, attitudes, and needs that are often not available to the individual for conscious investigation or analysis. Despite inaccessibility, they remain active and influential throughout life, and account for a variety of predictable and erratic behaviors. Held in abeyance during late childhood, psychodynamic predilections become volatile during adolescence as the individual is faced with rapid biological maturation, conflicts over dependence and identity, and the nuisance of reality.

The basic personality is established during the first six or seven years of life and is developed by the conscious and unconscious interactions with the first significant human, usually the mother. As a result, the quality of this first human relationship becomes the prototype for all other intimate relationships. As this first relationship is renounced during adolescence, a definite set of unconscious preferences, attractions, and revulsions emerge toward "types" of people. Although the types preferred may include physical and sexual attributes, the preference is determined by the psyche and is free of gender bias. That is, one's interaction style in the relationship (i.e., how one feels about oneself) is similar whether the partner is male or female. All individuals tend to be vaguely aware of people preference. Unaware of psychological contributors, they tend to describe physical or relatively superficial behavior traits. Careful inquiry, however, can help one become aware of certain unconscious needs, expectations, and response styles in significant relationships. The tendency toward selection of similar types of people is magnified by those who have experienced multiple divorce.

An attractive woman in her early fifties came to my office ostensibly to "straighten out her thoughts" about her pending divorce. Actually, she came to allay her guilt about divorcing her husband—her fifth— and to complain about his badness. As she became less defensive, I asked, "Would you please take a moment to think about how husband number five was similar to husband number four?" She immediately responded, "Oh, they were nothing alike. Dale had red hair, was tall and well-built, and was self-employed. Charley was shorter, had blonde hair, a pot gut, and a college degree." Before she went on, I interrupted with, "I don't mean the outside stuff. I was wondering how similar your *relationship* was with each of them." A long silence accompanied her contemplation. Quietly, she murmured, "There really wasn't much difference, I guess." "How then," I inquired, "was husband number four different from number three?" Impulsively she said, "They were much different! I told you about Charley. Well, Jim was the best looking guy I ever had. He was tall, dark, and handsome. He had a college degree too, but liked working with his hands, so he became a carpenter." "Yes," I said, "but how was the quality of your relationship different?" Her mood thickened with a silent depression, and she finally whispered, "I think it was pretty much the same." We repeated the interaction down to the first husband. Quietly and slowly, I said, "Strange, isn't it, how similar these relationships were for you? Prior to your first husband, do you recall ever having a similar relationship?" She sank into the chair with a moan. After a few minutes of noiseless tears, she firmly gripped the armrest, sat up angrily, and shouted, "Yes, dammit! I had exactly the same kind of relationship with my mother, and I couldn't wait to dump that lying bitch either!"

In addition to the psychodynamic forces influencing partner selection and marriage, the initial screening for a serious life partner is regulated by psychosexual and psychosocial factors.

THE ESSENCE OF ATTRACTION*

A flamboyant 68-year-old acquaintance, when learning of my work on mate selection, mischievously asked, "You mean there is more to it than sex? Hell, there must be. The first three times, I got married for sex; the last two times, it was for money." Although the sentiments were related jokingly, they correspond to long-recognized motives in human pairing. Sexual permission, economic responsibility, and care of offspring have been elements of marriage throughout human history. For example, connubial laws and customs in primitive cultures have dealt with regulating property and progeny. Social systems from time immemorial have designed laws to regulate the sexual impulses of their people. Since marriage in all cultures includes sexual permission, it is not possible to discuss motives for mate selection without first recognizing the pervasive influence of instinctive sexuality.

The energy for human mate selection originates in sexuality. Typically, when an individual accidentally or intentionally enters the perceptual field of another, there is an instantaneous, preconscious evaluation of attractiveness and sexual desirability. If the evaluation occurs at a distance, the general body type is first appraised. If acceptable, a slight erotic titillation energizes a closer inspection, which focuses on the hair, face, and eyes. When the overall evaluation is satisfactory, further interest follows. If the overall evaluation is not satisfactory, the individual is likely to be ignored or categorized along with other irrelevant "objects."

The potential for sexual satisfaction and conquest provides the basis for the human male pairing behavior. Because men are more easily aroused to a level of uncontainable sexual tension and are frequently more active in the pairing process, they tend to be less discriminating than women. Even a man who adheres to fairly stringent standards for choosing a serious life partner may capriciously lower or abandon them if a woman seems willing to offer him immediate sexual gratification. When carried out, such interactions can be described as infatuation, lust, one-night stands,

---

*It is important for the reader to realize that this section—and psychology in general, for that matter—cites *tendencies* in human pairing, which are valid *most* of the time. There will always be exceptions to these generalizations.

free love, or nearly anything else that describes such a state of affairs. Should a woman initially transmit "eager" signals as a lure, but later expect nonsexual indications of genuine affection as the man proceeds toward coition, the thwarted emotional arousal causes a temporary state of flux. Typically, he must decide whether she is worth the orgiastic delay. If she isn't, he leaves, often feeling hurt. If she is, he remains in the relationship and attempts to "decode her prerequisites"—i.e., to discover what he must do before she will agree to go to bed with him. To do so, however, he must remain in her presence for an unspecified duration. During that time, he must adjust his needs, attitudes, and behavior to conform to her expectations. When and if one or both individuals want the relationship to become more than what it has been during the early stages of interaction, tacit rules to determine how much the other person *really* cares, become predominant, which each must decode by behaving differently. Those relationshps that consist of a high number of covert rules and adjusted behaviors, particularly those behaviors adjusted by the male in order to acquire or maintain sexual fulfillment, are off to a destructive start.

Nobody likes to be manipulated. Thus, it is not uncommon for a woman to construct a highly idiosyncratic "love-testing" regimen in order to accumulate proof that her partner is not just using her. If he can successfully pass these tests, she concludes that he loves her, not just her body. Often, the tests are nonverbal because words can be inaccurate or even false when it comes to something as important as feelings of love. The common denominators of most love-testing are *endurance of hardship* and *willingness to tolerate emotional pain*. In short, the amount of personal sacrifice undergone for the partner tends to be the necessary prerequisite of "true love."

Because most people have been previously deceived about love either by parents, siblings, or lovers, simply being told that one is loved is seldom sufficient. As a couple's relationship progresses beyond simply the initial manipulation phase, they usually require nonverbal, behavioral proof that they are indeed special to each other and of primary importance to each other's well-being. It is the comparison of differential responses and the efforts of the partner that allow a person to conclude that he or she is more important to and more valued by the partner than anyone else.

Built into nearly all serious relationships is the *abandonment response* as a primary indication of love. If the person about to be abandoned doesn't apologize, make promises, and list amendments for change, he or she must not care. If the person abandoned doesn't show signs of trauma, rage, jealousy, depression, and other self-destructive behavior, he or she must not have cared. In severely neurotic and psychotic relationships, debilitating hardship, suffering, and suicide attempts tend to be the only indications of "love." Sick "love" is nearly always calibrated by gradations of suffering. In such a relationship, the thought process is: if you do what you don't want to do, or if you endure irrelevant and meaningless suffering just for me, you must love me.

Those couples employing the most devious, manipulative, and pathological tactics before marriage later endure the most heartache. Through the years, as reality slowly weakens the social facade and temporarily adjusted behaviors of courtship, the partners become sullenly aware of "not really knowing each other." For example, in a courtship where the man must conform to the woman's ideal by adjusting his behavior and verbalizations, the stage is set for later disappointment. Following a short period of marriage, after his sexual urge has been satisfied and interest in his partner lessens, so does his contrived behavior, which was once used to gauge his love. As he sheds some of his facade, his wife concludes that he doesn't love her, at least not as much as he once did. When this happens, the woman often feels deceived and exploited, while one of her greatest fears is realized: her husband's main interest in her may well have been sexual. Even if she is wrong, like any other woman requiring elaborate behavior adjustment in her partner during courtship, she will be disappointed. To avenge her hurt, many a woman attempts to thwart her partner's *modus operandi:* she strategically declares the bedroom as her battleground where refusal holds much of the power.

Contemporary courtship frequently includes living together, which would appear to provide a logical solution to the backlash of distrust. Perhaps, it is reasoned, the disillusionment would not be so great if couples were sexually "open and honest" from the start. The idea appears to be logical, emotionally healthy, and mature. Although there have only been a few studies on this subject, preliminary findings show that those who lived together during courtship are not any more satisfied while in the relationship, or after marriage, than those who did not live together. In fact, there is tentative evidence that the divorce rate is higher among those who lived together during courtship than those who did not.

The ideal of female attractiveness has remained fairly consistent throughout history and has been defined in terms of anatomical perfection. Historical accounts of female beauty include:

> . . . perfect symmetry in physical proportion. . . . Her legs must be long and slender, as should her face and neck. . . . Her chest should be capricious, her breasts firm and conical, her hips wide and her waist small—almost small enough to be clasped by the hand. . . . Her buttocks should be as firm and fleshy as her bosom. . . . Her hair voluminous and long, reaching to her knees and terminating in graceful curls. . . . Her lips should be red and bright and her teeth white. . . . Her hair and face should be clear, fair, and without blemish. . . . The surface of her body should be soft, delicate, smooth, rounded, and velvet-like to the touch. [Westermarck, vol. II, pp. 5–14] *

The perfected female body image is the envy of many women. Entrepreneurs earn billions of dollars annually selling products purporting to help women become more attractive and more desirable. Any physical feature too deviant from the perfected ideal is viewed as a deformity. Scars, crooked teeth, pimples, too little hair, too big a nose, too small a nose, too small a bust, too large a waist, too small buttocks, too large buttocks, and unshapely legs are a few of the anomalies considered "ugly." To many, the obese woman is anathema, an object of rejection and ridicule.

There is a close association between historical reports of male attractiveness (Westermarck, vol. I, pp. 462–469) and today's *machismo*. Conspicuous muscular development was highly valued in the uncivilized and war-making cultures in which survival was directly related to brute strength. Physical strength was particularly attractive to the female as it reflected the male's ability to conquer other men and consequently to protect her and to provide

---

*Quotations on pp. 8 through 12 are taken from *The History of Human Marriage*, vols. I and II, by Edward Westermarck. By permission of Macmillan, London and Basingstoke.

security. In the United States, the value placed on *machismo* and physical toughness is still prevalent in the undersocialized, lower socioeconomic class. Among the middle and upper classes, however, men whose major asset is brute strength are scorned. Intelligence, professional-social status, and economic prosperity have replaced physical bulk. Slenderness and youthful appearance are valued as they are suggestive of wealth, success, and virility. And, instead of musculature, male attractiveness in the middle class is now closely related to the ability to offer financial security, protection, comfort, and status to the female.

The role of males and females in pairing are extensions of phylogenic evolution. The historically less active role of the female, for example, originates in the primary sexual characteristics. Even in the lower levels of life, the ova are relatively few in comparison to spermatozoa, and are considered delicate, fragile, and in need of protection. Similar adjectives describe the female while caring for her offspring, as she and her progeny need protection and safety from the elements and predators. Conversely, the active thrust of millions of spermatozoa during coition, which seek out and attempt to penetrate the protected ovum, provide a basis for the active male role.

Westermarck, citing Darwin's *Descent of Man*, speculates about the activity role in pairing.

> . . . It is difficult to understand why the males should invariably have acquired the habit of approaching the females, instead of being approached by them. Perhaps the explanation may be that the seeker is more exposed to danger than the one sought after, and that the death of a male at the pairing time is less disadvantageous for the existence of a species than the death of a female. At any rate, we may say that the males should be endowed with strong passions in order that they may be efficient seekers; the more eager males leaving a larger number of offspring than the less eager. [vol. I, p. 456]

Demonstrations of a male's strength, courage, and power have historically been prized by females because they provide indirect validation of his ability to offer security and protection. In primitive societies, it was not uncommon for males to fight savagely for copulating privileges with the onlooking females, who were often sexually stimulated by the violence in the competition. The tranquility of many primitive tribes was occasionally interrupted by sexual passion and aggression as people ran amok during what could be called a sexual season or *rut*. The open sexual season, which has remarkable parallels to the daily mood prevalent in contemporary Western civilization, was a period of heightened anxiety, activity, restlessness, competition, and reckless aggression. During the rut, which occurred semiannually, both sexes adorned themselves with beads, feathers, rings, bracelets, earrings, conspicuous hairstyles, and variations in clothing to allure prospective partners. Dancing, loud music, and flamboyant coloration were aphrodisiacs. Coyness and resistance by the female were part of the courtship ritual and tended to further exacerbate male competition, violence, and war on other tribes. Aggression and destruction were rampant as males fought and killed for mating rights. Some females became uncontrollably aroused while observing competition among the males. Particularly arousing to a woman was the warrior who was willing to kill for her and then adorn himself with the opponent's head or scalp. Passion was a major contributor to head-hunting and war, as the braves needed to hunt heads and to kill to make themselves attractive. A young woman, it is reported, was so overcome with desire while observing a brave in a head-hunting dance, that she defied all social decorum, broke into the dance, and, clutching him, began to eat his loincloth (Westermarck, vol. I, p. 494).

Without stretching the imagination too far, it is not difficult to see what might be called "refined similarities" between the courtship rituals of primitive humans and what might be considered normal dating behavior of today. For example, there are parallels between competitive athletic games (which begin in the elementary schools), a tavern brawl, the subtle maneuvers at a disco, or the refined enticements seen at upper-middle-class executive office parties, and the rutting behavior of lower animals.

An exaggerated modern male ideal is sometimes depicted on television and in novels. Such a man lives in sumptuous extravagance with a harem of extremely attractive women. He is clearly the contemporary version of the early conquistador. He is not the victor in a violent bloodbath, but on the battlefield of materialism and capitalism: he has conquered all other males in the war of financial acquisitiveness. Hypothetically, the wives of the conquered should leave their deflated husbands to be cared for by—and to sexually care for—the victor.

COURTSHIP AND FOREPLAY

While presenting seminars on courtship and foreplay, I frequently find that I arouse anxiety in and am verbally attacked by certain participants. However, the ideas presented are usually not as disparate as they initially seem. The first idea that proves offensive to some is that men are typically more active and controlling in the initial pairing process. Some women overreact to this statement, for they believe that I am ascribing an all-or-none position to female passivity. Of course, this is nonsense. In fact, if one were to examine the activity-passivity continuum in sexual relations of those married over 15 years, it is not at all uncommon to find women significantly more active in initiating lovemaking than their partners. In the initial attraction-pairing process, however, males tend to be more active than females, primarily because of their more impulsive, immediate tendency toward sexual arousal and the tension that follows if the heightened drive is not satisfied. As the relationship proceeds, psychological factors determine who will be most dominant. Most often, dominance in a relationship can be reduced to who needs whom the most. In the initial phases of pairing, the male frequently needs the female in order to satisfy his impulsive sexual instinct. It is during this phase that men may appear to be more active and dominant. As the relationship proceeds, however, and the rules governing sexual activity become defined, an important choice becomes necessary. Either the relationship "deepens" as the couple moves to a higher level of interaction involving the more capricious emotional or psychological needs, or they decide to "not get involved," either keeping the relationship primarily sexual or terminating it.

Coyness prior to coition is observed in the females of nearly all species:

> The doe in her pairing time calls to the buck in clear tones that bring him to her side at once; then she, half in coyness, half in mischief, takes to flight at his eager approach, makes an open space, and

runs in a circle. The buck naturally follows and the chase grows hot and as exciting as a race of horses on a track. To the frequent high calls of the fleeting doe, are added the deep short cries of the panting buck; but suddenly the roguish doe disappears like a nymph into the thicket near at hand, and the baffled buck stands with his head erect and ears thrown forward; then we see his head lowered as he catches the scent and he too vanishes into the wood.

A similar sequence is noted in an anthropomorphic account of birds:

[The female] cuckoo answers the call of her mate with an alluring laugh that excites him to the utmost, but it is long before she gives herself up to him. A mad chase through the treetops ensues, during which she constantly excites him with that mocking call, till the poor fellow is fairly driven crazy. But she never lets him out of her sight, the while looking back as she flies and measures her speed, and wheeling back when he suddenly gives up the pursuit. [Westermarck, vol. I, p. 473]

Female coyness, in addition to its complex implications in human pairing, had a very basic and natural function in lower life. Antecedent to human foreplay, animal coyness increased the probability of pregnancy and the number in her litter. Well-planned resistance was clearly a mutual sexual stimulant. As the female resisted, the already impassioned male competed more strenuously to pass her "love tests," which served to further arouse her. Heightened arousal in both sexes causes mucus to flow profusely over the genitals, thus aiding in vigorous copulation.

In all animals . . . coition is not allowed by the female until some time after the swelling and congestion of the vulva and surrounding tissue are first demonstrated. . . . The prolonged excitement which follows from her coyness has another effect, which may be of utmost importance for the species; it increases the secretions of the sexual glands . . . so it does with the male because only when mixed with the prostatic fluid does spermatozoa gain full vitality. The profuse secretion of the prostate, resulting from prolonged excitement would give mobility to a large number of spermatozoa, than would be an increase in the prospect of fecundation. [Westermarck, vol. I, p. 496]

SCREENING FACTORS IN PAIRING

Reasonably mature individuals recognize pairing and family life as serious business. Through experience and education, they arrive at the belief that marriage is related to the pursuit of happiness, emotional security, completion, and peace of mind. Most individuals also know that a "bad" or "unhealthy" marriage is synonymous with emotional pain and misery. Consequently, emotional investment in serious relationships is usually committed slowly and cautiously over a period of time. (Casual sexual encounters, on the other hand, tend to be characterized by lack of emotional investment, recklessness, volatility, irresponsibility, and insensitivity to the partner's real needs. Such encounters are indiscriminate—nearly anyone will do.)

Ideally, people should have an open market from which to select a suitable life partner. In reality, this is not true. As shown in Figure 1, several social and psychological factors serve to restrict partner choice: (1) proximity in time and place, (2) social class background, (3) racial-ethnic-religious affiliation, (4) attractiveness limits, and (5) psychodynamic influences.

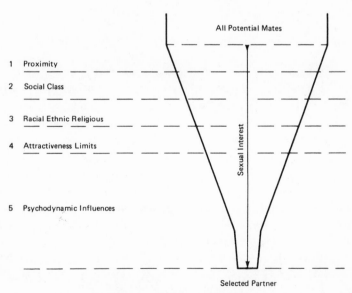

Fig. 1. Screening mechanisms.

The right side of the graph shows the sexual impetus, which might help the more restrained reader understand those who engage in numerous sexual encounters. Transitory sexual episodes are also governed by screening factors 1 and 4 (proximity in time and place and attractiveness limits). Even when heightened sexual passions are the sole impetus in a relationship, individuals must still be in the same place at the same time and be reasonably attracted to each other. In all human interactions, however, factors 2 through 4 serve as vigilant sentinels to eliminate undesirable and unwanted psychological foreigners so as to insure that the partner is "right."

Proximity in Time and Place

Before any relationship can begin, two people must be in the same place at the same time. Those who regularly traverse their social territory by traveling from place to place in the same community, or from city to city, state to state, or country to country, increase the probability of their meeting a potential partner. The active urbanite is apt to meet more prospective partners than the active rural inhabitant because of the greater number of people per square mile. The effects of the relative social isolation in rural areas are seen in the tendency for the inhabitants to marry earlier than city dwellers. Since high school is the major social arena in rural towns (followed closely by church functions), a young person's social contacts are markedly diminished upon leaving high school. The lower per capita divorce rate reported in rural areas is not so much a function of more satisfactory marriages as it is a function of social isolation. The fewer people impinging on one's social space, the lower the probability of meeting a prospective lover, whether single or married.

Proximity in time is a limiting function because of its generic relationship to age. Society dictates that couples should be approximate in age, with the man being about one to five years older than the woman. Men who marry conspicuously older women are deprecated as suffering from an alleged "mother complex," or some social or mental disorder. Women who marry men at least 10 years older are accused of harboring a "father complex." Even so, they tend not to be as socially impugned as the man who marries an older woman. In fact, some women, although they are reluctant to say so, are envious of the young woman paired with a much older man of wealth and social position.

The inability to occupy populated space greatly reduces choice in mate selection. A hermitlike existence, whether it is due to a preference for living in a wilderness cabin or other geographically isolated area, or to neurotic fear and social withdrawal, will reduce options. The institution of marriage has a similar effect in minimizing social contact. Those recently divorced or widowed who desire to pair again often expend extraordinary quantities of time and energy trying to enhance social space. In fact, following divorce or the death of a spouse, it is not uncommon for rural adults to drastically change their life-style and relocate in a larger community where there is an increased likelihood for social exchange. Similarly, the more discriminating individual from a limited social arena will attend college, or seek employment in a larger city, primarily to increase the opportunity for participation in a more expansive mating territory.

Social Class Background

Proximity in time and place is not an independent phenomenon— socioeconomic class ascription is a major determinant of opportunity and mobility. Despite differences in population density, individuals of middle- and upper-middle-class background living in rural areas have more social opportunity than individuals from the lower socioeconomic class residing in a large city. The socioeconomic differences, however, are not conspicuous at first. As depicted in Figure 2, the first 16 to 18 years for members of all social classes are similar in terms of independent occupancy of social space. Due to the limited sense of autonomy and independence that society expects for children and adolescents, satisfactory adjustment to the real world of adult responsibility is usually not possible until one leaves high school. Only after one leaves the protected milieu of adolescence and enters the adult world are one's psychological, emotional, and social resources challenged.

Figure 2 shows the similarity among the social classes in interpersonal opportunities up to the ages of approximately 15 to 17,

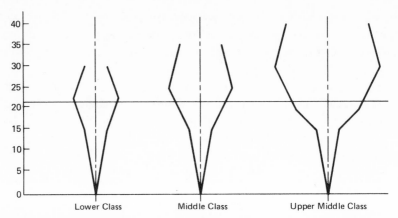

Fig. 2. Relative social distance and opportunity.

and the disparate opportunities following high school graduation. The left vertical axis represents age in years, and the bottom horizontal axis, distance from home. Members of the lower socioeconomic class not only remain closer to what they consider home, but they often obtain full-time employment earlier than members of the middle and upper-middle classes. The restriction in distance and time due to full-time employment minimizes the social arena from which to select a potential partner. When members of the lower socioeconomic class do leave parents, friends, and community in pursuit of higher education, careers, or better paying jobs, it is often with the unspoken intention that they will soon return. Most of them are pessimistic about raising their social position and become angry, paranoid, and jaded by inadequate "opportunity." Frequently, their lack of psychological reserve and the relative absence of their family's financial and emotional resources become obvious. Many return home after a short period to occupy the same limited space they had always known and attempt to find a mate with whom to settle down.

Young adults from the middle and upper-middle classes have access to an advantaged social and experiential arena not open to the lower class. These young people usually have sufficient psychological and financial resources upon which to draw, as they physically, and to some degree emotionally, separate from parents, friends, and community to seek higher education. During the critical years (approximately 18 to 25) when one is preparing for a professional career, absence from parents along with intellectual stimulation, aids in the development of psychosocial maturity. Being away from the security and familiarity of home in and of itself can help one develop ego strength because it requires individuation and separation from childhood dependency needs.

During the years away from home, there is substantial opportunity and freedom for one to experience a variety of self-determined activities that can be integrated into the psyche. If one has adequate psychological resources to help organize and integrate experience, even trauma can be absorbed meaningfully so as to promote emotional maturity. Whether one is able to use the advantages of time, place, and varied experience to increase the quality of life is entirely an individual matter. Generally, however, the increased latitude of time and space provides the potential for enhancing psychosocial maturity, which consequently ameliorates the chances of selecting a more suitable partner.

Individuals from the upper-middle class have potentially the greatest range of time and place in which to meet a prospective partner. Due to the increased financial reserve of the family and the wider range of distance available from home, the individual, figuratively, has the world at his (or her) fingertips. Young adults from the upper-middle class almost always attend college, and many go on to graduate school or prestigious professional schools.

Despite the potential for freedom of choice in career and mate selection, however, they are often victims of the law of diminishing returns. The advantages of time, place, and social opportunity among the upper-middle class can encumber the selection of a suitable mate. The critical years, in many respects, are often not governed by self-determined choice as much as they are by stringent socially and economically oriented familial expectations. In such instances, not only are professions, careers, and business ventures specified in advance, but further limitation is imposed by the fact that one must go to the "right" college, be seen with the "right" people at the "right" places, and eventually select the "right" mate from the "right" family.

Most people are unable to lend a sympathetic ear to the problems of the upper-middle class because "they seem to have it made" and are the envy of those who don't. Nevertheless, behind the closed doors of expensive homes in elite neighborhoods, genuine human beings exist with basic needs, anxieties, crises, joys, and sufferings similar to all other humans. Regardless of economic class, when all is said and done, people must learn to rely upon their individual psychological reserves. Sometimes, the wealthy are disadvantaged in the quality of their emotional life, as genuine psychological strength, which superficially could be described as "the ability to endure anxiety and sustained emotional stress," is enhanced by successfully overcoming the problems of everyday life. As people conquer daily conflict and become able to derive happiness from their reality, their crises become easier to handle. Since the wealthy sometimes use their dollars to protect themselves from external stress, or run away from it by travel and conspicuous consumption, they thereby miss the opportunity to grow from crisis. Deep within, the quality of their emotional life remains unchanged, even though their stress is temporarily eluded.

The second disadvantage of the upper-middle class is the relative absence of the simple pleasures in life. The "ordinary" person, because of financial necessity, is often able to adjust to his or her economic condition and develops ways to take pleasure in the simplicities of life. When one is accustomed to honey, there is little joy in sugar; when one is accustomed to life's bittersweet, a little sunshine is most pleasant. If one has been raised in a family where nearly everything has been relatively easy, the fine edge of appreciation for life's simplicities may be diminished. The simple, meaningful pleasures of an intimate relationship with spouse and family can become almost irrelevant as the husband, wife, or both invest all available energy in their profession and in meeting the exigencies of upper-middle-class living.

Another disadvantage of the upper-middle class, experienced primarily by women, is the exploitation of not only their sexuality, which is common among all social classes, but their heritage as well. Since men are usually the initiators in pairing and because their sense of worth, power, and attractiveness is closely related to professional status and financial means, many upper-middle-class women are never sure that they have not been exploited by an ambitious male. A very attractive and wealthy woman, while in the process of marrying her third husband, explained, "This time it is real love. It really is. He loves me, just for me as a person, not just for my body or my money. He loves me. It really feels good to know that someone can love me just for me." Her vocalizations were, in part, an attempt to allay anxiety over the possibility that her new husband might be more interested in her body and her dollars than in her personhood.

Social class is more than financial means, opportunity, and consumption. It is a life-style that also includes, in its basic sense, family history, socialization skills, occupation, wealth, attitudes, interests, and general sophistication about life and the world. Because social class correlates with an infinitude of attitudes and behavior, defiance of its boundaries is uncommon in mate selection. The undersocialized lower class, with its crudity, lack of sophistication, paranoia, hostility, and propensity for destruction, make those from the upper-middle class uncomfortable. Similarly, individuals from the lower class feel uncomfortable in the presence of "snobs" from the middle and upper classes. The animus connoted by the word *snob* is precipitated by envy, fear, and suspicion, for lower-class members are vividly aware of their disparate lifestyle. Such people often resent anyone who appears to have it easier. They believe that money "talks" and that wealthy families get all the breaks. To assuage the anxiety that exists from noticing and associating with one another, each class usually strives to maintain isolated habitation. For the most part, they live in distinct neighborhoods, interact only with people of similar background, gather in segregated social precincts, and disparage one another through jokes and diatribes.

Individuals of the middle class potentially have the greatest freedom of choice in partner selection. The greater population density is a contributing factor in and of itself, but there is also the freedom to traverse social class boundaries, which is not common for the lower or the upper-middle class. Freed from the severe deprivations and lack of opportunity of the lower class and the rigid adherence to the burdens of social and financial protocol of the upper-middle class, they have significant pairing latitude. This is not to suggest that the relationships are necessarily more satisfying, but, holding the degree of psychopathology constant across social classes, middle-class reasons for pairing tend to be less entangled with deviousness or hidden or predetermined social arrangement.

Racial, Ethnic, and Religious Influences

Racial, ethnic, or religious affiliation has always served to limit socialization and serious pairing. Brief sexual encounters, of course, are without boundaries. In fact, some individuals become passionately aroused by someone from a different race, ethnic group, or religion, in exactly the same proportion they are forbidden by parental and social decree. Recently, the limitations of these factors have been subdued by the humanistic movement, which, with its consciousness-raising efforts over a variety of social inequalities, has tended to minimize the stigma of miscegenation. Acceptance of racial differences, however, depends upon region, education, and, to some degree, urbanization. On the streets of Chicago, New York, or Los Angeles, little attention is given to a racially different couple. On the other hand, a racially different couple strolling arm in arm down the streets of some rural American communities should have second thoughts about doing so, unless they wish to expose themselves to personal harm.

The strength of ethnic-ideological identity and the natural exclusion via antagonism, projection, and displacement are demonstrated by the author's interaction with a client.

> He was an exceptionally bright and sensitive individual working toward a graduate degree in psychology. During our third session, he showed signs of irritation and impatience, which seemed connected. "What is it, please?" I asked. He responded, "This is only our third session, and I feel as though we have known each other for a long time. I feel as though you genuinely like me and care about me." I did like him, found him interesting, and cared enough to want to help him reduce his emotional conflicts. With increasing agitation and anger, he shouted, "Dammit, how can you like me so much? I'm Jewish!" Since he disliked others with dissimilar backgrounds, he had equal difficulty understanding that some people do not let it get in the way.

Observing the client interacting with others revealed that he elicited negative reactions from nearly everyone, which were most often a direct response to his own hostile and rejecting attitude. He had believed for many years that people had a negative reaction to him because he was Jewish. When he encountered other Jews, his response to them was more positive. Consequently, he received positive reactions from them. Despite superior intellectual and social ability, the client was oblivious to his own influence in social interactions and to the isolation precipitated by his rejecting attitudes. Unwittingly, he was continually processing, editing, rejecting, accepting, and psychologically negotiating and passing judgment within the first 15 seconds of social interaction. Following the sophisticated processing, his verdict was simple: he either liked the person, or he didn't. The new acquaintance was either acceptable or unacceptable, worthwhile or worthless, and he acted accordingly.

Attractiveness Limits

Everybody has unconscious limits of attractiveness with which to compare a prospective partner. Physical appearance is usually evaluated first. That a nice personality in a prospective partner is what really matters may sound appropriate, but seldom does one wish to date another because one has heard about his or her "nice personality." Most people, especially during adolescence and early in adulthood, spend considerably more time, effort, and money on their outward physical appearance than on personality development.

Attractiveness and desirability perception develop over the years by a subtle—and sometimes not so subtle—comparison of oneself to others. Elementary-school children can easily identify the most attractive members of their class as well as the most unattractive. By mid-adolescence, individuals are consistently able to recognize the "desirables" and the "undesirables" in nearly any social terrain, and they are sagaciously aware of how attractive they are in relation to others. Consequently, the attractive and desirable children and adolescents gather in cliques, which tend to exclude the mediocre and unattractive. A mediocre individual may wish to join the desirable group, but, more often than not, the request is denied. Desirable individuals are the most popular and sought-after. Those of equal desirability status are usually friends, because that is the social rule; those of lesser desirability seek to be in the presence of the most desired in order to reap vicarious status from the acquaintance. If a mediocre individual can be seen in the presence of a desirable, the mediocre temporarily derives a pseudo-sense of value and status. Until the rules are assimilated, some individuals attempt to accelerate their rise in the pecking order by being infatuated only with those who are more attractive. They learn, often by the cruelty of social derision, the upper limits of their own desirability and eventually find a proper place. There are times when an average or less-than-average individual is able to affiliate with those significantly more attractive. However, when this happens, the more attractive individual's preference tends to be determined by unconscious needs for inequality that often permeate the entire relationship.

From adolescence through early adulthood, individuals are pre-occupied with physical and sexual attractiveness (as are perennial adult adolescents). Several logical but complex factors contribute to the adolescent's preoccupation. The first is that he or she is in the developmental stage referred to as *biological pubescence*. Endocrinological changes between the ages of 11 and 14 elicit significant anatomical development, which forces attention toward the self, the body, and sexual characteristics. Since an adolescent's peers are experiencing similar changes, the prevailing emotional climate is one of narcissistic preoccupation with physical appearance and sexuality. Successful resolution of the narcissistic conflicts inherent in adolescence is an accomplishment achieved only by a minority. Pseudo-resolution may seem to be evident for many who are preparing for a career, working full-time, or raising a family, only because they are consumed by the task at hand. However, most adults retain more than a vestige of this preoccupation, and emotionally immature adults are virtually unable to evaluate themselves or a prospective partner on qualities other than the physical.

An additional factor in the narcissistic preoccupation of adolescents is that there are very few ways to be genuinely unique. When one is attempting to establish an identity apart from one's parents, nearly anything indicative of nonconformity will suffice. Since most adolescents are equally preoccupied, the logical modes of expression are those related to physical-sexual interests. The body and its adornments, then, become the only visible stage on which individual differences may be displayed.

Further enforcement of adolescent conformity is energized by massive separation anxiety. Few authors have articulated the importance of biological pubescence as a major and traumatic epoch of separation in normal human development. Adolescence represents a symbolic passage from childhood into adulthood, a rather tumultous transition that creates intense conflict, fear, anxiety, and personal problems. The unconscious desire to return to childhood for security, guidance, and dependence is turbulently at war with the conscious desire to avoid dependence. The emotional reality of separation, the sense of loss from a sheltered and protected childhood, and the unconscious desire to return to childhood are what generate the conspicuous signs of emotional instability, mania, depression, suicide, delinquency, agitation, and obvious moodswings in the adolescent. What adolescents believe they can no longer get from parents, they try to get from each other. Parental support and guidance tend to be replaced by peer pressure and peer conformity. During this tumultuous stage, when they need the most support, acceptance, understanding, and patience, many adolescents attempt to cut themselves off from adults and reject parental support in their awkward strivings for independence. To feel secure, they become surrogate parents to each other, and rely on peer groups for a sense of oneness, belonging, identity, family, and security. Frequently, emotionally disturbed youngsters who feel rejected by and alienated from their parents pair up while still in elementary school or early junior high so as to find an immediate replacement for their parents.

In my high school of several thousand students, everyone knew of the ugliest, most repulsive girl. Her name was Joan. She was awkward and cross-eyed, and had huge acne infections that the other kids referred to as "barnacles." In addition, Joan had stringy, oily hair, teeth that were yellow and crooked, and a perpetual body odor. From a poor family, her clothes were never in style. Moreover, Joan was of limited intelligence and thus took special classes.

For example, when Jim was infuriated with Bob he could get even by writing on one of the rest-room walls, "Bob was out with

Joan last night, and they f-----. He says he'll never go back to women." The girls did similar things. When Karen wished to avenge a personal conflict with Carol, the grafitti read, "Joan is Carol's best friend." There must have been 40 girls named Joan in the school, but everyone knew *that* Joan.

In retrospect, Joan was a very disturbed girl. Emotionally, she was needy and desperate to a point that her reality, social alertness, and social skills were severely impaired. Her needs for attention, recognition, and love were so great that she could be easily manipulated into pathetic situations. The more sadistic kids would befriend her for a moment, and then whisper in her ear that the captain of the football team had a crush on her. They instructed her that if she wanted him, then she should raise her hand during that afternoon's awards ceremony and wave at him while he was giving his acceptance speech. Joan did, and over 2000 kids roared with laughter, which finally forced her into cruel reality. When she cried from humiliation, no one cared. She was socially quarantined. Anyone close to her for any reason would risk an equally painful ostracism.

Inherent within the limits of attractiveness and desirability are specific, often idiosyncratic, social regulations. Physical size is an important social regulation, which all overweight people well know. As early as kindergarten, obese children tend to be impugned and eliminated from the mainstream of social activity. Nearly every elementary-school teacher can relate tragic anecdotes about such children who are the brunt of social derision. From adolescence onward, overweight females tend to be more socially ostracized than obese men. Because of the social regulations governing female sexual attractiveness and desirability, many obese women are embarrassed and ashamed because they are "not too desirable." In order to feel comfortable and less conspicuous, some "chubby" people pair with each other and engage in frequent competitive attempts to lose weight, often to little avail.

Socially, regulations of height also contribute to one's limits of attractiveness and desirability. A women who is much taller than the majority of men may be extremely attractive and desirable, yet men conspicuously shorter usually consider her "off limits." Although it is not usually stated that tall women must not pair with short men, the social mandate is markedly effective. Possibly due to residuals of primitive society, the male is nearly always expected to be taller, of greater anatomical breadth, and physically stronger than his partner in order to offer her security and protection. Regardless of how "unfair" it may seem, the obese woman, whether tall or short, and the short man, fat or lean, tend to be less desirable because of unspoken social regulations.

Idiosyncratic preference quirks are intriguing as there are few consistent patterns across couples. The quirks can be preferences in body type, hair color, darkness or lightness of complexion, etc. There are men who will not consider a woman who doesn't have a large bosom, shapely legs, a small waist, blonde hair, or firm buttocks. There are women who will not consider a man who is not dark complexioned, light complexioned, short-haired, long-haired, muscular, too muscular, too hairy, or not hairy enough. Most of the preference quirks are unconsciously derived from the relationship with the significant parent or parent surrogate. If a male has had a fairly satisfactory relationship with his mother, he will tend to eliminate women who are too much unlike her in appearance and idiosyncratic features. Conversely, if the relationship with his mother was unsatisfactory, but he was unaware of it because he did not feel free to express anger or negative feelings toward her, there is an unconscious tendency to eliminate those women who remotely resemble her. The quirks may be size, complexion, color of hair, physical appearance, or whatever stimulates emotional and mental associations.

Similar mechanisms operate in the female regarding her relationship to her father, or the significant male parent surrogate. Consider, for example, the young woman who was vehemently repulsed by the mere thought of being attracted to or making love with a dark-complexioned man. Because of her idiosyncratic quirk, she eliminated prospective partners who in any way resembled her dark-complexioned and abusive father, whom she unconsciously despised. Throughout childhood, she had been forced to repress her real anger and hatred for him. She compensated for it by consciously thinking of him as an ideal of perfection. The long endured rage toward him could not find direct expression but instead was unconsciously displaced upon all dark-complexioned males.

All of the preceding screening mechanisms narrow the choice in partner selection. Whether a relationship develops gradually or is "love at first sight"; unconscious psychodynamic needs; and the sense of urgency that occurs from the possibility of having those inexplicable needs met; these make up the experience known as *falling in love*. The health or pathology of those basic psychological needs is what determines the selection of a psychologically suitable partner. Relatively healthy individuals are unconsciously attracted to each other and can enjoy a healthy, satisfying relationship. (Nevertheless, sometimes healthy people are attracted to unhealthy individuals for external reasons, e.g., social status, wealth, last resort.) Conversely, emotionally disturbed individuals are also unconsciously attracted to each other, for only an emotionally ill person has the pathological conflicts and destructive impulses necessary to satisfy the needs of the other. Such a relationship is guaranteed to supply both partners with exacerbated continuation of the same heartache, pain, and conflict they have always known.

The unconscious silent forces of the soul, the deepest and most basic elements of emotional development, are the essence of one's ability to derive satisfaction from living. These psychodynamic forces work as a relentless gestapo, assuring each individual that the partner is in perfect accordance with this or her own deep, emotional and psychological needs. The energy and persistence of these forces are seen in the rage, panic, anxiety, depression, or confusion that occurs when a loved one leaves, deserts, or dies. Although unexpected partner loss may occasionally offer freedom and opportunity, most often it results in fantasies—or occasionally acts—of homocide and suicide, or in a life muted by a pervasive, agitated depression, or in a future that can never quite be free from sadness.

The remainder of this book details the unconscious forces of the human heart and their influence on partner selection.

2 / The First Relationship

The capacity for sustained, meaningful, and satisfactory relationships is governed by the degree of psychopathology in a child's first relationship. In Western culture, that relationship is usually with the mother, although it may also be with the father, a grandparent, sibling, baby-sitter, or anyone else responsible for the child's care. As the individual matures and emotionally separates from his* first love, a partial attachment develops to friends, teachers, dolls, teddy bears, blankets, animals, or anyone capable of offering security. These transitional relationships do not carry a full quantum of emotional investment, however, because the main attachment is still to the primary love object (mother)† and secondary love objects (family). During adolescence, as the primary relationship is capriciously relinquished, the individual frantically attempts to replace the lost love with a substitute. Separation anxiety, insecurity, and existential aloneness provide the energy and motivation for subsequent intimate relationships.

Extremes in the attachment-separation continuum are seen in the "seeking child" and the unmarried adult who remains at home with one or both parents. Seeking children are pre- and early adolescents who feel that their primary attachment was inadequate, unfulfilling, and tenuous. They are not consciously able to explain the inadequacies of their first relationship, as it is all they have known, nor are they able to confront or explain their disappointment, depression, and pain. They do, however, feel and respond to the ongoing anxiety, insecurity, isolation, worthless-

---

*Throughout this chapter and those that follow, unless specifically referring to a male person, the pronoun *his* should be interpreted as *his or her*.
†Whether or not the first relationship is with the mother, for purposes of simplicity, the word *mother* is used herein to mean the person to whom the child is first attached.

ness, and restlessness caused by inadequate attachments, and label their parents as insensitive, unloving, and old-fashioned. To satisfy the unfulfilled needs of the first relationship, the seeking child obsessively seeks what his heart tells him is missing. Separating from inadequate and unfulfilling primary attachments is not difficult, and the youngster finds it rewarding to be away from home for long periods. His desire to run away "because there is nothing at home" is an attempt to locate someone to fulfill his needs. Parental control and discipline are reacted to violently, for the adolescent interprets them as signs of insensitivity, rejection, and inability to love. When he leaves home to look for a benevolent replacement, the clever adolescent attempts to make the parents feel guilty by making accusations about their inability to care. Of course, the probability of the seeking child ever finding the fantasized relationship is woefully low.

At the opposite end of the attachment-separation continuum is the nonseeking, overly-dependent, overprotected, paranoid adult who is unable to relinquish the first love. He remains "at home" and feels obligated to care for the first love for life. The unspoken parental rule is that the child must forever care for the first love, out of decency and gratitude for all the heartache and suffering that person endured while raising the most difficult child. Pathological and devious parents are capable of developing numerous physical ailments in order to keep the child home and caring for them. At will, such parents are capable of suffering cardiovascular arrest, strokes, seizures, or fainting spells each time the child considers leaving home. Harmony is established only after the child has learned his correct place in life and committed himself to the care of the first love.

The faithful nonseeking adult remains at home and is frequently vexed with anxiety, stagnation, frustration, and resentment. Since he usually finds it necessary to forsake personal interests, emotional growth, and mastery to care for the first love, he remains perpetually immature. Some become impotent or frigid. The mother, keenly aware that her child might be lured away by sexual interests, began early to properly educate him about the wickedness and sinfulness of sexuality and people in general. As a result, the faithful child became too frightened to leave. Unable to function autonomously when separated from her, the child became convinced that the mother's admonitions were indeed correct. Put in bondage by distorted reality, fear, social ineptitude, and guilt, the nonseeking adult remains locked into a pathological symbiosis, and is thus prevented from seeking a partner.

Contrary to the seeking child who believes that nearly anyone can meet his emotional needs, the nonseeking adult believes no one can. Each is correct in his unconscious perception. Logic and proper perspective of reality are irrelevant because feelings dictate responsiveness to attachment and separation. Sexual expression becomes the *modus vivendi*. The nonseeker has repressed, denied, and sublimated sexual impulses to the extent that indeed the first love does provide more than could be provided by another. Some nonseekers become asexual through years of careful suppression and sublimation of erotic impulses. Some become obese in order to unconsciously disguise gender identity, which effectively extirpates sensuality. Others become self-righteous and condemnatory toward the licentiousness of youth, which provides vicarious release from their unrestrained and recurrent sexual tension. Conversely, seeking children use sexuality as dauntless proof for what they have always suspected: that nearly anyone can offer more "love" than their parents. For seekers, touching and being touched, holding and being held, rocking and being rocked, soothing and being soothed during transitory sexual contact feel more like what love might be than what was experienced at home.

Closely related to the nonseeking adult is the individual who, although married, remains more involved with the first love than with the spouse. Those who live in the same house as or geographically near their parents—because they become anxious and unhappy when too far away—provide a vivid example of the inability to separate from the first love. If the child returns home to the parents each time he is in conflict with the spouse, not only does the return undermine the couple's ability to eventually work out satisfactory solutions to conflict, but the message to the spouse is quite clear: no one can ever take the place of the first love. Every overprotected, overly-dependent child has had an overly-involved, overcontrolling parent who fostered such a relationship. Marriage to the overprotected, overdependent individual is usually unstable because the child is, in fact, still attached to the first love. Such an individual also unconsciously displaces onto the spouse much of the repressed hostility and resentment that he was unable to direct toward the overcontrolling parent. The unspoken (or sometimes spoken) message to the spouse is simply, "You will never be able to love me the way my mother [or first love] did."

The quality of the mother's relationship with her child is the most honest and revealing indication of her capacity for sustained intimacy. The ongoing relatedness, hour after hour, day after day, year after year, is the training laboratory in which the child learns what feels right and familiar in subsequent intimate relationships. It is in this relationship that he learns the indelible reality of that elusive construct known as love, and the feeling of being loved, which he will later unconsciously attempt to repeat with the partner.

STAGE ONE: THE FIRST YEAR OF LIFE

The quality of the first relationship is immune to good intentions—that is, the way the mother thinks it is, wishes it were, or pretends it is while in public. Because the child knows nothing else, he can only respond according to the way it *really* is.

The quality and intensity of the first attachment evolve through three stages. The first stage is equivalent to the first year of life, the second stage from one to approximately three and a half years, and the third stage from three and a half to approximately six years. The quality of the attachment during the first year is extremely critical, not only in regard to subsequent relationships, but in regard to "normal," versus psychotic, development. Void of the rudiments of healthy attachment—adequate security, dependency, physical and emotional comfort, protection, contact, the mother's voice—the child can suffer a variety of emotional and physical disorders. In cases of extreme maternal deprivation, where children have been raised in clean and sterile facilities, but without intimate human contact, the incidence of mortality is extremely high. Lesser degrees of maternal deprivation and inadequate attachment can result in severe psychosis, autism, chronic depression, developmental retardation, learning disorders, and high susceptibility to disease (Spitz 1966).

The quality of attachment is determined by (1) the readiness with which the mother responds to the child's emotional and physical needs, (2) the extent to which she is available and initiates interaction with the child, and (3) the emotional mood during the time she is attending to the child's needs. The interaction also involves transmission of her unconscious apprehensions over parenting, personal daily conflicts, and real feelings about the child. Since mother and child are essentially one emotional mass (symbiotic relatedness), the affective communications from mother to child are clear and powerful. The mother's real feelings hit the child's psyche with full force, as the child is yet without defense mechanisms. The feelings she transmits, which are absorbed by the unconscious, become the child's sense of self. The child's reality during the first year is the conscious and unconscious feelings of the mother. If the child is looked upon as unplanned, unwanted, and burdensome, the quality of his life will be much different than if he is considered planned, precious, and perfect.

The absence of a safe, secure, and trusting dependency upon the mother causes the child to later mistrust other people and to experience them more as inanimate objects. Without a secure and dependable attachment, the child tends to view the world as a mass of diffuse irrelevance that he is unable to meaningfully organize. Void of both intimate relatedness and his mother's substitute ego to protect him from overwhelming stimuli, the child automatically withdraws, and tends to become an island unto himself. Not allowed into his mother's heart, he builds invisible walls around himself in order to restrict social and environmental stimulation. Such walls prevent others from getting close and simultaneously prevent him from getting close to others, at least not any closer than he had been in his first relationship. If someone should attempt to get closer, the level of distrust and paranoia is sufficiently high that he will withdraw or attack to keep them away. The dissatisfaction and hurt of an inadequate first relationship is never totally forgotten even though specific events cannot be consciously remembered.

The first love's conscious and unconscious intentions are not always sufficient to account for the severe psychoses (autism) sometimes observed in children. This is particularly true when interviews with the family show the other members to be relatively healthy. Since it takes two people to be involved in any relationship, the child must be physiologically normal to be able to receive, process, and experience emotional love from the mother. During the past several years, I have had the disquieting experience of working with parents of autistic and psychotic children. As medical records were studied, and parents interviewed, a variety of physiological and neurological aberrations—particularly allergies—were noted, which had had the effect of preventing the child from receiving the mother's protection, care, and nurturance. Those children who experienced chronic pain during the first year, which the parents were unable to stop, were invariably the most disturbed.

Jared, a pathetically autistic child, had a bleeding skin rash (allergy) during his first 16 months of life. His heartbroken mother reported that the child cried almost continuously during his first year. He even whimpered in his sleep, and seldom slept more than two hours at a time. During his fifth month, he had begun to scratch the sores, causing profuse bleeding. Allegedly, the family physician did not seem too concerned. He believed Jared would outgrow the problem, and so encouraged the mother to ignore the infant's crying in order not to reinforce it. However, the pain was not stopped by anything the mother tried, and so Jared was unable to receive much caring, nurturance, or protection. In short, the physical pain was sufficiently intense and encompassing that for all Jared knew, his mother may have been causing it. Neither positive nor negative feelings could provide relief. The only sensations Jared could experience and introject were pain, suffering, and people who made no difference. Unable to enjoy a trusting, dependent, and secure attachment, the mother-child dyad failed at the first necessity of life.

Today, unlike severely retarded children who are often profoundly deformed, Jared is a physically handsome, almost beautiful child of seven. However, he is not toilet-trained, cannot speak, and has impervious, invisible walls around him. He cannot relate to people. When anyone attempts to get close, he throws back his arms and head, and releases a high-pitched scream while snapping his teeth and gazing at the ceiling. When he is not supervised carefully, he runs headfirst into walls or out into the street to butt the side of a moving car. Left entirely to his own, Jared would destroy himself.

Because of the immense pain suffered his first year, it is speculated that suffering and pain are his primary modes of interacting with life.

Tension reduction and the seeking of pleasure are not important to him, as they are to other children. Jared is not likely to get well or become "normal." Nor will he outgrow his disturbance. Perhaps the best one can hope for is the extinction of his self-destructive behavior and the conditioning of a rudimentary vocabulary. Jared no longer has allergies, but that doesn't seem to be of much concern.

STAGE TWO: ONE TO THREE AND A HALF YEARS

During the second stage, from 12 months to three and a half years, the child becomes more ambulatory, thus increasing distance from the mother. In addition to walking, talking, and exploring the environment, he begins to make other attachments. The quality of the child's interpersonal capability may be altered during this stage if a deliberate, conscientious effort is made to do so. The quality may be enhanced if there is a significant other in the environment, who is more responsive and more able than the mother to meet the child's emotional needs (e.g., more emotionally responsive adult, such as father, grandparent, older sibling). Although the quality of a child's first relationship can be mitigated during Stage Two, relationships of an inferior quality generally tend to be dissatisfying. If the child is capable of physical autonomy, he tends to avoid individuals incapable of the same quality offered in the first relationship as he perceives them as aversive and unfulfilling.

The symbiotic relatedness with the mother gradually lessens as the child becomes more physically able to do things for himself. Throughout the first few years, however, the child keeps a close eye on the mother and is careful not to let her stray too far from his sight or hearing range. When she leaves him for short or long periods, the child often cries, which is his attempt to maintain contact and reduce the pain and panic of the separation anxiety. Mothers who are extremely close to their child feel a similar form of anxiety when separated from the child.

Insecure, immature, and socially inadequate mothers, who are able to relate only to helpless, dependent children, tend to become panicked, embittered, and rejecting when their child begins the natural separation during Stage Two. Some mothers, in an attempt to replace the faltering relationship, desire to become pregnant again. Others enter a fairly severe depression caused by what they experience as loss. Still others seek employment or reestablish interests and relationships that were important before investment in motherhood. The less healthy mothers implement a wide range of devious tactics to frighten and traumatize the child, and make him feel guilty, thus undermining his developing autonomy and insuring a helpless dependence. The mother gets what she wants to some degree because she keeps the child; however, she also loses because her control and forced dependence are countered with massive resistance and hostility from the child she needs so much.

To the surprise of some parents, the child's allegiance to the primary attachment may switch to the father or to another in the immediate environment during this stage. The mother's ambivalence, her difficulty in letting go, and the blatant reality of having to discipline, control, and protect him from real dangers, occasionally cause her to become fearful and angry. At this time, the father, because he is usually not present much of the time and because he may be more accepting and more available to the child's needs, may emerge as the primary attachment figure.

STAGE THREE: THREE AND A HALF TO SIX YEARS

During the third stage, the child's capacity for intimate relationships becomes further entrenched; by age five and a half to six years, it is relatively fixed. If previous relationships, from the first on through several others in the child's existential arena, have been fairly healthy and secure, the child will later be unconsciously attracted to those who are capable of providing the same "type" of relatedness. Conversely, he will not be seriously attracted to those incapable of a similar caliber of relatedness.

By their sixth or seventh year, children have not only introjected the unconscious and conscious feelings of the primary attachment, but they are also influenced by the family constellation and its interpretation of culture. By the time children have reached age six, the parents and culture have also provided either an intentional or accidental ideal for them to emulate. The basic character of the child has been formed, and the family and culture serve as suppressors, channels, and reinforcers for acceptable expression of basic impulses. The child's sense of worth has now been established. From this point on, because he has introjected the feelings and attitudes of his primary and secondary attachments, his self-concept will be most difficult to genuinely change. He has also been equipped with the more sophisticated defense mechanisms—displacement, denial, and repression—and now has the psychological apparatus necessary to maintain and unconsciously repeat behavioral situations that validate and strengthen his feelings about himself and the world. **2109939**

The psychological equipment available for protecting and maintaining the real self is most complex. With denial and repression, however, one can survive the most difficult of human traumas and appear almost unaffected *on the outside*. Conversely, one can experience a most beautiful and meaningful human experience and remain equally unaffected *on the inside*. Even if an experience does challenge the way an individual feels about himself, he is usually able to negate and deny the learning potential of the experience so as to protect the self against change. One's sense of worth or worthlessness—mattering or not mattering—are genuine and pervasive character traits.

Since sense of worth is established before the child has the mental defenses to do much about it, it is most difficult to change later on, even when one deliberately tries to do so. Examples of the relative imperviousness to genuine change can be seen in many individuals who have been actively involved in growth groups, psychotherapy, or almost anything purporting to help one change. Many systems of therapy unintentionally attempt to help the individual deny his real feelings and to develop substitute *reaction formations* against the real self in order to look and behave "totally differently." Ostensibly, the individual does behave differently, usually in a manner opposite from his previous behavior, for the mechanism of reaction formation does not contain relative gradations but tends to require opposite behaviors and attitudes to fight against. As long as the client is convinced that he is nothing like he was and as long as he can get the strength to manage an opposite, self-deception (denial) will continue to work. A test of genuine change is to note what the person does when he is alone and away from those he wishes to convince.

Some children have little or no intrinsic worth or value to their parents, but instead are valued for a specific behavior. A fairly common example of a limited but specific sense of mattering is demonstrated in the following account:

> As early as Diana's fourth year, it was obvious that her parents val-
> ued her primarily for her physical beauty and attractiveness. Family
> life was sufficiently strained, and agitation and negativity pervaded the
> home atmosphere. The parents' discussions about their children were
> often tainted with mild agitation, hostility, and feelings of hardship.
> When they spoke of how pretty Diana was, however, their tone light-
> ened and they smiled proudly and positively. The little girl's primary
> sense of worth and mattering had been reduced to her appearance.
> When she was hurt or had experienced a crisis, and was thus in need of
> attention and support, she would go to her room, dress in her most at-
> tractive outfit, and then display herself before her parents. Since
> Diana's attractiveness mattered to them, they would stop whatever
> they were doing to praise her for her beauty. During those few mo-
> ments of unmitigated attention from both parents, she experienced
> positive feelings, which she interpreted as love. Although Diana's
> other talents were not ignored, her parents unconsciously focused on her
> attractiveness. She mattered, it could be said, for her body. Today, an
> exceptionally beautiful teenager, Diana is a major source of heart-
> ache for her parents because she now matters to others—for the same
> reason.

Overall, people have an uncanny ability for selecting others capable of a similar quality of emotional life. Tragically, those who
have experienced an insufficient, insecure, and tumultuous attachment, and who lack a sense of intrinsic worth, will later in life have
an unconscious propensity toward choosing a partner capable of
providing the same quality of experience. Consciously, the partner
may bear little external resemblance to the earlier attachment fig-
ure(s). Unconsciously, the psychological fit is almost perfect.

Pratt and Sackett (1967) reported a similar attachment and subsequent pairing preference in their work with laboratory-raised
rhesus monkeys. They found that monkeys raised in deprived
social-emotional isolation showed a significant preference for other
monkeys raised in deprived isolation. Monkeys less socially deprived—those raised in cages, for example—preferred those also
raised in cages. Monkeys raised with peers showed a preference for

others raised similarly. Furthermore, Suomi et al. (1970) found that normal monkeys chose normal monkeys for sexual partners, whereas lobectomized* monkeys selected lobectomized sexual partners.

CAPACITY FOR INTIMACY

Give me a dozen healthy infants, well formed, and my own specified world to bring them up in and I'll guarantee to take any one at random and train him to become any type of specialist I might select—doctor, lawyer, merchant-chief, and yes, even beggar-man and thief, regardless of his talents, penchants, abilities, vocations, and race of his ancestors. [John B. Watson]

Not long ago, a friend said to me, "You're not going to tell me that just because I get a headache or upset stomach at 11:30 each morning that my mother didn't toilet train me right, or removed me from the nipple too soon, or that she spanked me too hard, are you? I don't buy it." I assured him, "Of course I would never tell you that." Following a long pause and some apprehensive eye contact, I continued, "It's because she gave you an enema *and* beat you while you were eating that you have nausea and headaches at 11:30." After the laughter subsided, I proceeded to explain how the intensity, frequency, and the person's interpretation of early childhood experiences affect certain adult feelings, attitudes, and anxieties." While discussing the material with my friend, I was reminded that many people believe that one specific childhood trauma or tragedy can be the causative agent for a specific adult behavior and adult pathology. Although certain childhood traumata *may* shape and influence preferences and choices in later life, it is incorrect to assume that an early isolated experience can cause an isolated adult behavior.

Early childhood experience, because it determines how an individual feels about himself and the world, and because it determines capacity for intimate relatedness, is the basic foundation for the quality of living. Because it is easier to change or become sidetracked by exogenous interests than it is to change the real self,

*A *lobectomy* is a surgical operation in which the frontal lobes of the brain that are associated with responsiveness to affective stimuli are removed.

most people exert considerable energy in pursuing and accumulating things that make little or no difference. Since it took a significant relationship, commitment, and time during the first attachment to make a person what he is, it takes a subsequent healthy attachment and commitment in a relationship, over a substantial duration, to help an individual realize all he could be. Few forces are greater than the combined energy of two healthy individuals who are meaningfully attached and have a sense of purpose. Few, if any, of life's problems ever seem insurmountable to two people who are securely attached. Conversely, few forces are more destructive than the combined energy of two unhealthy individuals who live together but are unable to enjoy a secure attachment. Even the most trivial and transitory problems become insurmountable to two people enmeshed in a destructive symbiosis. Rather than provide a security base from which to grow, develop, and mature, pathological relatedness provides a medium through which the unexpressed destructive forces from childhood can be directly transferred to the partner who may or may not tolerate their expression.

The relatively fixed qualitative factors of human relatedness are seen as polar opposites in the following table:

Relationship Qualities

Healthy	Unhealthy
Trust	Mistrust
Closeness	Distance
Openness	Guardedness
Interdependence	Avoidance of dependence
	Dependency reversals

Each of the relationship qualities is experientially developed during the primary relationship. Because these qualities are components of intimacy, they are seldom observable anywhere but in an intimate relationship. That is, one can seldom know another's capacity for sustained intimacy by observing him outside his central relationship. Healthy relatedness cannot be fabricated or obtained by reading about how healthy individuals relate to each other. When an individual attempts a healthier relatedness than he can manage, it appears counterfeit and strained. Some individuals, particularly those who have participated in growth groups or who have kept abreast of the literature on personal growth, are able to acquire a style that approximates healthy relatedness. Nevertheless, they remain unable to relate sufficiently to their own partner. Although the real test has been failed, some people derive gratification by pretending they are what they really are not.

The qualities of the first attachment become notably stable after the sixth year of life. From then on, any encroachment on one's emotional territory threatens psychological balance. Because of the depth and pervasiveness of the relational qualities, feelings of anxiety and threat occur when a potential partner demands a higher level of trust, closeness, openness, and interdependency than was experienced in the first relationship. The anxiety signals danger to the psychological economy, and the individual will either fight or flee to regain emotional harmony.

TRUST–MISTRUST

The first characteristic to be tested in any prospective relationship is the level of trust in the partner. Those who have experienced a high level of trust and security in the first relationship tend to enter subsequent relationships with a trusting, positive, and confident attitude. Neither severely disappointed nor psychologically bruised, they enter new relationships easily and enthusiastically. Trusting individuals are repelled by those who are deceitful and unreliable. Unconsciously, they never assume that the prospective partner would wish to hurt them. Such an attitude is contrary to the distrustful, paranoid individual who has been hurt, rejected, and disappointed, in the first attachment. More often than not, those who have been bruised approach all tentative relationships suspiciously, expecting rejection, depreciation, and disappointment. Their hypersensitive social antennae are always scanning the actions and intentions of others, looking for anything to confirm what they already believe: that no one can be trusted.

Trust, similar to other qualitative characteristics, cannot be experienced to a greater degree than was experienced in the prototypic relationship. Although one can voluntarily become less trusting if necessary, one cannot trust at a greater level than that established during the early years. Nuclear trust serves as the regulatory valve for the emotional release of the other attitudes and feelings. The absence of trust in a relationship is apt to engender hostility, uncertainty, insecurity, emotional distance, anxiety, and lack of cooperation. In short, the relationship is void of positive relatedness.

When individuals incapable of trust pair, there exist two separate, anxious, and conflicted entities residing under the same roof. All that a relationship could potentially offer is not present. Due to the demands of adult reality and responsibility, and the varied and inconsistent feelings of daily living, numerous behaviors occur that the more suspicious person could construe as breech of trust. Because of the high correlation between trust, caring, security, and dependency, the resentful indictment, "I don't trust you," often means, "You don't care for me properly." Specifically, "I don't trust you" can be interpreted as "I have wants and needs and am dependent upon you for their fulfillment. When you don't meet my needs, or delay meeting them, or meet them begrudgingly or only when you want to, it is obvious you don't care." The natural tendency of the adult involved in a distrusting relationship is exactly the same as the infant's. When needs are ignored or spuriously met by the love object, the response is one of hurt, resentment, and anger. The child acts upon his frustrated needs by crying. If this active protest does not bring adequate need fulfillment, a period of depressed resignation follows in which he may intermittently cry in an attempt to have his needs satisfied. If the love object does not meet his needs, a hopeless detachment follows. The anger is still there, however, and the intention is, "The hell with it, I'll do it myself. I shall never ask for anything again."

Despite quasi-emotional detachment, people do continue to ask—although perhaps not for anything intimate, important, or directly related to their emotional needs, as to be refused could be too painful. Respect, courtesy, kindness, and consideration are irrelevant when vengeful demands become the medium through which requests are relayed to the partner. Unabashed, universal demanding is one of the more clever rituals used to restore the balance of trust and relatedness. Many couples, particularly those incapable of trust, or those in which one partner has recently been hurt by the other, tend to use demands as their only mode of interaction. Vengeful demands are a most functional and sophisticated tool; they should always be interpreted as an attempt to restore trust and relatedness to the system. It is the angry, hostile response that is meant to hurt and destroy the partner. Such a response is also a protection and distancing mechanism, as unconsciously the respondent does not expect the demand to be met. The self is thus protected against further hurt or involvement. Demanding is also a symbolic test of the partner's desire, interest, or readiness to restore relational balance. If he seems interested in meeting the demand and willing to do so, the anger is dissipated, and the couple can restore harmony. In many cases, the demand is attenuated to more reasonable proportions. However, if the partner shows no interest in the demand, or responds to the initial anger with more anger (which is what usually happens), the cycle is accelerated with more hurt, more mistrust, more distance, and greater demands.

Marge, a vivacious and charming client in the process of divorcing her wealthy husband, succinctly demonstrated the vindictiveness of her demands. She and her husband, Robert, had been in marriage counseling for over a year, and they concluded that their differences were irreconcilable. Marge had sought individual help from me because of a severe depression precipitated partly by her realization that her husband would never meet her needs. It was a classic case: the "successful" husband was more attached to his business and dollars than to his wife. Since Robert's main love affair was with money, Marge retaliated with extravagant spending. Shopping at such classy stores as Neiman-Marcus and Bloomingdale's, Marge regularly purchased a variety of expensive but unnecessary items. She had found her husband's primary vulnerability—his money—and was not about to relinquish her advantaged position.

Marge's moment of truth came during a session when she said, "David, the cost of living is rising so rapidly, I think it only fair that you raise your fees too." I responded, "That's quite all right. I am perfectly satisfied with my fees. Why do you wish to pay more?" Marge replied mischievously, "Well, Robert has lots of money." As she heard her own words, she became angry, and continued, "And . . . I just want to make the creep pay through the nose for my misery."

OPENNESS–GUARDEDNESS

Children are extraordinarily resilient during their early years. Despite emotional (and sometimes physical) abuse, they survive disparagement, rejection, parental insensitivity, and punishment markedly well. Because of their dependency needs, the relatively short duration of the abuse, and the positive emotional victuals that intersperse such abuse, children have a remarkable capacity for forgetting (i.e., repressing) unpleasant experiences. Following repression of the unpleasant experiences from the consciousness, children adjust their level of openness–guardedness to fit the realities of the family atmosphere and the primary relationship. If parents are unable to meet a child's needs and are overly critical, rejecting, punitive, or unstable, the child has little choice but to inhibit his receptivity. To survive emotionally, he learns to guard himself against criticism, hurt, scoldings, punishment, and emotional damage.

Children are born almost totally open to environment and social input. Spitz (1966), however, cites the physiological "protective barrier," which prevents children from being overwhelmed by stimuli that they cannot organize, block out, or dilute. As the child's natural protection barrier diminishes, his developing ego takes over the organizing function and blocks out, reorganizes stimuli and experiences so as to reduce anxiety and thus provide emotional comfort. From ages three and a half to six, however, the defense mechanisms of displacement, denial, and repression begin to operate. During these years, if the primary relationship is abusive and damaging to the child's feelings about himself, he has the emotional tools necessary to ward off full impact of the attack. It is at this age that children develop what most parents describe as "selective hearing." Children of the most critical, rejecting, and castrating parents develop a more severe case of "deafness," which guards the child against criticism and devaluation, and buffers the intensity of nearly all that is taken in. Severe guardedness in children tends to generalize to all receptive functions; for example, a high correlation exists between critical, nonaccepting parents and learning disabilities in their children. In pathological cases, all channels of the child's receptivity are constricted. Consequently, extremely guarded and defensive adults usually have the psycho-social maturity of children between the ages of six and eight. Within, they are only partially aware of their low strength, which engenders more guardedness. Their motive in life is not to open up and grow, but to guard and protect what little there is.

The guarded, defensive child becomes a chronically anxious and intimidated adult, unable to recognize or share his feelings or himself. Although he may be quite talkative about things and events, he becomes anxious when anyone shares feelings and emotions. If he is with a group of friends who begin to discuss emotions, he is apt to tune out, leave the room, or attempt to change the subject to something less personal. His feelings remain locked within, and they are not likely to get out. Such a person tends to reject feelings and emotional people in much the same way his parents rejected him. Debilitating anxiety in the guarded individual is highest in the confines of an intimate relationship. Never quite sure whether he will be rejected and impugned, he avoids close relationships and self-revelation in order to protect his depleted self-esteem. Others perceive him as vacant—it seems as if his emotional self is on vacation. He has eyes but does not see, and ears but does not hear, particularly where people, empathy, or anything emotional is involved. He is so cautiously guarded about his real self that he is void of spontaneity lest some of that real self sneak out. He rigidly attempts to control himself—and others in his family and his environment—so that no one can see that he is a human who might occasionally make a mistake.

The guarded individual is inherently destructive. Having been destroyed himself, he has a chronic inclination to devalue, reject, and inflict pain upon those in his immediate environment. The hostile-dependent feelings that he developed during childhood as coping mechanisms resurface with full expression in the marital relationship. For, despite the individual's compensatory exactitude and desire for perfectionism, his partner still sees many of his shortcomings. When anything other than respect and admiration are directed at him, he feels castigated and worthless. Minor reproof is experienced as condemnation. The repressed conflicts of his first relationship surface or become stimulated as he reenacts unresolved childhood patterns with a new antagonist.

In an attempt to cope with his easily hurt feelings, he either withdraws from the relationship or blames the spouse for not caring enough, all the while becoming even more guarded. He considers any attempt by the spouse to "discuss the problem" to be blame and further indictment, which hit the core of his emotional immaturity and low self-esteem. Depending upon his degree of socialization, he either lashes out with an infantile temper tantrum or further withdraws into himself and becomes more guarded and depressed.

In contrast, the open individual was raised in a totally different family atmosphere. Much of the natural openness, receptivity, and spontaneity with which he entered the world remains. Parents of open individuals tend to be mature, understanding, and accepting of a wide range of childhood behaviors, attitudes, and feelings. The child finds it unnecessary to guard and defend himself and his freedom of expression. With the relatively open range of acceptable behavior, the child learns self-confidence and realizes that he has intrinsic worth and value to his mother (parents). Because he has been valued and accepted, and because he feels a sense of personal worth, he brings feelings of security and self-confidence to all subsequent intimate relationships. Reproof and control by respected authority figures, and disagreements with others, especially the spouse, may be viewed as helpful because they carry the potential for correction, growth, and wisdom. Open individuals, because they have not been attacked and destroyed, have little need to hurt or destroy others, least of all the partner.

The anxiety and conflict that guarded individuals feel when required to reveal their feelings are somewhat similar to what open people experience when they cannot share themselves and their emotions. Because the guarded individual feels worthless and lacks confidence, he finds it threatening to share feelings that have the potential for rejection. Open individuals, because of self-confidence and feelings of worth, are not threatened by such sharing. In fact, they exhibit enthusiasm and eagerness at the prospect of sharing themselves with another. Not only does sharing bring relief to a person when he is stressed, but it also validates the worth of the self and brings the participants in the sharing closer to one another.

CLOSENESS-DISTANCE

The capacity for closeness parallels the development of nuclear trust during the first year of life. It may be altered during the early formative years by direct intervention, changes in the mother, or by changing the child's primary attachment figure. Most often, however, the child's ability or inability to feel comfortable and secure with emotional and physical closeness is unassailable by the time he enters the second grade. Developmentally, the frequency of intimate body contact, caressing, holding, gentle soothing, and touching decreases after the first year. As the child begins crawling, walking, and further separating emotionally and physically from the mother, there are fewer and fewer moments when the mother can transmit feelings of closeness by holding her child. Therefore, if the development of intimate closeness when the psyche is totally open fails, it will be most difficult to establish later.

After the first year, the normal child is a bundle of activity. Most of his hours are spent curiously exploring, manipulating, and mastering the environment. Any interruption in his busy day of active exploration is usually met with resistance. If the mother should want to hold or kiss him, she either waits until he is asleep or otherwise inactive.

After the third or fourth year, some children are too big to hold, or at least that is what their parents tell them when they are in need of physical and emotional closeness. As the child develops and naturally separates from the mother, she too disengages him. No longer accustomed to hovering over the child to protect and meet his needs, she may not be emotionally available or wish to take time from her schedule should he want to be held and soothed. As social reality intrudes, a five-year-old who is in need of holding or contact may be as reluctant to ask for it as his parents may be to give it. Clearly, experience has taught him that being touched and held by parents is not the thing to do.

Satisfying intimacy and closeness are experienced through a relaxed sense of passivity, receptivity, and trust in the love object. Closeness achieved by letting down the defenses and receiving physical touching, massaging, and soothing can be a most relaxing, curative, and restorative experience. Despite strong tendencies in our society—especially in males—to deny the need for touching and passive receptive physical contact, it remains a basic need, which most people try to integrate into the sexual experience.

Enjoyment of sex, however, may be a false indication of one's capacity for emotional closeness. Individuals who "can't seem to get enough of each other," particularly in courtship, and who find it necessary to touch, hug, kiss, poke, and walk hand in hand, sometimes interpret primordial eroticism as capacity for closeness. When an adult has been deprived of ongoing relatedness, he has a restless yearning for emotional and physical symbiosis through a vigorous and aggressive copulation whereby he desires the mucus of the partner to be assimilated into the self. A more accurate appraisal of a person's capacity for closeness can be determined from an analysis of his behavior after orgasm. The high number of people who "hit-and-run," or become anxious or depressed, or need to be alone following intercourse bear testimony to their difficulty with comfortable closeness. The restorative, healing function of intimate sexuality is lost when either partner is incapable of resting in a tension-free, almost symbiotic, physio-emotional relatedness with the other following intercourse.

One's eventual (adult) capacity along the closeness-distance continuum is not established *just* by physical closeness with the mother, but by her ability for closeness and emotional investment in her child. Mothers usually cannot be any closer to their child than their own first loves were to them. Certain mothers withhold emotional investment and closeness from their child because they do not want to be bothered by his reciprocal involvement or because they cannot bear the inevitable loss. Some mothers withhold closeness because they have learned that the closer they are to the child, the more time and energy he consumes. If he is left alone and ignored from the start, they reason, he'll take less time and energy later. Although this logic sounds feasible, it does not work that way. What is more apt to happen is that the child will contrive incidents to get his parents involved in his life. If he is critically deprived of closeness, he is likely to become accident-prone or illness-prone to get mother to hold, touch, and caress him. As adults, some individuals who have not been able to enjoy satisfactory physical closeness make frequent visits to physicians, chiropractors, massage parlors, and/or prostitutes. They also engage in repeated sexual encounters to receive a sense of physical closeness without being threatened with emotional vulnerability.

The mother's capacity for emotional and physical closeness is recorded by the child's psyche early in life. Immune to language, experimental investigation, and objective analysis, the emotions accompanying the first love will not be forgotten. On the contrary, they will forever affect an individual's confidence and attitudes about himself and the satisfaction he derives from human relationships. They will provide a subjective measure of intimacy with which prospective partners will be compared. The capacity for closeness and the enjoyment that the child received from his mother as she delighted in kissing, caressing, and soothing him are forever recorded in the child's rudimentary memory. He will not be able to explain why, but, in all subsequent relationships, it will be uncomfortable for him to accept less. Conversely, the distant individual, because he has experienced less closeness, will feel uncomfortable around those capable of more.

Several years ago, a young, college-educated couple named Karen and Joseph came to my office with their eight-month-old baby boy, Steven, to get help for his almost continuous whimpering and crying. When I picked up the child, it became obvious that something was wrong. The closer I put Steven to my face, the more agitated he became. He struggled vehemently and threw himself back and almost out of my arms to "keep his distance." I repeated the sequence of picking him up, holding him, and bringing him closer several times, with the same reaction. That is, he whimpered quietly while left alone; as he was picked up and brought closer, he began to scream loudly, for his acceptable distance was at arm's length; brought closer, he cried loudly and squirmed strenuously. I asked Karen to repeat the maneuver. When she got the same response, I asked Joseph to repeat the exercise. The child's response was identical each time. Karen, apparently seeing my concern, exclaimed, "Oh, hell, why don't we throw the little shit in the toilet!" She knew she had revealed an important clue to the child's behavior, even as she covered her real feelings with an apologetic, "I was only kidding."

As we began the session, I learned that Karen had recently remarried. Joseph was not the baby's biological father—Karen had been impregnated by her first husband, whom she despised. Unfortunately, his child served as a tangible reminder of a tumultuous past. Attempting to construct a new life for herself, Karen was unable to feel anything but hurt, anger, and resentment toward anything that reminded her of her first husband.

Following several sessions, which focused upon helping Karen verbalize and work through her hostility toward her first husband, she was able to release her vengeance, consolidate, and begin the job of developing emotional and physical closeness with her son. In the office, she practiced gently picking up Steven, deliberately trying to transmit good feelings, while forcing him against her face and bosom. Joseph helped with what might be called "loving restraint," while Steven actively fought the emotional intrusion. As the child became fatigued, however, he was unable to continue the fight and so began to relax and to experience a calm, comfortable security until he fell asleep. When he awakened, he again protested when his mother tried to bring him close, but not nearly as much as the first time.

Throughout the following two weeks, Karen practiced her attempt to establish closeness with her child. Although his protest was initially ferocious, it was relinquished during the first week. During the second week, she was able to hold him closely against her face and bosom. He cooed and smiled as he relaxed in his mother's arms, sensing security and tranquility. He was also able to touch her face and breasts, and to become a passive recipient of her affection. Mutual enjoyment of each other began as his scathing cries of distance, separation, and aloneness ceased.

When one has been distant and to some degree detached throughout development, intimate closeness is not only threatening but offensive. To impinge upon the limits of one's emotional territory not only raises anxiety to a level of near panic, but may generate a variety of hostile reactions similar to those of a physical rape. The individual experiences a sense of threat, vulnerability, and invasion to which he responds by becoming more distant. The increased distance insures against anyone ever getting close to him again. Since closeness is painful and revulsive to the distant individual, he is not likely to select a partner who differs greatly in capacity for closeness. Unconsciously, persons capable of an intimate, close relatedness are offended and annoyed by the emotional vacuity of those who are not.

INTERDEPENDENCE

Avoidance of Dependence

Over the years, whether conducting workshops on the psychodynamics of partner selection or teaching courses on personality theory or psychological testing, I find antagonism and resistance to be most evident whenever I'm discussing issues related to dependency needs. Not too surprising is that, at the mention of dependency, most of the males vocalize adamant opposition and repugnance. Many of the women interpret the defensiveness accurately. They seem to know that, in the male's defensive negation of dependency needs, there lies a reasonable basis of truth. Such women tend to remain quiet at such workshops, knowing how threatening the issue of dependency is for most males in our society. Those women who believe the aphorism, "The only difference between men and boys is the price of their toys," seldom express those feelings around men. They have learned that, whatever the expense to themselves, they should never threaten a male's intelligence or his self-esteem by telling him he may be an overgrown child. However, whether one is male or female, the degree of awareness and acceptance of one's dependency needs, as opposed to their denial, avoidance, or compensation, separates the emotionally mature from the immature.

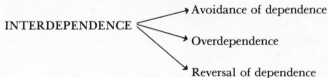

Becoming conscious of avoided truth about the real self, which an individual has consciously worked to deny, creates anxiety and anger. Some psychologists believe people should be able to cut through years of denial and overcompensation by making a list of psychological characteristics or adjectives that they are sure they do not have. However, the person who says, "I am *not* hostile, I am *not* weak, I am *not* dishonest," for example, may very well be all of those things. Many people consciously develop a perfectly opposite reaction formation against their real feelings. Even suggesting that, deep inside, people might be different than what they are outside is met with antagonism by those who cannot bear to have the emotional truth brought so close to their consciousness.

Defense mechanisms serve to ward off external and internal reality, thus protecting delicate, vulnerable, real feelings. To be imploded with external and internal reality is a brutal experience, which intimidates one's emotional stability. The well-integrated psyche takes over as moderator of conscious and unconscious experience, and automatically denies, represses, and compensates for all feelings that may threaten the emotional economy. To further complicate this process, the quantum of emotional pain and anxiety that would ordinarily be directed at the self if the truth were known is instead projected outward onto people and objects.

Consider, for example, a stereotypical, outwardly tough, don't-give-a-damn construction worker who expends most of his energy doing jobs that appear to demonstrate his strength and stoicism. Such activities prove to himself and—he hopes—to others that he is not weak, but strong; not helpless, but powerful; not fearful, but fearsome; not a sissy, but "a real man." After work one day, he met his buddies at a bar where he bragged about how much he got done in one day. While boasting, he engaged in arm wrestling and proceeded to drink the others "under the table." As he meandered boisterously throughout the darkened shadows of the barroom, going from the pool table, to the bar, to the pinball machines, he came face to face with a known homosexual male. At once he was overwhelmed by who he is inside, which he had worked hard to deny. Instantaneously, he retaliated in an effort to protect the conscious interpretation of self from the real, unconscious truth. To restore his own emotional balance, he attempted to destroy the messenger of brutal psychological reality. Without thought or provocation, he began to beat up the homosexual while yelling "you goddamn sissy, you fag, you weakling! I'm going to kill your ass!" It took three men to keep him from injuring the homosexual. The power of his internal conflict had existed for a long time, but had been directed toward accomplishing "masculine feats" of strength.

After this episode, the construction worker, because of a history of acting out, was referred to me for psychological help by the county judge. After several months of treatment, he was able to feel trusting and open enough to allow into consciousness what he had been denying for years. Deep within himself, he did not feel strong at all, but weak. He recalled that, as a child and early adolescent, he was called "fatso" and "mama's boy," because he would run to his mother in tears when he was scared or humiliated. He remembered the time at age 15 when he decided to work out with weights so that no one would ever push him around or tease him again. Almost from that moment on, he developed a reaction formation against his real feelings by attempting to be tough, athletic, and emotionally impenetrable. Anything less than his annealed facade left him feeling childish, powerless, and weak. Many times throughout the early sessions, it was not difficult to see that he was responding emotionally to many issues we discussed. Later, as he was able to let down some of his defenses, I asked why he could not let out some of his gentleness and warmth. He responded, "Because I've always been overly sensitive and I tend to cry easily, and I'll be damned if I'd ever cry in front of another man. I cried a lot when I was a kid, and everybody called me a sissy."

As he became more able to accept the unconscious forces within, his own dependency needs also surfaced. Within a short time, he was able to let his wife know how much he needed her, which is what she had been wanting to hear for years. He became a more gentle and loving husband and father. As he resolved his inner turmoil and began accepting himself beneath the level of his reaction formations, he became a more responsive husband, a more enthusiastic father, and far more understanding of homosexuals.

Reasonable mature adults invariably have fewer and less rigid defense mechanisms. Consequently, they are more accepting of themselves and others primarily because their parents were more accepting of them. They are also able to accept nearly all of their real feelings with minimal denial, anxiety, embarrassment, or trauma. They are the more comfortable individuals who have begun life with a trusting, secure dependency upon a nurturing, available, and reliable parent. Acknowledging that one has a reasonable level of dependency is experienced neither as a threat nor as something that must be fought against or denied. Healthy adults are both capable of and recognize the need for reciprocal interdependence. Thus, mature adults, who are capable of trust, openness, and closeness, are attracted to each other. They have little difficulty in depending upon each other fully and willingly, particularly in times of crisis and stress. The simple act of letting go, to become temporarily dependent on a partner capable and willing to provide the nurturance, support, gentleness, and sense of worthiness and security that was once provided by the first love, is the foundation for satisfactory pairing.

Everyone is born helpless and dependent. The mother (or first love) provides the child's basic nurturing needs. As she decreases her effort and supplies, substitutes are provided. For example, as the breast and nipple are discouraged, the bottle and solid foods are encouraged. As the bottle and spoon-feeding are discontinued, drinking from a cup and self-feeding are encouraged. With each separation from mother come more responsibility, more insecurity, more freedom, and more dependency surrogates. If the first relationship is healthy, the child introjects a sense of mattering and support provided by the first love. As a result, the valued child exhibits a conspicuous sense of well-being as well as a reduced *need* to clutch the mother each time he is scared, insecure, or overwhelmed. His coping and organizing capacity (i.e., ego strength) are relatively high.

Inevitably, the healthy child moves away from the mother, returning when he needs her security to restore his emotional balance. Parents who have accepted their own dependency needs usually do not discourage such a return, regardless of the child's age. Since healthy parents had their own needs met rather than denied, they recognize the importance of meeting their child's needs. One of the most paradoxical developmental truths is that ignoring, denying, punishing, or side-stepping a child's needs makes him *more* needy, not less. The child may attempt to punish himself, or to deny or ignore his basic dependency, but later in life these needs will surface in full force.

Similar to the construction worker who was unable to repress his homoerotic feelings in the presence of a homosexual male, are the parents who climb the walls when their child displays unabated dependency needs. Many times over the years, I have had the opportunity to witness what I call *dependency panic*. A parent's dependency panic typically occurs at home, at social events such as picnics, in the supermarket—almost anywhere but in my office. Most often, it occurs when a parent is depressed, agitated, alone, and in a general state of low strength. The parent's low strength has been caused by unconscious feelings of alienation, and the conviction that no one really cares. Secretly, the parent wishes he had someone strong to love him, take care of him, and to be dependent upon. Even the kindest, most sensitive, and mature parents are not capable of offering much emotional comfort to their children when they themselves are stressed. Often, they insist that their child "grow up" or "get away" when what the child needs most is to cling to the parent with a helpless dependence.

The full force of the dependency panic is stimulated when the child's seemingly endless crying penetrates the deepest layers of the parent's psyche. The crying renders the parent incapable of denying his own tearfulness, helplessness, and need to be nurtured. Much like the worker who attacked the gay "intruder," the dependency-panicked parent wishes to destroy the messenger child who brings the parent's most painful unconscious needs into awareness. Sadly, a child's helpless crying has caused some parents to abuse and even kill their child as a desperate attempt to stop the intrusion.

Some adults, although bombarded with the reality of their dependency needs, have been rigidly socialized against acting out. So they act in. Instantaneous depression, migraines, backaches, headaches, or other somatic complaints and illnesses allow a temporary and socially sanctioned regression. While ill, they have social permission to be as helpless, irresponsible, and dependent as their child. Their pain and hostility are very real, but are directed inward so that no one can see them, thus preserving the integrity of their conscious self-perception. Interpretations from spouse, children, or friends that the illness might be psychosomatic are rejected as violently as the homoeroticized male rejected the gay person. To convince disbelievers that their illness is not psychosomatic, such people sometimes get sicker, thus commanding nurturance, caring, and protection from family, neighbors, and physicians, who after a while tend to give reluctantly.

Overdependence

In contrast to the person who must endlessly avoid awareness of his dependency needs is the individual who perpetually avoids or distorts reality in order to remain overly-dependent. The overly-dependent adult has frequently been an overprotected, unconsciously rejected child. In addition to serving as a special, idiosyncratic symbol for the mother or the family, the overdependent adult was made to feel guilt over assertive self-expression by an overcontrolling parent. The special purpose that the child's existence symbolized is deeply buried and often inaccessible to analysis. Sometimes, a child represents a stabilizing force in a faltering marriage, or a hope for the parents' unrealized dreams, or a vicarious lover to the parent of the opposite sex, or a scapegoat for the family pathology, or continuation of the parents' name and heritage, or proof of the father's virility, or someone to love the unloved parent. Sometimes, he represents the only reason the parents remained together.

Whatever the reason for the child's symbolic specialness, it loses its impact as he matures and begins to resist parental control. To preserve the symbol in the child, parents find it necessary to inhibit the child's natural abilities, desires, and ambitions. Parents also suggest that the child could not get along without their guidance. Throughout the early years, the child learns that mother is right, and to receive her love it is necessary to be extremely good (i.e., to be submissive). The hurt and anger that accompany all forms of oppression of one's natural expressiveness does not find release in overt retaliation against the parents. Consequently, the child forces himself to swallow the pain and suffer quietly, often through a variety of obscure somatic complaints.

The specialness is preserved in the child through guilt and affection for the child's "goodness." Typically, the child goes through life overcontrolled, denying reality and his own feelings in order to prevent punishment and censure. His omnipotent and omnipresent parents remain overinvolved in his life. Important decisions are made by the parents, while insignificant decisions "could possibly be handled by the child himself." Phobias, anxiety, severe depressions, and psychosomatic symptoms are preferred mechanisms for coping with stress because "they don't hurt anyone but the self." Unable to make decisions or to assert themselves for their own benefit "because it is selfish," overcontrolled people are relegated to a life of passive, overdependent submissiveness. Their fantasies are filled with grandiosity and sadism, which frequently become confused with their distorted and idealized conception of reality. Helplessly dependent, they are attracted to self-righteous and autocratic ideals and individuals who promise to care for them exactly as their parents did. They usually find partners who are willing to control, punish, and make them feel guilty, but who are unable to see in them the original specialness that evoked the parents' positive relatedness.

Closely related to the "special" child who is overly-dependent and who expects that someday he will be valued for that vague sense of specialness, is the narcissistic individual who creates his own semblance of external specialness to compensate for underlying feelings of blandness, nothingness, insignificance, worthlessness, and incompetence. Blatantly rejected (usually by both parents), as he grows older, his only recourse is to rely heavily on autostimulation and autoerotic fantasy. Because he feels insignificant, he promises himself that "no one will ever treat me like nobody again." Set on automatic pilot toward this self-fulfilling prophesy, he becomes egocentric and self-absorbed to the point where there is little or no strength left to be genuinely concerned with the feelings or welfare of others. Mildly rejected before age 3½ and severely rejected or ignored thereafter, his relational style is to render people as worthless and to ruthlessly use them for self-gain. The relentless internal drive that pervades his entire character often leads to unusual accomplishments and success in terms of social recognition. Inside, however, he does not have the capacity to enjoy his life or accomplishments. His successes are empty symbols that "prove" to himself and everyone else that he is not what he really is.

The narcissistic individual appears to be dependent upon no one, but is dependent upon everyone—at a distance. He attempts to win the admiration and affection he never had by accruing possessions and fame, which he believes everyone wants. Due to his pompous vanity and emotional emptiness, however, he is often rejected and scorned by those he needs most. Proud of his achievements, he uses them merely as indications of power to cover the shell of emptiness. To further compensate for his real feelings of nothingness, the narcissist strives for a position of control, power, and aggrandizement. Eventually, he fails at what he really needs for contentment, mainly because he cannot relate to the people he desires to own. In his presence, his subordinates may pay him deference, but, behind his back, they sneer at him and attempt to undermine his interests because they resent being treated like objects. Due to his insatiable need for dependence, the narcissist makes infantile demands upon his employers, spouse, or children for the attention and caring that he did not receive from the first love. His subordinates pay superficial homage, which is void of feeling, but which is better than nothing.

When narcissistic individuals accelerate to positions of power, they usually surround themselves with empty, detached automatons of similar ruthlessness. Emotionally healthy individuals leave their employ, or are fired because they fail to show proper respect and admiration. A meaningful relationship or satisfactory marriage is not possible for these people for they are incapable of positive relatedness. Even minimal closeness induces anxiety and an almost overwhelming panic because of fear that the intimate will see the vacancy beneath the facade. The narcissistic individual can only relate from afar and usually pairs with empty but glamorous individuals whose primary role is total devotion, submission, and blind compliance. For example, narcissistic men unconsciously desire gorgeous robots similar to the electronic slaves cited in Ira Levin's novel, *The Stepford Wives*.

Narcissistic women take one of two routes in their pairing. Most often, they pair with a passive-dependent man who has deep feelings of insignificance and ugliness. His self-esteem is temporarily elevated by his attractive and self-centered partner, while she receives a captive partner who worships her and is of little threat to her frail self-concept. The second, and less common, route is to pair with an equally narcissistic man. Invariably, the relationship is stormy and chaotic because narcissistic people need to have other, less conspicuous people worship and obey them.

Reversals of Dependence

Dependency needs can also be reversed. This is commonly done by those who long for dependency but avoid it, because they have no one to depend on, they have always been in the "rescuer" role and/or they are too paranoid to be dependent. Reversals are most common among helpers of people, such as physicians, lawyers, nurses, psychiatrists, psychologists, social workers, teachers, and clergy. Unable to accept their own dependency needs, some helpers deny them, develop a pseudo-sense of superiority, and proceed to let the unfortunate know that they couldn't function without their help. Although basic feelings of inadequacy, powerlessness, and insignificance do not vanish by wishful thinking, they can be partially denied by forcing others into a dependent role. If one cannot be interdependent with his spouse, he tends to unconsciously force those who are in need of help into a humiliating role of coerced dependence. The message transmitted to the client or patient is that the omnipotent helper is in charge, should be feared, and can make things happen. The possessiveness observed among such helpers when their clients, patients, students, or congregation wish to find another helper is a classic example of how dependent the helper is upon the one in need. Irreversible damage may be done to the client or patient by a helper who is unable to be interdependent upon colleagues who are more competent or specialized. To ask a colleague for help is to confirm the inadequacy, powerlessness, and worthlessness that they deeply feel, but deny.

Reversed dependency can be observed in many marriages. The more unhealthy the need of one partner, the greater is the likelihood that the other partner* will be menaced into the role of a helpless, worthless victim.

Psychologically, the more unhealthy partner feels highly inadequate and desires to be taken care of, but is too mistrustful to be dependent. Consequently, he tends to force his partner into a passive, helpless dependence and derives gratification and pseudo-self-esteem from such one-upmanship. Over time, however, after seeing his spouse so helpless and dependent, the truth about his own real dependency begins to penetrate his consciousness. Similar to the construction worker who attacked the homosexual when his own unconscious was threatened, the more dominant spouse begins to turn his anger toward the partner. His anger surfaces regularly because he is certain the partner does not love him

---

*This partner is often reasonably healthy. Frequently, healthier people can be easily maneuvered because they have a high ability to trust.

properly. The anger is further heightened by the realization that he will never get the "love" he so badly needs.

When a child is born, it is helplessly dependent upon a nurturing and responsible adult for its emotional and physical survival. As shown in this section, children who cannot make a secure initial attachment to a significant adult either become psychotic, or, in extreme cases, may become depressed, give up, and die. As adults, we are also dependent upon the caring of at least one primary attachment figure in order to feel complete and psychologically comfortable. Over the period of time from birth until one establishes a central relationship with a partner, one's capacity for intimacy is determined by the quality of the first intimacy. It is commonly recognized that one needs social and intimate relationships to feel enthusiastic about life. It is not so commonly known that the capacity for intimacy is relative. The more trusting, open, and satisfactorily dependent the first relationship was, the greater is the likelihood that one may later enjoy a sustained and satisfactory relationship with a mate.

3 / Characterological Influences

There be three things which are too wonderful for me, yea, four things which I know not: The way of an eagle in the air; the way of a serpent upon a rock; the way of a ship in the middle of a sea; and the way of a man with a maiden.

Proverbs 30:18-19

While writing this book, it was necessary for me to structure my days with a firmness of discipline not known since graduate school. To reward myself for this torment, I stopped each morning for coffee at a local restaurant. While sipping my coffee and reading the daily newspaper, it was not uncommon to be asked why I "wasn't working." When I replied that I had taken six months off to write a book on the unconscious motives behind mate selection, a variety of reactions were elicited. Almost everyone thought it an intriguing subject. Some proceeded to talk about the pitfalls of marriage and of their own desires to return to the "good old days" when their relationship was more passionate and had fewer responsibilities. Others, the self-proclaimed psychiatrists, thought it necessary to "set me straight" on the subject, and talked at length about the reasons people pair, while I listened amusedly. Some exclaimed, "Geez, that's really an interesting subject. I can hardly wait to read the book so I can figure out why I got married!" A few labeled me as mildly diabolic for meddling in the sanctimonious will of the Lord.

Overall, I was surprised to see the number of people willing to share fairly personal issues without the slightest provocation. A recently divorced individual, for example, struggling to hold back his tears, said, "God, before I divorced my wife, we fought everyday about how miserable we made each other. Now that I've been divorced a year, I know what it really means to be miserable. I'd give my right arm to be with her and the kids." Tears trickled down his cheek as he continued. "But, she remarried a few months ago, and now I'll never get her or the kids back." Empathizing with his pain, I touched his hand and looked him in the eye. It seemed clear to him, I think, that I understood, and he sauntered away.

Troy, a successful businessman, upon hearing the title of the book, said excitedly, "I was nothing before I got married. I was barely making it through college and was really a goof-off. I was quite a mess, but when I met Julie, I immediately knew she was what I needed to be complete and to help get me moving. In fact, I don't know if it's normal or not, but ever since I was fourteen I looked forward to the time when I could get married and have a family of my own." Then, he shared his theory about how opposites attract. Although he was unable to specify what he meant by "opposites," he was aware that, psychologically, he and his wife were much different.

There are two common hypotheses regarding attraction and partner selection. Some theorists speculate that opposites are attracted to each other and have the most satisfactory marriages. Others believe that those most similar have the highest possibility for a satisfactory relationship. In actuality, each is partly correct, depending upon whether one is postulating external (social) factors or internal (psychological) factors. It was shown in Chapter 1 that individuals similar in social class background, intelligence, education, attractiveness, and purpose in life are more apt to meet and eventually pair. The "social" theorist, then, is correct in assuming that *similarities* attract. In Chapter 2, the qualities of human relatedness were presented. It was shown that the more *similar* individuals are in their capacity for intimate and genuine relatedness, the more apt they are to be attracted to one another. Thus, the "psychological" theorist is also correct. In this chapter, the character *opposites* that are found in all satisfactorily paired couples are presented.

The elated compulsion toward another, labeled as "love," is motivated in part by the fact that the partner meets unconscious needs and in part by finding a replacement for the lost first love. Unconsciously, people have a powerful attraction to those whose character structure is exactly opposite their own. Feelings of wholeness, unity, power, and direction reported by those in love evolve from the attachment to, and symbolic possession of, an individual with opposite character traits. The emotional fit between two individuals with opposite character traits provides each partner with what is missing or underdeveloped in his own personality. The completeness realized by a perfectly opposite fit offers the potential for emotional security, satisfaction, and a stable energy base from which to grow and develop. Fairly healthy to mildly neurotic individuals who have been satisfactorily paired over a number of years become conscious of the opposite character traits of their spouse as their greatest asset, a complement to their own emotional stability and maturity. Conversely, emotionally unhealthy individuals view the opposite character style of the partner as the nucleus of disharmony and conflict. Because paranoid features are present in all pathology, such people often interpret the opposite character styles of the partner as deliberate harassment, insensitivity, and validation of suspected incompatibility.

THE OPPOSITES

Character traits are similar to one's capacity for intimacy—both are resistant to deliberate change. In fact, the capacity for intimacy, although highly impervious to natural alteration, can be changed through psychotherapy or traumatic experience more easily than can basic characterological response patterns. Fundamental character styles develop early in childhood and are reinforced throughout life. They are the confluence of heredity, physiology, psychology, and environmental factors. Each character trait is part of a larger constellation, which I call the *character style* or *response style*. Simply stated, the two character styles that hold mutual attraction for one another are (1) depressive types and (2) manic types. The remainder of this chapter delineates the unconscious necessity of oppositional character traits for growth and development. In addition, it discusses the inherent problems encountered in living with an individual who on one hand is unconsciously necessary and on the other hand may be, consciously, antagonistic. The destructive component of each of the traits will also be discussed.

Character style is most evident in the way one copes with anxiety, conflict, and insecurities, irrespective of where one is or whom he is with. Very early in life, usually by the time an individual is eight years old, he develops a pattern of coping that is carried for a lifetime. As the constituents of the manic and depressive character styles are delineated throughout this chapter, many readers will recognize their personal styles and the style of their partner. In addition to the basis of intimacy that determine one's capacity for sustained positive relatedness (p. 38), the opposite character traits of the partner provide each with the incomplete or underdeveloped personality factors necessary for psychological growth and maturity.

Figure 3 shows the six character opposites found in nearly all satisfactory relationships. Individuals in the healthy to mildly neurotic range of adjustment have the uncanny ability to select a satisfactory partner with a perfectly opposite character style. That is, the partner's initial response to crisis, anxiety, stress, and conflict is conspicuously different from his own. When oppositional character styles are bound by a secure attachment over time, an emotional balance is struck that helps each become more than

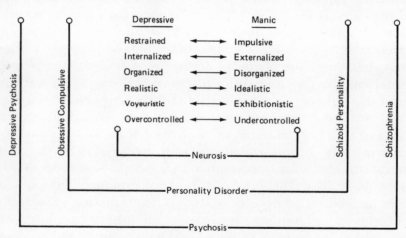

Fig. 3. Opposite character features.

what he could have been alone. For example, depressive types are unconsciously attracted to manic types, and vice versa. In the severely neurotic to personality-disordered range of adjustment, obsessive-compulsives are attracted to the schizoids and vice versa. In the psychotic range, depressive psychotics and schizophrenics find each other most attractive. Thus, as suggested in Chapter 2, people unconsciously select partners who have a corresponding degree of health or pathology. The manic types (i.e., schizoid and schizophrenics), however, more frequently display their symptoms and therefore *appear* more disturbed than their spouses, whereas depressive types (e.g., obsessive-compulsives and depressive psychotics) tend not to show behavioral disintegration even under extreme anxiety and internal pathology. Therefore, socially and behaviorally, they appear to be more healthy and appropriate than do their manic partners, especially when they are away from "home."

Healthy to mildly neurotic individuals are attracted to each other, while personality-disordered people are attracted to other personality-disordered individuals.* Similarly, psychotics are usually attracted to psychotics. There is more than a morsel of validity to the worn-out maxim, "Tell me who your friends are, and I'll tell you all about yourself." A depressive neurotic, for example, may be initially attracted to a schizoid personality but will eventually become aware that something "isn't right." The schizoid, due to a relatively continuous state of overt anxiety, activity, loose thought associations, and overall unpredictable and unstable behavior, would tend to overwhelm a healthy-range depressive. Similarly, something would "not feel right" for the obsessive-compulsive personality while becoming involved with a schizophrenic. Neither would feel the "click" of the relational qualities despite the initial psychological attraction for one another.

Some years ago, while consulting with the staff of residential treatment facility, I had the opportunity to work with many adolescent patients and their therapists. Most of the patients are now in their twenties, and I occasionally hear from a few of them. Debbie, who was extremely schizoid as an adolescent, and is still

*See Chapter 6 for a detailed discussion on the levels of psychological adjustment.

working on her growth with professional help, calls me every few years to share her recent struggles and victories. The last time she called, she shared a noteworthy example of preconscious ambivalence about relational qualities and character traits. "Do you remember Dan? Well, I still go out with him occasionally. We have a good time and all that, but I am not in love with him. It just doesn't feel right. I'm kinda mixed up though, because deep inside something tells me he would be best for me. But he doesn't turn me on the way Steve does. It's the weirdest feeling. Something tells me if I keep getting better, I'm going to really fall for Dan. But right now, it's Steve. I also know the worst thing I could do is to be involved with Steve, but it feels right." Preconsciously, Debbie is aware of the discrepancy between Dan's and Steve's levels of health. Dan, being fairly healthy, was unable to provide enough pathological material to give her the right feeling. On the other hand, Steve, who was borderline psychotic, is crazy enough to provide Debbie with what she presently needs to feel right. Because she is exceptionally bright and sensitive, Debbie knows something is "wrong" but can't quite place it. Something within also tells her Dan is healthy and that someday she might be ready for him.

The specific traits included under the generic *depressive type* and *manic type* are closely related but distinct facets unconsciously required by the psyche for emotional completeness and balance. Depressive types are emotionally restrained, internalized, organized, realistic, voyeuristic, and overcontrolled. The depressive psyche finds its missing components in the manic who is as impulsive as the depressive is restrained, as externalized as he is internalized, as disorganized as he is organized, as idealistic as he is realistic, as exhibitionistic as he is voyeuristic, and as in need of control as he is controlled. Disturbed individuals, of course, nearly always have a distorted sense of reality. In severely disturbed couples, because of their chronic state of emotional turmoil, the realistic-idealistic trait must be cautiously considered, as each grossly distorts whatever "reality" they perceive.

MANIC AND DEPRESSIVE TYPES

In satisfactory marriages, the manic partner tends to cope with anxiety, insecurity, and conflict by conspicuous activity. Whether the activity takes the form of verbalization, excessive chatter, physical work, or other muscular involvement, the purpose is the same: to deny painful anxiety in an attempt to secure emotional equilibrium. Reasonably healthy manics are able to restore emotional balance fairly easily because imbalance is usually related to events in external reality. Unhealthy manics, on the other hand, are seldom able to obtain emotional harmony from their activity because much of it comes from chronic intrapsychic conflict and crisis. The only time they feel emotional harmony and calmness is with the aid of alcohol or drugs or while asleep. The manic types need a mild humdrum of activities in which to invest their excessive anxious energy. Because of their emotional responsiveness to a wide variety of stimuli, they may be seen as enthusiastic leaders who "never seem to run out of energy." They enjoy being active and, in fact, are unable to settle down. Nearly everything they do is done quickly, and their underlying sense of urgency sometimes causes them to judge less anxious individuals as lazy or lethargic. External reality does not necessarily force them into a frenzy; internally, however, they need to hurry in order to keep ahead of (i.e., deny from consciousness) anxiety and feelings of guilt.

Manic types are easily bored and notably restless. Nearly always in a mild panic, they quickly become agitated and depressed when circumstances force them to slow down. Clinically, their high energy and activity level, in addition to warding off anxiety, also serves to ward off an underlying depression, which manic types begin to experience as soon as their activities diminish and which they refer to as "boredom."

Because of their high activity level and effervescent mannerisms, manics tend to be relatively conspicuous. The presence and recognition of others is rewarding for manics as they often delude themselves that they are interesting and unique. They frequently admire themselves for these qualities, which others may or may not see. Since manic types are propelled toward immediate action when exposed to emotionally arousing stimuli, there appears to be a direct, reflexive, and almost open channel between emotional stimulation and activity. Unable to contain impulse, they tend to act or speak first and sometimes think later. In less socialized individuals, whose activity preference is more physical than verbal, their behavior exposes their infantile development. Schizoid and schizophrenic individuals from the lower socioeconomic class, for example, show their physical expressiveness in violent temper tantrums, episodes of turbulent verbal attack, and unrestrained physical "acting out." Even healthy-range manics recognize frustration over their expressive impulses and wish they could be less expressive. Desirous of an alliance against their own acting-out, poor judgment, and in essence, themselves, their compromise is to pair with someone who is characterologically opposite.

For every manic in a satisfactory relationship, there is a depressive who provides a contrary and stabilizing balance. Depressives are frequently unaware they are depressed, even though they are able to acknowledge a relative emotional blandness or uneventfulness, which they prefer to call "maturity." Similar to the manic who is not always hyperactive, the depressive's mood is not *always* anemic, hollow, and flat. In fact, at times, he might be excitable and spirited. His primary reflexive tendency, however, is toward emotional squalor.

Psychologically, the depressive's immediate response to anxiety, threat, and insecurity is to attempt to block it from conscious thought by intellectual processes. Affective stimuli are seldom experienced as emotions or feelings, but as massive painful intrusions, which must first be analyzed. Piece by piece, detailed information about emotional events is stored in the memory and slowly dissected for logical and intellectual analysis. As each fragment is emotionally defused and rendered harmless, additional details are sought for further organization and examination. Such facts are the necessary barrier to emotions. They prevent genuine feelings from penetrating the depressive's consciousness. Only after emotions have been reduced to nearly harmless trivia are they allowed in. Depressives do not have the open stimulus channel of the manic, nor can they throw emotional stimuli out of the psyche for relief. When asked how they feel about something, they tend to offer minute details about an emotional event or to respond with an automatic "fine" because they seldom know how they really feel. They usually know they are boring, and so they are attracted to and identify with a manic partner, who also wants and needs emotional arousal in order to prevent boredom and depression.

When their emotional stimulation is too intense, depressives frequently become unable to organize, shut out, or de-emotionalize the input. Because of their history of attempting to handle their emotions by intellectual overcontrol, they have difficulty mastering emotionally charged issues. Because of their fear of emotional arousal, they are seldom able to grow and mature. Unable to successfully integrate emotions and intellect, they have little choice but to become dull, lethargic, detached, and withdrawn in situations requiring an immediate emotional response. If their spouses or children, for example, display unmodulated emotion, depressives automatically withdraw and come out only after it is safe.

The most severely disturbed depressives become caught by their own defenses. Due to the years they spent shutting out emotions with their overworked intellectual controls, something tragic occurs. They may have indeed blocked emotions from consciousness, but in the process they have also shut out feelings of pleasure and vitality from their lives. For some, living has been reduced to a stagnant blandness, which they claim to enjoy more than being controlled by emotions as some people are.

Established first as a defense against anxiety and overwhelming emotion, intellectualization has worked too well. For the severely disturbed depressive, all emotional input has been obfuscated by fact, details, and self-deceptive logic. Living has been reduced to apprehensive toleration. Dead inside, these individuals become annoyed and even enraged by anyone in their environment who is too alive. Their children are made to feel guilty and/or are beaten into the same quiet submission that precipitated their own vapid emotional lives.

Disturbed depressives may be busy, industrious, and fairly energetic as long as arousing emotional experiences do not intrude. They do not accept surprises of any type gracefully as they are unable to control and organize the input so that they can deal with it "properly." Emotion that enters their awareness too fast tips the psychological equilibrium off center to such a degree that they become even more frightened. During rare moments of loosened intellectual controls, they panic at the thought of how easily they could let go of all controls and become the helpless children they are inside.

When emotional situations are too provocative, the depressive carefully seeks an overload of nonessential details and facts to camouflage the original emotion and keep it from entering the consciousness. Thus, the intensity of the anxiety—caused by too much emotion—is negated. In about the same proportion as the manic attempts to fight off anxiety by ignoring realistic facts and essential details, the depressive carefully gathers more knowledge and more information. This intellectual preoccupation prevents feelings from penetrating consciousness. Nevertheless, there exists a relatively continual state of emotional pain. In cases of severe pathology, the level of pain is sufficiently high that the intellect must work hours of overtime, assiduously churning ideas, facts, and laborious details. When a sudden emotional situation impinges in full force, the psychosystem becomes overloaded, and one of those rare but memorable temper tantrums occurs. The deeper the pathology, the more frequent the tantrum must be to alleviate mounting tension. Because emotions have as much trouble being released as they do being recognized, an agitated depression is almost always present, which taints nearly all of life's experiences.

Despite their "mature" exterior and firm behavioral organization, depressive types are no more emotionally mature than manics in a similar range of adjustment. In fact, their stoicism alone is a major clue to understanding exactly what it is they are trying to protect. They are convinced that feeling and emotional display are out of place and immature. As any schizoid individual can acknowledge, arguments with an obsessive-compulsive partner carry an underlying theme of condescension and righteousness. Righteous individuals believe that it is not only wrong to feel, but also to ever admit they are wrong in an argument. Expression of emotion is not only frightening, but it is also viewed as morally, spiritually, and psychologically "wrong." Some of the more sadistic obsessives rile their already too emotional schizoid partners so that they can then disparage them for being so "unstable." They obtain a temporary lift in self-esteem because they are "too well adjusted to cry and feel."

John, a bright, obsessive-compulsive lawyer came to me for psychotherapy because his physician had partially convinced him that his stomach irritation and colitis may have had a psychological origin. Although he refused to believe it, he came to me anyway in order to prove his doctor wrong. As is typical with obsessives, the sessions were dull and boring because of the lack of affect and the underlying sadistic hostility that override any positive feelings between patient and therapist. Finally, after several sessions, I shared with him what he had believed all along. I said, "You know, I never told anyone this before, but I am really the crazy one in need of help. How would it be if you became the therapist and I became the client for a few sessions?" Since he believed that the problems of the world were due to the fact that people were immature and stupid, my breech of professional protocol readily confirmed his biases. I sat in his chair, in the same way he did, and tried to identify his feelings. When I was able to experience some of his pent-up emotions, I felt overwhelmed, scared, and tearful. As a few tears rolled down my face, he interrogated me with a harsh, "Why are you crying?" I tried to understand the feelings so I could share them, but I could not. So I replied, "I'm not sure. As I tried to empathize with how you might feel, I became terrified and tearful." As I reached for a tissue, he began to sob. Shortly thereafter, the moment of truth came when he said, "That's why I try never to feel anything. I'm so damn miserable inside, I'm afraid if I feel anything I'll become uncorked. If I ever started crying, I might never stop."

Because of their more satisfying childhoods, depressive types in the healthy to mildly neurotic range are not nearly as pained and hostile as the obsessive-compulsives or the depressive-psychotics. Generally, depressive types can be understood in terms of their relationship with their parents. More often than not, the depressive has identified with one or both of his depressed parents. For example, if the father was a depressive, he too had to limit emotional input to keep himself together—had to suppress by punishment and guilt the natural liveliness and spontaneity of his child. In addition to fearing the depressive parent, the child learned that his own value was in "being good," which meant quiet, orderly, clean, and cooperative. In essence, his goodness was based on being a nonperson. Parents appreciated the child more when he was not there—not physically and not emotionally. (Metaphorically, he was appreciated more when he was "dead" than alive.) Consequently, while under stress, the adult depressive does what he did during childhood: he becomes quiet, orderly, meticulous, and emotionally absent as a maneuver toward emotional restoration.

An examination of the marital relationship of Troy, the successful businessman, cited earlier in this chapter, shows that his wife,

Julie, is as depressive as he is manic. Troy's emotional responsiveness sometimes causes him to become carried away. As he presents grandiose intentions to Julie with the enthusiasm and optimism that only a manic can muster, she becomes overwhelmed, anxious, and emotionally constricted. She efficiently organizes his input while soliciting detailed information. By the time she has the input properly sorted, Troy's enthusiasm has been reduced to a manageable level, and he too can see things more realistically. Left entirely to his own, he would be swept away by currents of his own enthusiasm. Because of the poor judgment exercised in all states of mania, he would more than likely have made irreversible and possibly damaging errors over the years. On the other hand, Julie, left to her depressive devices, might have cautiously organized to the point where opportunities would have been lost. Her low level of risk, along with her overly-cautious and deliberate thoroughness, would have rendered her life dull. Julie and Troy are an excellent match. Over the years, in order for Julie to keep up with Troy's activity level, she has had to become more active and emotionally expressive. Conversely, he has become less manic, more thoughtfully organized, and reportedly more efficient. In less than 10 years, each has helped the other become more complete, self-reliant, and emotionally mature.

RESTRAINED-IMPULSIVE

Because depressive types think first and feel later, and manic types feel and act first and possibly think later, there is an automatic counterbalance effect in most successful marriages. Impulsivity, however, is not strictly limited to the manic types, as depressives unconsciously desire days of conspicuous elation in order to alleviate persistent tension. During these times of mania, they may be even more animated than their comparatively impulsive partner. Their short-lived impulses tend not to involve increased disclosure of personal feelings, but are associated with materialism instead. When depressives become enthusiastic and energetic, their underlying fear of people remains, while energy is directed outward, often in the form of impulsive spending. They may buy things for themselves, their family, their spouse, or anyone important to them. Giving gifts, for some depressives, is the only medium available for expressing affection toward the partner.

In some relationships and within certain families, the depressive-restrained adult is disparaged by the partner and children for his conspicuous inability to give emotionally. The physiological tightness, emotional restraint, and uncontainable hurt is frequently experienced by the spouse and children as hostility, anger, and hatred. If the restrained parent is the father, the children naturally fear him and endeavor to avoid contact because they astutely detect his underlying agitation.* So, within his own family, he is often ostracized and despised. Feelings very similar to what made him the way he is are relived. In order to feel worthwhile and valued at all, he needs to place himself in a position of pseudo-omnipotence, tightly controlling his spouse and children by physical threats or economic deprivation. He is not aware that when he is away from home or out of sight, his spouse and children join forces to conspire against him. They not only become more impulsive and recklessly jovial, but they blatantly express their hostility for the father by lampooning his behavior and belittling him.

The overriding atmosphere of fear and hatred toward the depressive-restraining parent lends itself to a perplexing determinism for the next generation. If the restrained parent is the father, for instance, the underlying fear of and anger toward him force the children to unconsciously identify with the more impulsive and manic mother. Because of their fear of the father and their mothers' antagonism toward him, the children become overly attached and dependent upon her. They are well aware that father is a stick-in-the-mud, and it is difficult for them to identify with him when the mother considers him to be of low status and little value. Consequently, they overidentify with the mother and become manic-impuslive types. Unconsciously, the pattern for future mate selection has been established. The manic-type children will be attracted to a partner who is characterologically comparable to the despised and feared father.

Although the manic-depressive dichotomy is observed in the majority of marriages, it may not apply to all relationships. In some emotionally disturbed individuals of pairing age, the hate for a parent runs so deep that they deliberately try to avoid anyone remotely similar to that parent. Clinically, there is not much differ-

---

*Restrained mothers are discussed on p. 74.

ence between individuals who hate their parents and those who, because of hate for and from their parents, hate everybody. When the hate between parent and child is vocalized, the child might make a stubborn commitment to never marry anyone "like my mother" (or "like my father"). To avoid parental likeness, he may deliberately make an error in mate choice in order to prove to himself that they are not what they are. For example, a schizoid individual may stubbornly denounce his attraction for an obsessive-compulsive because he is too much like the consciously despised parent. Instead, he may pair with another schizoid, knowing full well that "it isn't love." Without the opposite characterological checks and balances, the relationship will be inherently stormy and destined for failure. Likewise, an obsessive-compulsive may stubbornly denounce his attraction for a schizoid and pair with an equally stubborn obsessive-compulsive. Their relationship will not be as temperamental as that of two schizoids, but it is sure to be empty, monotonous, desiccate, and perfectly predictable.

The impulsive spouse can seldom understand that the restrained partner would like to give spontaneously of the self, but cannot. Sometimes, problems are exacerbated when the more impulsive individual (here, the wife) becomes frustrated by her husband's restraint, especially while under increased stress, and she accuses him of withholding affection. Threat and anxiety are thus heightened, which forces the restrained husband to pull in further. Occasionally, he may be cajoled or pressured by guilt to *act* more spontaneously or more demonstratively, but it is only an act. Even if his behavior simulates displays of affection, real feelings are withheld except for anger, which sneaks through when one is forced to give what might not be there to give. There is no question that willpower and positive thinking are useful in attempting to remove barriers between people. Trying to change basic character traits by begging, cajoling, or threat, however, is not possible.

Most impulsive spouses are unaware that their restrained partners are inherently resistive. Attempts to change the restrained partner automatically require the same tactics employed by the parents years ago. For example, now, as then, he will respond to threat and pressure by increased resistance and stubbornness. The impulsive spouse is usually unaware that only slightly beneath the partner's surface there are genuine feelings of low self-worth and a great deal of pain. Whenever he tries to change the restrained spouse, his message is exactly the same as it was when stated by the parents, "You are no good the way you are; you must change to be better." For the restrained spouse, acknowledging the need for personal change would represent proof that he was wrong, bad, and worthless all along, which is what he already feels. To protect himself from such an awareness, he must adopt more restraint, orderliness, compulsivity, and righteousness. The compensation is never satisfactory but to give them up would leave the individual with less esteem and more pain.

Material possessions, such as money and other symbols of power, are often an issue between restrained and impulsive partners. If the restrained individual is the breadwinner, he often equates giving love with the giving of money or possessions. Because of insufficient self-esteem and self-worth, to give oneself away would be to give nothing. However, to present a symbol of love through something he has sacrificed for or earned, is to give what he values. It may also represent all that he has to give. More often than not, the restrained breadwinner has difficulty giving even material possessions to spouse and children. When he does, however, he expects them to love, appreciate, and obey him. When spouse and children show inadequate appreciation for his gifts (which they often do), he is angered and frustrated. To not value and appreciate his gifts, is to not love and appreciate him. The underlying theme of retentiveness, with the concomitant attitude of rejection, are what spouse and children respond to, not a few material gifts that are usually given with compulsory injunctions and expectations.

While writing the preceding paragraph, I recalled a family-therapy session that illustrates the attitudes of a restrained father. Psychoanalytically, restrained individuals are said to be fixated at the anal stage of development. Thus, restraint, retentiveness, orderliness, and perfection are labeled as *anal traits*, as they are related to characteristics of the anus.

While in a family session with a charming couple and their three children, it was obvious to me that the husband was the restrained individual, while his wife was the impulsive-expressive counterpart. All of the children were psychologically healthy and expressive, with a tendency toward impulsiveness. As the session moved toward the real issue, the mother and children tried to convince the father to "love them better" by expressing and giving of himself rather than material gifts. As the family let down some of their barriers, all of them became tearful, both out of pain and out of joy that they were finally working on the important issues that would help them live more harmoniously. They all stood and hugged each other while the wife apologized, "Honey, I'm sorry if you feel we are all ganging up on you, but I just want you to feel more alive and more a part of our beautiful family. I know you love me and the kids, but we want you to be more expressive and to tell us you love us sometimes." Everyone seemed elated at this point as they could tell father was listening and responding. The mother continued, "Your money and your job are fine, and we appreciate how well you have taken care of our material needs, but we want more of you as a person." It was emotionally moving for me too as I experienced their energy, affection, and hope for tomorrow. One daughter, a spunky teenager, severed the intensity with a perfectly timed and cogent anal insight, "Yeah Dad," she said, as she got closer to him, "We don't want all your shit, we want you!" The laughter dispelled the tension that is always present during moments of psychological truth. When the father smiled at his daughter, he understood, and, when she looked at him, she knew he did too.

In families where the mother is the most restrained and the father more impulsive and expressive, the children tend to gravitate toward the father as they grow older. Because he is more expressive, more active, and often more giving in interpersonal relationships, the children tend to rely on him and enjoy him more than the mother. Her hostility and antagonism toward her husband, whom she views as a rival, frequently heightens as she loses her children. This is particularly evident when she is obsessive-compulsive and he is in the schizoid range of psychological development. Since young children are brilliantly attuned to their parents' unconscious attitudes, they are driven away by their mother's anger, tightness, and rigidity, and propelled toward the father, who needs his children, sometimes too much. His children enjoy being around him because, when he is in a good mood, his infantile personality and impulsivity are displayed before them. He thus becomes "one of the kids," and with little effort is able to relate to them on their own level.

As the restrained mother "loses" her children, one of her fears becomes realized: she is unlovable, inadequate, unworthy, and boring. She thus becomes more bruised, more doubtful about her abilities, and more hostile. Her unconscious hostility toward her husband is expressed by frequent episodes of passive aggression, refusal, stubbornness, and frigidity.

Because the husband is already more impulsive, and because men in general tend to become more easily aroused sexually, the wife is able to acquire a pseudo-sense of omnipotence and esteem by refusing sexual relations. She achieves minor relief from her hostile impulses by refusing her husband's advances while simultaneously observing his erotic need for her. Since, deep within, she feels unwanted, unlovable, rejected, and unworthy, she is able to derive a sense of being wanted, loved, valued, and needed in about the same proportion she is able to frustrate and have power over her husband.

She is, at one level, aware that she is a "cold" individual who doubts her ability to attract anyone. When her husband approaches her, she sets up the most brilliant of all psychological maneuvers. She creates a double bind to which her schizoid husband, because of his childhood, is already much too susceptible. When he makes sexual advances toward her, she accuses him of only wanting her for her body. Because sex is physical as well as emotional, there is enough truth to her accusation to cause him to be deeply hurt, frustrated, and more in need of human contact to heal his bruised esteem. He therefore attempts to make her feel guilty and to "force the issue" by being excessively rough and impulsive when she does give in. Because she is usually frigid and does not enjoy intercourse, she accuses her husband of being dirty, oversexed, exploitative, and insensitive. From her viewpoint, she creates a classic double bind: "If you really loved me, you wouldn't want to have sex with me."

As the more devious, obsessive-compulsive wife becomes aware of her own dubious logic in the sexual argument, she becomes capable of a myriad of vaginal difficulties. Encompassed within her genital problems is the message that the husband, in his "fit of animal urgency," has damaged delicate vaginal tissue with his despicable penis. Vaginal problems serve two important functions in this instance. They tend to provide medical justification for the wife's previous refusals and simultaneously make the husband feel guilty for his sexual interests, thus validating the vengeful self-righteousness observed in all compulsives. Exceptionally persistent and hostile obsessives who believe that their partner does not love them can even create the need for a psychosomatic hysterectomy.* In such cases, the message is the same, but the ante of self-destruction has been raised to a point of no return. The removal of the vital reproductive organ serves as proof that "she wasn't lying" all those times she refused her husband because she was sore or infected. Beneath the surface is her unspoken, "See the pain you caused with your sexual desire and penis. Perhaps now you will love me just for me, not just because you want sex.

Depressive types are unaware that their manic partners behave the way they do to protect the vulnerable self. When anxious or threatened, depressives pull in further and become angrier when no one comes to provide caring. The manic types push out in an attempt to find anyone or anything that will help repair the bruises and restore balance. The depressives may be considered *internalizers*, while the manics may be considered *externalizers*.

INTERNALIZED–EXTERNALIZED

Internalization and externalization are psychological *processes* that people use to cope with anxiety and threat and also to maintain or restore their self-esteem. When emotionally bruised, internalizers have inadequate defenses against real or assumed attack and punish themselves further with an almost continuous state of depression. Deep within, internalizers are aware of their low self-regard. Whether they are, in fact, as valueless as they feel is inconsequential because they have felt that way since childhood.

---

*I have observed many couples who have changed their interactions with one another following hysterectomy. Overtly, the woman seems more satisfied with the relationship, while the man might develop such psychosomatic symptoms as rapid weight gain. Nevertheless, the area of psychosomatic vaginal difficulty and hysterectomy needs further psychological investigation. This investigator does *not* wish to imply that all hysterectomies have a psychological origin.

When threatened, they become conscious of their feelings of low self-esteem, and immediately withdraw to ward off further anxiety. Secretly, they hope someone with more energy and higher esteem will *come to them* to provide support and understanding. Their internalizing function is clearly an attempt to gain emotional support from others without having to ask.

Due to their unusually low toleration for anxiety and tension, externalizers continually battle to fight off conscious feelings of low esteem and underlying depression. Because depression is painful, the externalizer's activity level is heightened as an avoidance maneuver. Typically, externalizers exert enormous quantities of physical energy to escape inner tension. Their activity level, talents, and whirlwind of projects and plans are multipurpose. The primary purpose is to remain busy enough or noisy enough to prevent conscious acknowledgment of anxiety. While externalizers are busy, the majority of their tension, hurt feelings, anger, and unresolved conflicts can be channeled into productive or not-so-productive activity. Externalizers need people and activity to avoid being alone with themselves. When no one is available, their anxiety and boredom can be almost intolerable.

In disturbed manics such as the schizoids and schizophrenics, the inner turmoil is so high that the person becomes totally absorbed in a nonstop workday. Sometimes, such people need as many as 18 to 20 hours a day to avoid awareness of their intrapsychic disharmony. Life for them is an energetic pandemonium, which almost always involves a full day of activity that in some way is people-related. Their day ends in nearly total exhaustion, which forces them into immediate sleep. However, they usually awaken very early so they can "get going." Immediate sleep prevents the person from thinking about his condition, thus further avoiding conscious notice of anxiety or the underlying depression. Sometimes, the disturbed individual may be unable to unwind at the conclusion of the hectic day, and requires drugs or alcohol to slow down the tumultuous anxiety.

In order to maintain and enhance his self-esteem, the externalizer needs people to believe in him, value him, and admire him. They are the actors in life who are busily enmeshed with their environment, which nearly always includes other people. Under severe anxiety and threat, they *do not pull in* and depend on others to come to give them support; they *go out* in a trial-and-error method and actively seek admiration and caring from people, successes, and social involvement. The more limited individuals may go to great lengths to plan an event or participate in a project that promises but a morsel of attention, because it may temporarily enhance their self-esteem. They tend to feel valued and worthwhile when they are doing something that might result in recognition. Living and enjoying day-to-day experiences is not possible because they are in a hurry to engage in activities that in some way provide recognition or promise for tomorrow. Recognition proves to the externalizer that he is worthwhile, which provides impetus for further perfunctory involvement. Alas, externalizers remain relatively immature because of their ability to deny inconvenient features of reality.

Everyone needs to be needed. The internalizer pulls in, hoping someone will come in after him and bring him out. The act of coming after him reinforces his self-worth. The externalizer is able to avoid reality and consciously disavows anxiety and feelings of low self-esteem. To ward off conscious anxiety, he goes out toward people and attempts to prove to them and to himself that he is highly desirable. Unconsciously, some basic needs are met, and each person becomes more complete in a successful relationship. For example, when an internalizing wife pulls in, the externalizing husband goes after her because fulfilling his need to be needed raises his self-esteem. In that interaction, both are restored. When the externalizer needs support, he is able to distort the reality and deceive himself by aggrandizing his own importance to his spouse.

Ecclesiastes 4:9 simplifies the importance of opposite character dynamics in raising self-esteem and strength in a marriage. "Two can accomplish more than twice as much as one for the results can be much better. If one falls, the other pulls him up: but if a man falls when he is alone, he's in trouble."* Since coping with anxiety and issues of low self-esteem are present throughout daily life, one can easily see why aloneness and emotional destitution exist between those improperly paired.

If two internalizers pair, how does the impasse get restored? Who will make the first move? Whose self-esteem will be raised by making the first helping move toward the equally threatened spouse?

*From *The Living Bible*, copyright 1971 by Tyndale House Publishers, Wheaton, Illinois. Used by permission.

Conversely, when two externalizers pair, the relationship is nearly always competitive, destructive, and mutinous admidst the scramble for admiration and support. Two externalizers will not hold up well together nor are they likely to have a satisfying and stable relationship.

Internalizers are shy, self-conscious, quiet, introspective, withdrawn, and universally attuned to rightness and wrongness of social behaviors. In group settings, they typically remain unnoticed because they fear calling attention to themselves. Throughout life, they have conformed to conventional social protocol and are astutely aware of appropriate and inappropriate behavior. As children, they may have been sufficiently withdrawn so that their parents remember them as "no trouble at all." During their early years, the internalizers were well-behaved, rather modest individuals who were frightened of parents and authority but acquiesced to their demands to avoid censure.* Because of their self-consciousness, attendance at social events makes them anxious and sometimes physically tired. Physical symptoms such as headache, digestive problems, and back pain are common responses to anxiety. Consciously aware of their anxiety around groups, some rationalize it away by "preferring to be alone." Internalizers usually have little to say while in a group because they are afraid that whatever they contribute will either be wrong, unimportant, or open to criticism. Their behavior and social graces tend to be exact and perfected as they quietly derive esteem by comparing their "good" behavior against the "bad" or inappropriate behavior of others.

Small social groups provide an excellent laboratory for identifying the internal and external individual. The anxiety that enshrouds all unfamiliar social settings forces each to become more of what he is. The externalizers are both conspicuous and necessary in small social groups as they are usually the life of the party, dissipating their social anxiety by jocularity, whoopee, and the ability to entertain with sportive banter. If the mood of the party lulls, they will enliven it by creating activities to excite the others. If the party still seems dull, they feel responsible, guilty, and bored, and slowly become subdued by their underlying depression.

---

*During adolescence, they may have acted out because of social pressure or retaliation against their earlier background; however, deep inside, their internalizing tendencies persisted.

Adroit planners of social events are aware of internal–external character traits in successfully paired couples. In party planning, spontaneous comments nearly always include something like this: "We must invite Sharon and Bob for sure. A party just isn't a party without them. Isn't Bob a guy! He just sits there and lets Sharon carry on. They sure are mismatched!"

Internalizers are apt to keep emotions bottled up inside as long as they can. They tend to be passive and submissive, and to rigidly comply with rules of social convention. They are not apt to directly assert themselves against authority, nor are they likely to overtly complain to authority, although quietly they may be most resistive. In extreme cases, an internalizer's self-esteem is so low that he believes he has no right to complain. Some believe that any form of self-expression is complaining. Not only does complaining never do any good, but it is also wrong. Internalizers seldom deal with anger and hurt openly and appropriately because they learned early in life that anger and hostility are the most intolerable, destructive, and vile of human emotions. Decent people not only do not show anger, but they are too healthy to get angry in the first place; instead, they "turn the other cheek." In their quiet suffering, internalizers obtain a mild form of relief and enhanced self-esteem from belief in their righteousness. From their parents they have learned that they are good when they suffer quietly.

When overt verbal and behavioral channels of expression are not available as release mechanisms for anxiety and anger, the destructive constituents of these energies turn inward against the self. Minor degrees of unexpressed anger are seen in resentment and mild depression, while unexpressed feelings of a greater magnitude are manifested in more severe and continuous depression and somatic complaints. Headaches are the most common symptom of unexpressed anxiety and anger, followed closely by stomach ailments and lower back pains. When the severity and duration of unexpressed hostility and anxiety approach pathological proportions, and the individual is not able to overcome stringent social upbringing by expressing those feelings, he sometimes obtains temporary relief through the destruction of a specific organ. The unconsciously selected organ then becomes the focus of hostile emotional energy. Among males, ulcers, circulatory and respiratory problems, lower back problems, and heart attacks tend to be the most common physical expressions. Females suffer headaches including migraines, problems of the reproductive organs, and certain types of tumors.

Internalizers are seldom internal all the time. Their immediate, often unconscious impulse is to withdraw and thus shut out threatening stimuli. However, if the social milieu is conducive to and safe for expression, even vicious feelings can be unleashed. Clinically, children are frequently scapegoats for the internalized parent's misplaced hostility. Since young children are comparatively powerless, their retaliation is not feared by the adult who needs to express pent-up aggression. When the internalizer's feelings need release, any of the child's (or spouse's) behavior that was enjoyed or tolerated yesterday can become the impetus for a tantrum. In pathological families where there is an abundance of pent-up rage and unresolved conflict, children serve a most useful purpose. Since children are so actively involved in living, they offer an unfathomable resource for the displacement of their parents' hostility. Frequently, the parents, despite feelings of guilt, rationalize their displaced aggression by labeling it "punishment" or "discipline."

In both adolescent and extremely immature adult relationships, it may not be possible to detect which individual is the externalizer and which is the internalizer, especially among the learned and more socially sophisticated. In addition, published articles on mental health—suggesting that well-adjusted people are assertive and not-so-well adjusted people are passive (internalized)—further confuse the issue. Some people negotiate their flight to emotional health by pretending to be more assertive and expressive than they really are. Deep within, however, people can only be who they are, and so those who try to externalize anger usually reveal themselves through an inappropriate expression of aggression. Each time these individuals overreact with pseudoaggression, they are, if only for awhile, able to convince themselves that they are nothing like they are.

Pseudoaggression is a natural defense against basic feelings of passivity and internalization tendencies. Deep within the "tough guy" who at every opportunity must prove how strong, nonfeeling, calculating, and fearless he is, and who claims to be the "meanest bastard around," is frequently a whimpering teddy bear. For instance, after their husbands' adolescent energy burns out (usually between ago 30 and 40), wives often become painfully aware that their once-upon-a-time ruffian needs more care and attention than a two-year-old. Age and reality have nullified the energy necessary to maintain his facade. The wife thinks her husband has changed and is no longer himself. Little does she realize that he has not really changed at all. He has merely become himself.

Externalizers are earmarked by their comparative audacity, lack of inhibition, seeming self-confidence, extraversion, and verbosity. Deep within, their real feelings may be quite opposite; due to defiance of reality and to social convention, however, they use external events to acquire internal supplies. Parents sometimes describe their externalizing child as troublesome, sassy, and somewhat defiant. Under fairly stringent parental oppression (e.g., physical control or guilt), the more conspicuous behaviors of the externalizer may not emerge until the individual is away from home and has the freedom to be more active.

Externalizing women who were raised by oppressive and restrictive parents often pair with equally oppressive husbands. Because inhibition of expression is not part of the basic character of such a woman, her life can be most painful and dissatisfying until she is able to break free and become more expressive. When she severs the bonds of control, she derives significant gratification in her acting-out (which is often sexual) and feels more complete and alive than ever. Confusion and disorientation are to some degree lifted, but the longitudinal influence and effort of oppressive parents remain as punitive as ever. The guilt accompanying the acting-out can be traumatic if a woman becomes involved in indiscriminate, almost compulsive, extramarital relationships in an attempt to both expiate her guilt and convince herself that she is not "hung up" but free. The oppressive and righteous husband is traumatized at the discovery of his wife's acting-out and may want her to get psychiatric help for her "illness."

Since anxiety, threat, conflict, and issues pertaining directly to self-esteem are realities of the human experience, successfully paired couples frequently have within their relationship the necessary healing powers for emotional restoration. The internalizer covets the social skills and ostensibly confident attitudes of the spouse and derives comfort and gratification from identification with the spouse. Conversely, the externalizer needs the internalized partner to admire, value, and, in some cases, worship him in order to maintain self-esteem. The healing and restorative system can reverse itself, however, and approach pathological proportions when the partners are unhealthy or when a crisis annihilates the balance of the system. If the internalizer is in the personality-disordered or psychotic range of adjustment, or is damaged by the behavior of the externalizing spouse, the hurt and unresolved conflict will prevent him from offering consistent admiration, acceptance, or even recognition to the partner. If balance cannot be restored by all that has worked previously, the externalizing spouse may seek emotional supplies outside the marriage. A vicious circle then begins: the externalizer moves outside the relationship, paying less attention to the internalized partner, who attempts to control the externalizer, thus driving him further away. Due to the negative mood at home, the outside relationship (e.g., friends, lover, business) becomes more appealing and is invested with more energy than the marriage. Although the couple may remain married, the real attachment is elsewhere.

Within the pathological range of adjustment, basic human needs and expectations can seldom be satisfied because of their duration and intensity. In these relationships, the curative aspect of the internalized-externalized traits found in healthy relationships cannot operate. Instead, the same tendencies may be used to facilitate psychological and, in severe cases, physical extermination. Within the personality-disordered and psychotic range, the externalizers, rather than coming to the rescue of their internalized spouses, can easily destroy them. Their low toleration for stress, along with their astute social ability, manipulative qualities, verbosity, and inability to delay painful impulse, force these externalizers into almost immediate attack upon the spouse. Their relentless blaming, through verbal and sometimes physical attack, is meant to annihilate the partner, and it does its job well. Such unhealthy externalizers cannot be successful in their efforts, however, without perfectly opposite individuals who are capable of introjecting their hostility.

There are hundreds of thousands of "relationships" in which the disturbed externalizer feels compelled to destroy the internalizing partner. Although the conscious intention may be to blame or get even with the partner, it is difficult to predict the extent to which the damaged internalizer can absorb anger and destroy his or her own bodily organs. Clever externalizers have been known to maintain the attack until the only appropriate solution for the internalizing spouse is to die. Whereas the healing qualities of a healthy relationship are powerful enough to precipitate miraculous cures for both emotional and physical ailments, the hostility of an unhealthy relationship is commensurately devastating and can facilitate death.

ORGANIZED–DISORGANIZED

Mark and Shirley got caught in a downward spiral of hurt, anger, resentment, frustration, and destructive relatedness, which had gone on for five days. Previously, their upper limit of antagonism and separateness had been three days. Although neither of them really wanted their quarrel to continue, the timing had not yet been right for them to restore a mutual feeling of caring and emotional well-being.

After the third day, marked behavioral changes could be observed in each of them. Mark became very precise, organized, and automatic; he also became nonfeeling and machinelike. Things out of place—his son's bicycle on the walk, a wet towel on the vanity—annoyed him greatly and added to his resentment for Shirley, whom he expected to keep things in place.

Shirley's behavior also changed. Ordinarily, she was well-groomed and pleasant, verbal, and empathetic. In addition, she was usually a neat and efficient manager of her home and three children. Shirley took pride in her competence as a wife, mother, and homemaker. Mark and the youngsters also enjoyed her efforts, and appreciated them as much as children and husband are able.

On the fifth day of the fight, however, Shirley slept late, instead of getting the children's breakfast and helping them to get ready for school. They missed the bus. Mark had to feed the children, find their clean clothes, and drive them to school. He was late for work.

Shirley, looking haggard, remained in a housecoat nearly all day. Feeling emotionally exhausted, she moped about, watching television game shows and soap operas and eating great quantities of junk food. When Mark came home, he had a brief "tantrum" at what he saw.

He scolded Shirley, who tearfully retreated to the bedroom, and chased the children outside. Then he began to clean the house, slamming cabinet doors, complaining to himself, and hurling silent four-letter invectives at Shirley's laziness. The more he cleaned and vented, however, the better he felt. An hour and a half after he began, Mark's resentment and anger had nearly vanished.

Meanwhile, Shirley, who was crying in the bedroom, could sense Mark's hostility as he slammed his way through the house. She had seen him "carry on" many times before, until she learned to retreat to her room. After a while, Shirley dozed off, and, when she awoke, she felt much better. She showered, dressed, and sheepishly meandered into the kitchen. There, everything seemed bright and sparkling, and in place. The children and Mark were eating dinner, and for some reason life didn't look so dismal anymore. When Shirley joined the dinner, the children gave a sigh of relief that their mother was back to normal. The evening was fairly pleasant, even though Mark and Shirley were unable to look at each other. When the children went to bed—a little earlier than usual—Mark and Shirley apologized to each other and began to talk about what had happened. For reasons unknown to them, their lovemaking that night was extraordinarily emotional and meaningful, as it had always been when the balance of caring and closeness was restored to their relationship.

Mark and Shirley's adaptive mechanisms and processes had operated no differently than they had during earlier conflicts. This time, however, Shirley had never been so disorganized and Mark had not been quite so hostile. During the quarrel, there were a few moments when she thought she could pull herself together, but they did not last long enough for her to mobilize her depreciated resources. She could not legitimately care about anything. Shirley knew Mark would eventually come home, "bitch at her," carry on for awhile, and then organize the household. She also knew she would feel better after the place was cleaned up and after she had cried and slept awhile. Since those were the rules of their restoration ritual, neither Shirley nor Mark paid much attention to the process. After all, it had been that way ever since they could remember.

Although the organized–disorganized traits observed in satisfactory relationships provide a restorative dimension to a marriage, they can also be an ongoing and conspicuous irritant. Despite the psychological necessity for these opposite traits, they are the impetus for recurring conflict. Each partner remains unaware that the manic becomes disorganized and disoriented under stress while the depressive becomes rigid and more organized. Even though the process and reactions are predictable when a couple is angry or anxious and seem worlds apart, each prefers to believe the other is deliberately trying to antagonize. Typically, the superorganized depressive gets a perfect opportunity to exercise his self-righteousness by condemning the disorganized partner for not attending properly to the important issues in life. The disorganized spouse, although hurt by the insinuation, becomes equally retaliative because he feels more well-adjusted than the uptight spouse who often seems traumatized over misplaced trivia. And on it goes, until the couple can restore balance to the emotional insurgence. If they can't however, their relationship may become earmarked by agitation and resentment that cannot be resolved.

Healthy to mildly neurotic individuals are more inclined to accept the "shortcomings" of the partner's character. In fact, they often tease one another about their quirks. A disturbed partner, however, is unable to find any amusement in the spouse's rigid character style. Each is convinced that the partner, when it is best to be logical, either falls apart or becomes rigidly organized. Because the underlying hurt and hostility are so close to the surface, neither partner is likely to appreciate or adapt to the relatively predictable response patterns of the other. Clearly, they cannot learn to appreciate each other's differences.

Relatively healthy individuals such as Mark and Shirley are able to make positive use of their organization-disorganization traits. Inherent in the term *healthy* is the ability for positive relatedness because of the existence of trust, openness, and mutual interdependence. With a good capacity for intimacy as a base for a couple's symbiosis, they are able to accept each other for who they are, even while ensnared in temporary conflict. Emotionally resilient, they are able to forgive and forget. The forgiveness allows again an emotional vulnerability to one another, which secures the return of closeness and positive relatedness. Sustained tension and occlusion of their positive relatedness becomes painful for each because life is conspicuously void and more anxious without the emotional connectedness to the partner.

As we have seen, the manic-disorganized individual is typically the one most able to give of the self while in conflict, whereas the organized-depressive is more restrained. Under significant and prolonged stress, however, when the manic partner becomes too disorganized and helpless, the organized individual finds it necessary to act on the environment, thereby giving of the self. Under conditions of sustained anxiety, the organized individual has little choice but to compulsively restore order to the environment in order to reduce anxiety. In doing so, he is able to provide exactly what the disorganized spouse needs. The deliberate acting on the environment stimulates the healing process. The disorganized spouse realizes that the partner is indeed giving. It is the *act of giving* during periods of compulsive organization that reverses the downhill spiral.

It has already been shown that depressives become more organized under stress. A more detailed psychological account of that process reveals that the establishment or orderliness is an aggressive maneuver that helps to dissipate hostility and anxiety through physical activity. For example, self-esteem is restored when a depressive wife is able to carry out the return of everything in the immediate surroundings to its proper place. Such an organized partner will readily mention how much better she feels when everything is organized. The disorganized husband, on the other hand, who is accustomed to having people give (admiration and love) to him because of his efforts, is now able to receive from the organized partner. He interprets the wife's giving of external organization to their lives as valuable love, which raises his self-worth and helps both of them become revitalized. As emotional balance is gradually restored, the underlying resentment is further absolved by verbal, psychological, and physical intimacy.

Emotionally disturbed couples exemplify the extreme of the organized-disorganized trait. Under even minor stress, disturbed depressives rigidly reject anyone who or anything that upsets established mandates. Not even minor deviations from rules of order are allowed as the individual becomes more conspicuously controlling to keep from coming apart. As the disturbed manic-type spouse becomes more disorganized, he becomes more resentful, more hostile, and more aggressively responsible so that things won't get too far out of control. Hate and hostility, which are the manic's greatest fears, surface, which forces more disorganization and loss of control as he attempts to restore balance. Because disturbed individuals are deficient in the basic relational qualities, trust is not possible, nor is openness, closeness, or interdependency. The hurt, anger, and destructiveness that could be resolved in a healthy couple cannot be easily reversed in the emotionally disturbed. Resentment and hate are omnipresent forces that may persist for days, months, or years. All too often in such relationships, destructiveness is all there is because developmentally that is all there ever was.

Continuously threatened and agitated by anxiety, anger, and resentment, emotionally disturbed individuals are unable to trust or forgive. The mistrust residuals of their first relationships are carried over to contaminate subsequent intimacies. They cannot accept others' apologies for the insensitivities and accidental inconsistencies that result from being human. They interpret such accidental insensitivities and breeches of how they expect others to behave as deliberate impudence that is neither forgivable nor forgettable. Deep within, their own feeling of being hurt and their desire to hurt others are projected outward into the partner. Therefore, if the partner does not keep his word to the letter, the disturbed individual considers it an unforgivable violation and valid proof of the partner's intention to harm and disparage. The basis for mistrust has been set, and it is unlikely that the relationship will ever mature into something healthy and satisfying.

Under threat, depressive types almost always become less expressive, more intellectual, and more rigid and organized. Manic types, on the other hand, almost always become more expressive and more disorganized when threatened. Consequently, the disorganized spouse who desires to communicate with the organized partner amidst conflict will not have much success. As he tries to communicate, his thoughts, feelings, and words will be sufficiently disoriented so that the tight, organized spouse will not be able to understand what the partner is trying to say. The organizer will listen attentively to the words and miss the emotional intention, while the disorganized spouse tries to communicate through emotion and pays less attention to the exactness of the words. The organized partner hears the words and misses the music; the disorganized spouse hears the music yet becomes more disorganized due to the confusing lyrics.

No fewer than half-a-dozen times each year I have the opportunity to work with inherently bright, articulate organizers who, out of necessity, become functionally retarded in the presence of their disorganized spouse. Most often, these are obsessive-compulsive males and their schizoid wives. Capable of organizing and managing large successful businesses during the workday, these intelligent individuals protect themselves from attack, manic disorganization, and emotional chaos at home by developing effective, invisible, sensory inhibitors. While at home, they see nothing, hear nothing, say little, and seem like excellent candidates for the back ward of a state hospital. Unable to separate the meaningful from the meaningless intentions of their spouses nor the relevant from the irrelevant ramblings, their option is thus to perceive and process nothing. To be open to the emotional intent from a schizoid or schizophrenic soon makes one psychologically, disoriented or, in some cases, physically ill. For the obsessive-compulsive who needs exact organization, the loose thought associations and rambling verbalization of the partner are computed as "useless data," and the partner's program is subsequently aborted.

> At the coaxing of a school nurse, a middle-aged couple came to my office to discuss their teenaged son. The receptionist brought the couple in, introduced us, and then informed me that I would have to speak louder because the husband had a hearing problem. When I looked at him, he had that mischievous grin often worn by children who are "caught in the act." The wife then discussed her son, the school, herself, her husband, and her family, in disoriented fashion. With her high-pitched whining, loose thoughts, and inappropriate affect, I had the urge to stuff Kleenex in her mouth. Her ramblings, as well as the underlying hostility she exhibited toward her husband, made it easy for me to understand why everyone thought he was somewhat deaf. In fact, over the years he had had three hearing aids—and had lost every one!

Disturbed, obsessive-compulsive organizers and their schizoid, disoriented partners are nearly always entangled in a venomous subliminal battle designed to simultaneously hurt the partner and protect themselves. Overt battles often erupt when the enemy is tired, vulnerable, or has relaxed his vigilance. Most disturbed couples employ cold-war tactics (both conscious and unconscious), primarily so that they can remain married, while their friends, relatives, and neighbors will be none the wiser. In fact, such couples have found a functional compromise between their different styles of thought and communication. The disorganized individual, for example, *must* chatter about nearly everything and anything without logic, coherence, transition, or visible external stimuli. Sometimes, when a couple has worked at it, the fleeting verbalizations of the disorganized partner can be considered creative, amusing, or interesting by the obsessive-compulsive spouse who has learned to deliberately ignore the emotional intent. If he can appear to be listening to every seventeenth word or so, then an acceptable communication system has been established. Most obsessives, however, are unable to be that loose. Intellectually, they cannot follow nor expediently deaffect the spouse's chatter. Their civilized compromise is to develop a deafness to the massive bombardment of what they consider irrelevant, repetitious nonsense. Even the most brilliant depressives, capable of handling a multimillion-dollar business, can appear to be retarded in their own homes when their disorganized partners try to communicate with them.

Zealous graduate students training to be family and marriage counselors believe that if they can help a disturbed couple communicate, the couple will "become better" and live happily ever after. Although such a positive attitude provides more hope than does pessimism, many students eventually feel depressed and guilty when, for instance, after eight weeks' counseling, a couple's situation seems to be unimproved or even worse. Eager to change the world, such students overlook that most couples have already done the best they can with what they have, considering where they have been. A couple's noncommunicative cold war develops by trial and error over the years and is a functional adaptation they use to protect themselves from each other's wrath. The enthusiastic students, however, convinced they know what the couple needs, inadvertently side with the more verbal and often disorganized partner, and then cajole the other partner into becoming less of what he is and more of what he isn't. The added pressure and anxiety serve to make that partner feel more inadequate, insecure, and anxious, to which the depressive's favorite response is more constraint, obstinacy, and rigidity.

The reader can probably envision the pandemonium that occurs when two disturbed manics pair. In such mismatched couples, the excitability and emotional expressiveness lack a suppressive counterbalance necessary for relationship stability. Without the counterbalancing effect of a significant spouse, who is capable of holding down exaggerated verbal expressiveness, the relationship tends to be anxiously out of control. If the couple, however, chooses to remain paired "until death do us part," each partner is likely to become attached to someone or something outside the relationship that has the potential for suppressing emotional impulses, thereby offering a feeling of psychological stability. Sometimes, the outside attachment is a friend, a relative, a lover, a therapist, or a potential people-helper. The outside attachment may also be in the form of an extreme emotional investment in an occupation that has the potential to direct one's life through a forced role conformity or excessive demands on one's time. The primary attachment may also be a religion or philosophy, which has the integral function of forcing impulse control. Some manics become attached to the accumulation of money. If they devote themselves entirely to the purpose of material acquisition, nothing else is important. Emotions, people, children, and spouse are all irrelevant while one is being controlled by underdeveloped inner controls.

One can also imagine the highly eroticized and tempestuous love life of two manic types. While working with couples over the years, it has become obvious to me that two manic types are often drawn to each other strictly out of their desire for sex. For such couples, a compromise is attempted but never satisfactorily accomplished. They try to tell themselves that the problems caused by their lack of security and stability are worth it because of their vigorous sex life. In actuality, however, the underlying resentment and anger accumulate, and they frequently hate each other. Because each tends to discard intellectual or logical controls when emotionally aroused, their relationship is characterized by an impulsivity that can easily become destructive. The deluge of free-floating anxiety and aggression—which is heightened by mutual criticism and rejection—does not allow either to feel trust or security. Consequently, the relationship cannot mature, nor can either grow and psychologically profit from their involvement. Without the influence of opposite character traits, two manics get caught in their own anxiety and hostility. They have little option but to destroy each other, as well as their children.

One need not be too imaginative to speculate about the life-style of two mismatched depressive types. They may, in fact, have an overly stable and secure but stagnant relationship; however, without a disorganized manic type to add an energetic sparkle to counterbalance the theme of cautious self-oppression, each partner may suffer a hastened emotional or even physical demise. Due to the theme of self-destruction in depressives, when paired, they often grow very old, very fast. (Even when chronologically young, they are usually attitudinally old and stifled.) Growth is unlikely in such depressive couples because of their avoidance of risk-taking and inability to enjoy spontaneous experience. When one's life is organized to the extent that new experiences and the mastery of them are not possible, one's self-esteem and self-confidence must remain low. Mismatched, depressive types may appear to live a quiet, conflict-free existence, but that state of affairs can hardly be called living.

REALISTIC–IDEALISTIC

Humans cannot bear very much reality.   T. S. Eliot

Over the years, it has been increasingly obvious that, in daily living, one's reality is limited to the experiences prevalent in the immediate environment. An individual who places a high priority on growth may need to expand his reality, which frequently requires one to leave behind familiar surroundings in exchange for a new set of experiences. Any major alteration in one's reality that causes a substantial separation from the familiar carries the potential for further growth, as well as for regression and deterioration. The anxiety and pain of separation from the familiar are what keep some people committed (or married) to another, or living in the same area, or working in the same occupation, even when that situation is neither satisfying nor productive. Because life's anxiety is sufficiently high, most people are unwilling to *deliberately* increase tension by separating from familiar reality.

It is the habitual phenomena that formulate the emotional homeostasis within a marriage. Thus, when one partner tries to change the rules, expectations, or desires beyond certain unspoken limits, the other frantically attempts to hold onto previous reality and militates against change.

Consider, for example, an incident from the lives of Abe and Lenore. Abe, a wheeler-dealer, was nearly always attempting to make one kind of deal or another in an overall scheme to "strike it rich." Lenore, on the other hand, was deliberate, conscientious, and cautious with her money. She was content with the money that they had. Naturally, they had frequent arguments about his impulsively seeking high-payoff schemes and her need to be satisfied with what they had.

One day, Abe located what he was sure was the "deal of a lifetime," which would make them wealthy. He tried to coerce Lenore into signing a bank note, which he needed in order to make a sizable real-estate investment. To secure the loan, however, they would have to obtain a second mortgage on their home. He knew that Lenore would be opposed to the deal, but he believed that if he could get her swept up in his enthusiasm, she might let down her guard and sign the note. While emotionally aroused, Abe could easily discard important limitations of reality, and in this case he overlooked some important details in the seller's contract. Caught up in his own mania and by his desire to get rich, he misinterpreted some very important legal contingencies. In fact, if the investment were resold at the price Abe expected to get, he would actually lose money. When he brought the papers home to Lenore, she automatically attempted to counterbalance his enthusiasm for she was extremely anxious about taking out a second mortgage. Under threat, she naturally sought more truth, more information, and, from her perspective, more reality. To get more data, she carefully read the seller's agreement, including the fine print. She also studied the mortgage agreement painstakingly. To allay her anxiety, she *needed to know* everything there was to know about what mortgaging her house would mean to their financial security. As Lenore read on and located important loopholes in Abe's idealized perception of the exact amount of money he thought he'd make on the investment, Abe became furious. Eventually, however, he softened because the final analysis showed that they might have lost a great deal of money and possibly their home.

In nearly all successful relationships, many arguments are launched because the manic partner tends to idealize while overlooking the essentials of reality, and depressives tend to rigidly adhere to an overly-cautious and overly-factual approach to their perceptions of "reality."

Despite numerous attempts by the depressive partner to convince the spouse of his faulty perceptions or unrealistic intentions, manic types never seem to perceive reality in a way satisfactory to the partner. Depressives within the healthy to mildly neurotic range eventually learn to adapt to the partner's distorting of "reality," and may even find such behaviors amusing or stimulating. Some couples have developed a system whereby the manic partner's idealistic plans are discussed in detail, exaggerated, and then eventually abandoned. Talking about illusions of grandeur in detail seems to help the manic partner add a dimension of reality to his other impulses.

Disturbed couples, however, view the battle between realism and idealism as deliberate defiance and further indication of incompatibility. The intensity of their incompatible behavior may reach a point where each believes that the only solution is divorce. Unfortunately, neither is usually sufficiently realistic to recognize that each is likely to pair with exactly the same type of individual again. Although the name, age, occupation, and demeanor of the new partner may be completely different, his soul is likely to have more than minuscule familiarity.

The realistic and idealistic factors in mate selection are understandable when one examines their development. Deep within themselves, depressive types do not want to be so self-conscious, realistic, and appropriate. They often wish to defy social and parental convention, but are afraid to express these feelings in anything but fantasy. As developing children, they were inhibited from being spunky, curious, active, definite, aggressive, and somewhat uncontrollable. Such inhibition was due either to oppressive parents, an overload of guilt, fear of losing their parents' love or a complex matrix of parental ideals that served the same purpose. Because of continuous early oppression of spontaneity and the later identification with equally restrictive parental ideals, the realistic, depressive individual is afraid to defy his upbringing by being what he was trained not to be.

The realistic depressive paired with an idealistic partner derives gratification from two sources. First, he has a partner with whom he can identify. The partner's defiance of reality provides vicarious gratification because of the depressive's own deeply buried desire to do or think similarly. Some depressive types unconsciously encourage their partners toward more idealism and greater grandiosity because it enables them to vicariously participate in those behaviors they have been taught not to participate in. The second area of gratification for realistic depressives is the availability of a conspicuous personification of all that they were taught not to be. Because they have often overlearned the exactness of social "reality," these individuals get a sense of enhanced esteem, albeit destructive, when they compare their own righteous inability to stray in thought or deed with their partner's idealism and "badness."

Childhood development is more subtle and complicated in idealistic, grandiose individuals. The parents use the child to act out some of their own unconscious conflicts and desires. In a very unique way, the child can be an expression of the parental relationship and so is the embodiment of large quantities of free-floating anxiety and ambivalence. Typically, the parents encourage the child to be all the things that are desirable in society, however, the nonverbal (unconscious) message from the parents, encourages the child to defy all that they were telling him to be. Consequently, the child becomes quickly confused under stress and can easily defy reality when emotionally aroused. An accidental side effect of all the confusing parental messages is that the child becomes hypersensitive to the unconscious, subtle motives of others. Unable to trust what the parents said, the child learns to trust what was nonverbal as the real intentions of human behavior.

As children, the idealistic types could not comfortably please their parents because their messages were too ambivalent. As adults, because of their deeply inculcated feelings of rejection and anxiety, they often develop a myriad of conspicuous skills in order to win the love and approval that they could not feel as children. Their fantasies and unrealistic plans are always related to accomplishment or acquisition of something (or someone) that will help convince them they are lovable. Because deviations from "reality" are most often associated with being "crazy"—which is how they feel inside—their unconscious attraction is toward a partner who appears stable and sane. In the case of a disturbed couple, however, after a short period of marriage or sometimes in courtship, the idealist learns that the partner is actually unfeeling and uncommunicative.

Spouses seldom understand that if their manic partner is anxious or bruised, it is psychologically necessary for him to generate grandiose ideas in order to temporarily escape threatening reality by falsely elevating himself. The moment that self-esteem is raised, so is the ceiling on idealistic plans, and the intentions become even more unrealistic. For instance, two manics are most amusing when planning an event. As they stimulate each other with their anxiety, enthusiasm, and defiance of reality, what started out as a molehill becomes a mountain. Alas, such a mountain is rarely climbed.

More often than not, frustration and anger surface when, for example, a realistic wife interferes with her idealistic husband's grandiose strivings. Aware that her idealistic partner has glossed over relevant facts that would change the end result, the wife proceeds to point them out. His bubble thus burst, the idealistic husband becomes emotionally deflated and hostile. As the wife absorbs his anger, she is hurt and baffled by the attack, which seems out of proportion to the infraction of having merely pointed out a few tidbits of reality. Conversely, the idealist cannot understand why the wife finds it necessary to ruin the pleasure associated with his exuberant plans. After all, it was just an idea. Each knows something like this has happened before and will more than likely happen again. Neither knows why.

Emotionally disturbed couples seldom resolve the realistic-idealistic opposition in their relationship. In the first place, "reality," whatever it may mean to them, is capriciously altered by the intensity of their unmet emotional needs. Due to the pain caused by the many thwarted needs and aspirations, external events and responsibilities (reality) become irrelevant. Each partner begins to see what he needs to see, and to believe what he needs to believe, in order to survive. Second, their high level of anxiety, threat, hostility, paranoia, and insecurity, along with their low self-esteem, tend to subvert the couple's already vitiated ability to trust one another. Because living with another person reveals his insensitivities and inconsistencies, disturbed couples are seldom able to accept and adjust to the frailties of being human. In order to ease the psychological pain, the disturbed idealistic partner will continue to try—and often will—carry out his grandiose intentions, while his partner will exert considerable effort to prevent things from getting out of hand. Unable to tolerate the intrusion of detailed inquiry, especially when the "iron is hot," the idealistic partner may become secretive and even devious to prevent the partner from interfering in his attempts to raise self-esteem and magnanimity. Because the depressive-realistic partner has nearly always felt somewhat worthless and left out, being lied to is too close to what made him the way he is. The deviousness in the relationship tends to shatter their already questionable ability to trust. Nevertheless, their inabilty to be trusting, close, open, or interdependent now has valid justification.

VOYEURISTIC-EXHIBITIONISTIC

Within the forces of unconscious motives for partner selection, there exists a peculiar constellation of opposite attitudes, behaviors, and feelings. For the purpose of this section, I will label these character opposites *voyeurism* and *exhibitionism*. Because these words are used regularly in clinical psychology and by the general public, it is necessary to mention that, in the present context, the words are devoid of strict genital meaning. For example, one need not ever have exposed himself (or herself) to be considered an exhibitionist herein, nor need one have gone peeping in windows in order to be called a *voyeur*. Herein, *voyeur* will mean one who tends to vicariously participate in the activities, risks, desires, impulses, and promptings of one's partner. Eventually, such an individual could be considered the *reactor*. By *exhibitionist*, we will mean the more expressive, emotionally responsive individual who seeks out others and who needs them to sanction his behavior. This individual is considered the *actor*. In all satisfactorily paired relationships, one individual—the voyeur—tends to observe life from a second row seat. This partner carefully observes, criticizes, and sometimes reacts emotionally to the exhibitionist partner, who is nearly always on stage.

Some exhibitionists deny the eroticism in their need to be seen and heard. Because of religious, social, or moral conviction, they remain unaware of the seductive quality that pervades their personhood—despite their obsession with the opposite sex and sexuality! They are also blind to the many sexual connotations in their language and attitudes, as well as of the erotic tincture in their heterosexual interactions. Sadistic exhibitionists delight in teasing and arousing their audiences (or partners). Their self-esteem is then temporarily raised when they refuse the aroused partner or audience and then condemn the unusually high number of "immoral people" who make sexual advances toward them.

Most exhibitionists are aware of the eroticism in their strivings for social recognition. Despite the social taboo against being self-centered, many exhibitionists tend to be unaware of their self-absorption and the amount of time and energy they spend on themselves in order to symbolically "seduce" attention (love) from others (parents). Since adolescence, being noticed has been an integral part of their social reality. Whether the recognition is positive or negative, constructive or destructive, is irrelevant. Because the social shaping of an exhibitionist is dependent upon the ability to accumulate recognition from groups of voyeurs, a deep-rooted dependence upon recognition from others becomes necessary in order to "feel right." The exhibitionists' basic craving for nurturance and recognition, which are often scattered among several people or groups, helps them to appear relatively independent. Deep within, however, they tend to feel annoyed and "unloved" when they are without conspicuous voyeurs to reinforce their needs.

Exhibitionists who have limited talent, opportunity, or mobility become anxious if they lose their audience, such as when their friends move away or cease to admire them. They don't recognize that their agitation and depression are directly related to their dependency upon voyeurs and to their feared loss of love. Left to their own devices, exhibitionists seem to profit little from the natural life phenomena that tend to help other people grow and mature. Instead, when anxious, lonely, angry, or depressed, their first impulse is to seek out friends or nearly anyone else and proceed with their "act" in order to gain recognition and support. Sometimes, to their own surprise, their underlying eroticism surfaces forcefully. Fantasies become heavily imbued with sexuality, while sexual encounters, which are attempts to elevate the self, reduce aloneness and avoid the pain of depression. Frequently, their partners become annoyed and frustrated when they realize that, no matter how hard they try to make their exhibitionist spouse feel special, their love and support are seldom enough.

Voyeurs tend to be only partially aware of their overdependence upon their partners. They are almost oblivious to the even stronger dependency needs of their exhibitionist partners, who, while receiving ample recognition from outside resources, can foster the delusion that they "don't need anybody." Beneath the surface, voyeurs derive vicarious elevation of self-esteem, potency, and worth when others value their exhibitionistic spouses. For example, the voyeuristic male enjoys a symbolic erection and a feeling of potency when other men find his exhibitionistic wife desirable, especially if she is "virginally seductive" and unwaiveringly faithful. A voyeuristic female sometimes derives gratification from identification with her exhibitionistic husband's accomplishments. Such living through another often forces an anxious dependency. Her identification with him is partly derived from her knowledge that other women may value her "possession" and may even wish to submit themselves to him. Nevertheless, the man is *her* object, and much of her gratification comes from knowing that others admire and are envious of her as the "owner" of the valuable "property."

The enigma found in all character opposites is this: exactly that which is unconsciously needed by one's psyche to complement itself and to facilitate growth is exactly that which one avoids in order to remain secure. It is thus little wonder that one can be dimly aware of that inexplicable need for the traits of one's spouse, while simultaneously recognizing that they are the apex around which most struggles evolve. Consider, for example, a fairly common occurrence between attached couples, as exemplified by Anita and Zachary.

While at a party, the exhibitionist (in this instance, Anita) needed to "get around" in order to display herself. Because of her problems with idealism and reality, the drinks, the hypnotic music, and the elevated mood loosened her already weak controls, causing her to enjoy the evening "too much." As Anita got "carried away" with flirting and exhibitionist antics, Zachary, her voyeuristic husband, became anxious over his belief that she might abandon him for a new lover. On the way home, anxiety, threats, and anger surfaced as the couple fought about whether Anita had made a fool of herself. Anita vehemently defended her right to have a good time. Zachary called her loose, lusty, and inconsiderate. She labeled him jealous, rejecting, and boring.

The accusations were, of course, correct, but the fight was unfair. For, rather than acknowledge their real feelings, the couple attacked each other with subsurface truisms, which invariably exacerbate threats, anger, and defensiveness. Nevertheless, each was aware that fights similar to this were recurrent. Each was sure the other was at fault. Each knew that they would struggle with the same issue again.

Noncommunicative couples, too frightened to share their feelings with each other, may declare themselves too mature or too emotionally healthy to quarrel. Instead, they agonize inside to prevent an outside struggle. Social events are avoided for any number of seemingly illogical or unacceptable reasons. For example, the voyeuristic husband claims he doesn't feel like going out, while the exhibitionist wife complains because her audience has been severely restricted. As hostility and resentment build, the voyeuristic husband is held responsible for the restricted life space. When tension between them becomes severe and verbal communication sparse, the exhibitionist wife may move out alone seeking display, affiliation, and support. The voyeur remains at home, trying not to think about what his eroticized partner might be doing.

In disturbed couples, the voyeuristic-exhibitionistic traits represent a harsh and destructive counterbalance, which neither partner experiences as helpful or enjoyable. Because disturbed individuals already feel *more* inadequate, *more* insignificant, *more* impotent, *more* helpless, *more* rejected, *more* ignorant, *more* alone, and *more* paranoid than those in the healthy to mildly neurotic range, their propensity toward voyeurism and exhibitionism is also more pronounced. Due to their crippled capacity for sustained positive relatedness, emotionally disturbed couples are forced to go outside the relationship to find whatever they believe to be missing. Disturbed exhibitionists, regardless of the size or status of their audience, cannot make up for the deep feelings of rejection experienced in the first love. Even though the disturbed voyeur needs the partner's erotic display to elevate self-worth, the need backfires because such display increases the possibility of losing that valuable object, the partner. The exhibitionist's flirtatious antics overwhelm the already precarious capacity for positive relatedness, while jealousy and anger accelerate. The war over trust-mistrust, in which each battle serves as further evidence of their incompatibility, continues until the emotional or legal divorce.

Voyeuristic-exhibitionistic patterns can be observed as early as the sixth year of life. Elementary-school teachers are astutely aware of those children who prefer to be part of the audience and those who prefer to be part of the show. Some teachers pride themselves in their ability to help a child "come out more" during the academic year to become more of a participant and less of an observer. Children who are especially talented in the more visible activities may appear to defy their voyeuristic tendencies while they are in the process of becoming more exhibitionistic. Deep within, however, they remain true to their basic core. When allowed to be themselves, they are clearly voyeurs—albeit more confused than if they had been left alone.

During biological pubescence, voyeuristic-exhibitionistic tendencies may be altered and further developed. As adult genital sexuality comes into the forefront, eroticism and seductiveness are added to the adolescent's repertory for acquiring recognition and enhanced worth. In adolescence, some voyeurs reluctantly conclude that looks, glamour, and preoccupation with external events may not be the most important aspect of life and so invest their energies elsewhere. Exhibitionists, on the other hand, conclude— even if they must grossly distort reality—that, in some unique way, they are important, good-looking, or especially endowed. They remain narcissistically invested in themselves and expect others to notice their special qualities. The entire self becomes an eroticized instrument for the purpose of exploiting recognition from voyeurs.

The voyeur-exhibitor character opposites form a complete psychological system for those couples who are satisfactorily paired. For instance, an exhibitor husband has within his domain a loving partner who values and cherishes his display. In addition, the couple's basic trust is sufficient to endure any outside voyeurs the husband might need in order to maintain a satisfactory level of self-worth. The voyeuristic wife, on the other hand, is genuinely accepting of the partner. She learned long ago that it is more comfortable not to be so conspicuous. She also has her own valuable object to admire, applaud, and identify with. Within the healthy to mildly neurotic range, the character traits are relatively modulated and inconspicuous to the untrained observer. Behind closed doors, however, the system is complete, and mutually satisfying.

This symbiotic system works fairly smoothly in terms of reciprocal need fulfillment until one or both change the "unspoken" agreement upon which their relationship was established. If the exhibitor, for example, has violated the basic trust or bruised the voyeur, the voyeur automatically withdraws notice and attention, and ignores the actions of the exhibitor. Without the voyeur to admire him, the exhibitionist's repressed anger, feelings of rejection, and hostility quickly surface. The underlying hostility of the exhibitionist remains on or slightly below the surface, and the couple gets stuck at an impasse. Despite attempts to get back to where they once were, however, it can never be the same. Something important and basic is lost when nuclear trust is violated. It is doubtful that either partner can become close to the other again without professional help.

Betty and Pete, a couple in their mid-forties, came to me for help with their relationship. Pete, the exhibitionist, was extremely depressed because Betty was fed up with him and had filed for divorce. Despite Pete's sincere attempts to emotionally reach her, she had constructed impenetrable shields to protect herself from being further hurt by him. Realizing that they could not even tolerate being in the same room, I saw each of them individually for a few minutes.

In the first session with Betty, I said, "It's obvious that you feel extremely hurt and want absolutely nothing to do with your husband. Would you tell me what happened to cause such agony?"

"When we first got married," she replied, "I enjoyed being with him. Pete was always so energetic, so carefree and fun-loving, and I needed that because I have always had difficulty being carefree. My life until I met him was overburdened with feelings of responsibility. After a few years together, however, I realized that Pete was just a big overgrown baby. Not only did he need my attention all the time, but he also needed the attention of other women. He knew when we got married that I could never handle his having an affair, but he did it anyway. It seemed as though he needed more and more affairs over the years. Now I'm just sick and tired of living that way. It's too hard to be around him and to be lied to and deceived time after time. I just want out."

The impasse in their marriage had occurred many years earlier. As I talked with Pete, it became apparent that he and Betty had had marital problems before he had ever had his first affair. After that affair, Betty was so hurt that she could neither forgive nor forget what Pete admitted was a "terrible mistake." To avenge the breach of trust, she refused to discuss the problem and had shut him out of her life. She also refused to go for professional help. After three years of being shut out, Pete began to have love affairs in order to get the emotional support he needed to feel human. Little did Betty realize that, by shunning Pete, she was encouraging the behavior that caused his initial violation of her trust.

A discussion of the voyeuristic-exhibitionistic character traits is incomplete without addressing the function of that elusive but ubiquitous force called *guilt*. The devastating influence of guilt is nearly always inaccessible to introspection and self-analysis, which is why it is so powerful.

The guilt in the voyeur and in the exhibitionist may be likened to two children playing in a park after they have done something wrong. From out of nowhere, a fearsome voice says, "Hey, you two, stop it! You are wrong!" The voyeur altruistically replies, "*I* didn't do anything wrong, *I* was only watching. *He* did it!" To which the exhibitionist replies, "*I'm* not going to take all the blame. *He* was here watching all along. Besides, *he* told me to do it!"

Deep within, both feel guilty. One individual, however, acknowledges his guilt, for he prefers not to be the actor or to call attention to himself. The exhibitionist tends to use overdramatization and denial through conspicuous, repetitious displays of the self in order to prove to others he is not wrong or bad. His guilt is mitigated when he can convince (or manipulate) others to behave similarly. His unconscious attitude is, "See, I must not be so bad if others are doing it too and are approving of me!" When guilt is too pervasive, the exhibitionist overtly rejects anyone who does not believe or behave as he suggests (or demands). As others comply, his guilt is temporarily dispersed, and feelings of well-being and confidence are momentarily enjoyed.

Healthy couples profit readily from the voyeuristic-exhibitionistic traits. When the effects of the successful counterbalance have been incorporated by each partner, the voyeur feels less guilt over being conspicuously expressive and assertive. The exhibitionist, on the other hand, may rely less upon others to serve as the sole index of personal worth. In other words, the voyeur becomes more exhibitionistic, and the exhibitionist becomes a bit of a voyeur.

As a therapist, I find it refreshing to interview couples who have successfully lived together for a decade or more. Each will recall the earlier days when neither was intrapsychically comfortable, and their life together was hectic and somewhat insecure. Each tenderly values and appreciates the other for providing the necessary missing ingredients. Each values the other for the love, acceptance, and support offered, particularly in times of struggle. Each has indeed become more mature, complete, and self-sufficient, and together they have achieved the comfortable state of affairs called *emotional maturity*.

TO CONTROL OR TO BE CONTROLLED

The last, but in no way least, of the opposite character traits contributing to the unconscious motives of partner selection is the need to either control or be controlled. Because being controlled and resisting control are among the earliest conflicts in human socialization, they are primitive and continuous considerations in nearly all relationships. In that first relationship, the individual learns the most effective way to get his needs met and to deal with the control of his overpowering parents. Some children learn that they are better off acquiescing to parental control in order to receive the necessary victuals. Those less fortunate come to realize that their needs are unimportant and that they are selfish to expect very much. Their compromise is to expect little or nothing from their parents or life.

Other individuals, because their basic nurturing needs were not quite satisfied, consistently learned to manipulate authority figures as well as their peers to get what they needed. Thus, they became perceptive detectors of the inconsistent moods of the first love. Knowing when the mother was most receptive to giving what was wanted, the child employed subtle manipulations to get her to give it. Sensitivity to both the conscious and unconscious motives of others is what contributes to the social sophistication and smoothness of manic types. Experienced clinicians, for example, will attest to the brilliance of schizophrenics in detecting the unconscious moods of their therapists. Like surrogate parents and surrogate spouses, such clinicians have been embarrassingly manipulated by manic-type patients. Therapists also recognize that manics need to first be controlled in order to mature emotionally. Similar to concerned parents and spouses, therapists too are met with a full dose of hostility in their attempt to suppress the manic's expressiveness and impulsive behavior. Depressive types are especially attracted to individuals who are somewhat disorganized, overly emotional, and easily confused. Unconsciously, they are attracted to manics because they can be "loved" for that aspect of themselves that is most pronounced, their control. Due to the relationship with their overcontrolling parents, depressives can easily provide structure, control, and righteous guidance for their partner who unconsciously requires these qualities to function more effectively. To be the controlling force over another offers the depressive a feeling of omnipotence and righteousness not at all unlike that which was once experienced by his parents.

Because depressives have been overly controlled, they tend unconsciously to want to control others. Righteous control over another also provides a cleverly disguised but socially appropriate vent for some of the hostility caused by parental overcontrol and restriction of expressive impulses. Each time the depressive is able to correct the partner's erring ways, his position of oneupmanship temporarily elevates his worth and esteem.

In an emotionally disturbed couple, each individual feels so worthless that there is a continuous battle over who is best and who is worst, or who is "rightest" and who is "wrongest." Almost every interaction is critically evaluated by the partner in order to detect errors about which to impugn the bad guy. In marriages where hostility is kept buried beneath the surface, it is not uncommon for the righteous depressive to covertly encourage the partner to act out, that is, to have an extramarital love affair. Then, when the bad guy gets caught, the innocent partner can bathe in uncontested righteousness, which adds immeasurably to his control. The power struggle can seldom be successfully resolved because, to the righteous, infidelity is *the* unforgivable sin—it is magnanimously forgiven but never quite forgotten, as both well know. Even within the healthy range, couples battle over power, because neither partner is willing to be humiliated by giving in to blind submission. Despite the manic's unconscious need for specific limits, he will violently resist what he unconsciously needs for his personal development. Thus, some degree of conflict over power exists in all relationships. Left to the couple's own devices, however, they are unlikely to be resolved easily or gracefully.

Depressives appeal to manics initially because of their quieter mannerisms and lesser desire for social recognition. The manic interprets the depressive's quiescence and inhibition as approval of his own grandiose behaviors and ideas. He also views the depressive's inhibited verbal expressiveness as a welcome change from the confusing messages he experienced in the first relationship. Unconsciously, the manic believes he has found a loving alliance to provide affirmation for everything he is, but has been afraid of. It is this factor that, in time, often surprises the partner. Because of the support they experience in the attachment to the depressive partner, some manics eventually regress to an adolescent stage of development and begin to act out. For some people, those adolescent impulses, which were marginally suppressed before marriage, surface only after the manic has established an attachment to a stable depressive type.

The depressive's quiescence, to which the manic is initially attracted, most often turns out to be a major irritant. After marriage, the manic eventually discovers that the "backseat" taken by the depressive during the early stages of the relationship was not approval at all, but rather the rudiment of emotional reticence and expressive impoverishment. Although these qualities were most important at the relationship's start, the monotony of responsible, adult living causes the manic to need more support, more attention, and more evidence that he is loved. Over the years, as the manic discovers that the depressive partner cannot be emotionally expressive, a major shift in relatedness occurs. Because manics have difficulty containing themselves under stress, they usually castigate the partner for not caring enough. When the manic becomes aware of how much he needs continuous support, he simultaneously discovers that he is not in control of the relationship at all—he is being controlled by a silent partner. To need love, support, and recognition so badly from someone who cannot provide it is the epitome of powerlessness.

The desire for control, as well as the subtle and not-so-subtle avoidance of control, are elements in all social interactions. If a person is accustomed to active, manipulative control, he is likely to feel uncomfortable with anyone else who is competing for active control. Conversely, if an individual is accustomed to passive control, he will usually feel "at home" among those who need to be active. Depressive types often use a passive-subtle form of control because parental pressures and guilt were too powerful to resist. They got what they thought they needed through cooperation and compliance. Manic types, on the other hand, use an active-manipulative form of control. They were the individuals who felt rejected and misunderstood by their parents. To get what they wanted, they found it necessary to actively manipulate parents or other power figures. For the manics, parental control was sufficiently inconsistent that, as children, they could never be certain why they were being controlled. When control was enforced, it was usually done with enough parental ambivalence and anger that the child learned to associate controls with rejection and deprivation.

A somewhat contemporary example of ambivalent control can be observed in parents who have made a commitment to be "super-parents." These are couples who dislike the way they were raised and promise themselves that they won't be anything like their own parents. Thus, they read the how-to-parent books and try to model themselves after the ideal parents presented.

One such couple came to my office for consultation because Amy, their two-and-a-half-year-old daughter, was retaining her feces for a week or so and then relieving herself in various places around their house. As we examined the subtleties of parental control, it became obvious that both parents believed their daughter would be psychologically damaged if they controlled or refused her. As a child, the mother had felt extremely rejected, and she despised her parents' control because it made her feel that they did not love her. To insure that Amy would not feel rejected, she was convinced that she must only give huge quantities of "love," which to her meant letting the child do exactly as she pleased. She was sure Amy would feel rejected if she was asked to sit on the potty against her wishes.

A typical two-year-old, Amy did not care to waste valuable exploration time constrained on a toilet and resisted initial attempts to make her do so. The epitome of her mother's ambivalence became obvious. On the one hand, she didn't want to reject Amy, while on the other she was extremely angry because Amy wasn't trained and had relieved herself whenever she pleased at various inconvenient places around the house. Her ambivalence was increased because she could not express her anger and frustration toward Amy; if she did, she believed she would be doing the same thing to Amy that had been done to her. Beneath the surface, however, the mother was angry at the child. Despite her overly-permissive, oversolicitous attitude toward her daughter, her real feelings came through loud and clear.

The mother said that she had told Amy that she wasn't angry at her, but she wished she would do what she was told and sit on the toilet. I stopped her rather abruptly and said, "I wish you would quit trying to be a supermom by denying feelings of anger. In fact, it is obvious to me that you are mad as hell at your daughter." The mother seemed shocked when she realized what she was doing because she had read about ambivalent messages in one of her books on parenting. She realized that she was in fact mixing words of love with feelings of anger. She was also projecting her own hostility over having been controlled and rejected onto her daughter by assuming that Amy would hate her if she controlled her.

I told the parents to quit worrying about Amy's toilet training and to let me worry about it for awhile. I then asked the mother to record the number of minutes a day that the toilet-training problem would ordinarily cause her to be disgusted with Amy and herself. I also asked her to take note of any cues the daughter gave to indicate she had to go to the toilet. (Both had said earlier that her face reddened and she grunted when she had to go.) After the second session, I told both parents to send signals of genuine affection to Amy while they held her on the toilet for 15-minute intervals at least three times each day. On the second day of the program, Amy relieved herself while on the toilet. At the end of the first week, she was essentially trained.

This example of parental ambivalence may appear trite, but the confusion experienced by the child, however, is what creates later problems over being controlled. In addition, hidden messages between the content of *what* is said and the intent of *why* it is said are sufficiently complex that the child has little choice but to attempt to decode the real (unconscious) communication rather than just the words. The conflict areas in which ambivalence can be experienced are many but the results are nearly always the same. The child accidentally becomes attuned to the unconscious motives of the parents and often learns to mistrust the words. The severity of the ambivalence determines the degree and ease of psychological confusion in the child.

Manic types are the most conspicuous members of society. They are most apt to vocalize their dissatisfaction—and, frequently but indirectly, the conviction that they are unloved—and then to act on those feelings. At each level of their psychosocial adjustment, manic types are frequently the recipients of an unconscious love-hate ambivalence, which precipitates their high level of anxiety, insecurity, and desire to quickly express themselves by acting out. As shown in the preceding case history, love-hate communication to the child is not direct or verbal, but indirect and nonverbal. The child, to protect himself from the destructive "vibes" emanating from his first love, has to become extrasensitive to beneath-the-surface clues. In addition, he is left with a permanent, heightened sensitivity to acceptance and rejection by others. For example, schizophrenics are seldom able to receive approval or acceptance from others because they most often look for signals of hostility, and rejection. Normal-range manics also have trouble with acceptance and rejection.

Most manics have been raised in an overly affective and insecure environment where more than a fair share of blame was dumped on them. Even though they attempted to fight it off, much of the blame was introjected. The quality of the environment forced the child to protect himself by prematurely detaching from the emotional vulnerability of the first love. In order to psychologically survive the ambivalence of the first love, he developed a sense of pseudo-independence and began to disperse his childhood dependency needs outward onto peers and various accomplishments that provide recognition. The love, acceptance, and stability unavailable in the first relationship were sought from the peers instead. Some necessary constituents for personal growth, however, were left behind. The need for control, which can both reduce anxiety and add security, was lost. The ability to be satisfied with one central relationship was also lost.

The unconscious need to blame the first love (and thus, the eventual partner) for not providing enough of the right kind of love is characteristic of disturbed manics. Unable to see that no one person can satisfy all his needs for recognition and acceptance, which were provided earlier by his peers and audiences, the manic's affection hunger causes him to be unhappy with only one relationship. The more clever manic elevates himself to a position of social power, where he can receive sufficient recognition from others. When he does, his relationship with his partner often goes more smoothly. In other cases, support and approval from outside sources provide the manic with more than is available at home. Often, the relationship will break down further and may be eventually abandoned.

Most manic types have a convincing rationalization for avoiding control. Unconsciously, they harbor more than a modest residual of ambivalence from their first relationship, which can be summarized as, "If you love me, you will let me do as I please. If you try to stop me from doing as I please, you must not love me." One can see how easy it was for the mother to back off from exercising control when the child accused her of not loving him. One can also see how easily this tendency is transferred to subsequent relationships.

Manic-type males provide an excellent example of the "if you love me, you'll let me" maneuver. More often than not, they wish to act out, either sexually with one or more woman or by carousing with "the boys." Their more basic desire, however, is to avoid overwhelming responsibility and to acquire more emotional supplies than can be obtained at home. When a depressive wife questions her manic husband's activities, he retaliates by accusing her of mistrust and misunderstanding, and then tries to make her feel guilty for even questioning him. He concludes somehow that if his wife really loved him, she would not mind his outside interests. About the only thing more incredible than such irrational manipulation by manic men is the number of their wives who cooperate.

Despite their unconscious need for external controls, manics are instinctively resistant to people who tell them what to do. Whether that resistance reaches their conscious awareness is unimportant. Because of the ambivalence of the first love in setting consistent limits, issues involving authority, submission, and injustice are continuing themes in the life of the manic. The unresolved childhood conflicts over who controls whom, hypersensitize the manic to any personal or social issue in which there is the slightest hint of unconscious similarity to "insensitive" or "unjust" authority. Deep within, they need to be taken care of (and controlled) by one who is more powerful, yet loving. Consciously, however, manics have trouble allowing their partners much control over them because to do so automatically stimulates feelings of helplessness, as well as their deep dependency needs, which they are always trying to deny.

An additional psychological force in all manic types is their underlying feeling of being crazy and stupid. Because manics tend to first respond emotionally rather than intellectually, others often accuse them of being stupid or crazy. For example, not long ago, a tornado alert sounded while I was browsing around a large shopping center. While the siren wailed, I observed a young mother who was obviously petrified. Her husband was panicky too, but was working at not showing it. One of their children, a boy of about six, became frightened and began to cry loudly. Then he ran over and clung to his mother—which is probably what his father wanted to do! The father looked angrily at his son and yelled, "You crazy little bastard! Wipe those tears away, and quit acting so damn stupid!" He felt better immediately and proceeded to lead his family out to the car. The small boy had clearly served as the emotional barometer of his family. When his parents were angry or anxious, his capacity for responsiveness caused him to absorb their feelings and express them physically. He obviously didn't know why he did, nor is he likely to find out. Ask his parents or siblings, however, why the boy behaves that way, and they would no doubt reply that he is obviously crazy—and pretty stupid, too.

In about the same proportion that manics need to be lovingly controlled in order to grow, depressive types need to defy some of the overcontrolling aspects of their development, take more risks, learn to be more "selfish" and more spontaneous, and to generally be more expressive by acting out some of their fantasies. Exactly what the psyche needs to begin the movement toward greater emotional maturity is manifested through certain characteristics in the partner. Specifically, the depressive types *need to lose control*, preferably under careful guidance, in order to realize that the world will not come to an end if they let go a little. However, the process is not that simple because, under stress, which is often the only time depressives might naturally lose control, they "instinctively" become more controlled and thus less spontaneous. Instead of trying out new behaviors, they return to their well-inculcated mode of response. Depressives are unconsciously attracted to more expressive, responsive partners who will act out and thus express their own pent-up emotions for them. In disturbed relationships, the depressive is crushed to learn that the emotional expressiveness of his partner can also be turned into a hostile, relentless attack against him.

Depressive types tend to be hard on themselves because of their deeply ingrained sense of social and moral responsibility. They are particularly attuned to the "craziness" in their manic partners, and, depending upon the level of health in the relationship, they may label it either "creative" or "sick." To the depressive, "crazy" describes nearly any behavior or attitude that isn't listed in their "manual of socially acceptable behaviors and attitudes for the supernormal." Depressives are reluctant to realize that in order to further mature and to enjoy life to the fullest, they must first get a little crazy. Most depressives will fight against spontaneity and loss of cognitive control as vehemently as their partners resist being controlled. The depressive perceives that to be a little crazy is to act like nearly everyone else against whom he compares himself. His punitive superego and feelings of righteousness are much more powerful than his desire for growth. Besides, left to his own dynamics and defenses, there is not much room for improvement; after all, the depressive is already conspicuously stable, mature, rational, well adjusted, and uncrazy. Craziness is for others, that is, those more similar to the spouse.

Jerry, a bright, manic-type graduate student, hesitant about his impending marriage, came to my office for one session to discuss his "blind spots" and his motives for marriage. "I went with quite a few women before Judy, but after a few months I dumped them because they seemed like more trouble than they were worth," Jerry began. "How so?" I inquired. "Well, in all the relationships I had the weirdest feeling we were competing for something. All discussions—even those about nothing—turned into vindictive arguments, which never quite ended. Any conversation, no matter how it began, eventually turned into a fight. Yeah, that's it, we always seemed to be trying to prove a point so we could prove each other wrong. There always had to be a winner." "Who wins most of the arguments now?" I asked. "Now," he said, "we really don't argue. We have discussions that are almost always meaningful, and we seldom get to the point of heated argumentation. Besides," he began to laugh, "Judy lets me get my way most of the time." Aware that he revealed something important, Jerry smiled and, with a look of anticipation, waited for me to interpret what he'd said. As we concluded the session, it became clearer to Jerry how some of his more basic needs were being met in his relationship with Judy.

As suggested in the preceding example, what people consciously respond to and believe they need may, in fact, militate against their emotional growth. The manic, for example, needs to develop realistic inner controls through being judiciously controlled by a loving and consistent significant other. To acquiesce to control, perhaps for the first time, is often a frightening experience—it reveals one's vulnerability and dependency. For, if the truth about him were ever disclosed, so the manic thinks, for sure no one could ever find him lovable.

Healthy to mildly neurotic individuals are usually able to adjust to power conflicts in their relationship. Due to the positive relatedness carried over from the first love, each partner feels valued and needed by the other. Ensconced in a trusting atmosphere of empathy and caring, each feels open to the other. Despite some mild resistance, each becomes open to experiences that facilitate growth. Pathological individuals who feel that no one cares and that they don't matter to anyone are almost always in a power struggle. There is a natural and predictable human phenomenon that forces those who feel the most insignificant to seek positions of power. For, to control others is *to matter*. That's why spouses seem to hassle each other the most at exactly the time they should be doing it the least. When one partner feels he doesn't matter to his spouse and children, then control, whether constructive or destructive, is better than nothing.

Since this book exposes the primitive and in most cases parasitic motives for human pairing, it is appropriate to conclude by exposing the most common and brilliant manipulative stratagem of the manic for controlling the spouse. All reasonably intelligent manics are capable of manipulating the partner through pseudosincerity, confusion, irrelevance, guilt, and the final play on the partner's vulnerability to righteousness and intellectual propriety. In order to understand the manipulation, it is necessary to recall that manic types have extraordinary sensitivity to the unconscious vulnerabilities of others. The more disturbed the individual, the greater the sensitivity. With their sensitivity and verbal expressiveness, manics have a natural interest in any kind of salesmanship or politics in which deviousness or manipulation is required. Friendliness, pseudo-sincerity, and confidence are the first tactics they employ. The unconscious message relayed is that everything is fine, in control, and that they are trustworthy. It always helps if they can make the spouse or victim feel that he or she is the most important person in the world. (They manipulated their parents the same way.) As soon as this is accomplished, the next step is to pull the opponent into the manipulation by getting him to agree to nearly anything. This is the most interesting maneuver because they astutely scan an entire range of totally irrelevant issues in a matter of minutes, hoping to find one item of interest and agreement. What they say is not important. Getting the opponent to take an emotional interest and to agree with them is the point. Deviousness becomes apparent at this point because the manic will say anything to get the opponent sucked in. When the opponent becomes emotionally vulnerable, the battle is nearly over. The seduction then becomes a matter of protocol.

When a couple is in conflict and their needs and resentment surface, the manic (in this case, the woman) becomes slightly disoriented in her attempt to disarm the intellectual controls of the depressive husband. The husband, who is trying to intellectually follow her irrelevant garble, becomes totally confused. In the depressive's attempt to logically follow illogical thoughts, he becomes disoriented and emotionally open. At this point, the manic presents her punch line clearly, which is usually accepted because it is the first element of intellectual logic in the entire argument. To accept the manic wife's argument is less painful to the depressive than is the emotional and intellectual confusion caused by her ramblings. He accepts the manipulation in order to become unconfused. Milton Erickson (see Jay Haley, *Advanced Techniques of Hypnosis and Therapy*) isolated this process as a powerful technique of hypnotic suggestion in overcoming patient resistance. Manic types have the market on the technique, as they come by it naturally. The gimmick that secures control is to play on the guilt of the partner. The partner, already too susceptible from the first relationship, feels foolish and shameful for his lack of cooperation.

In a disturbed couple, the depressive individual soon becomes "wise" to the manic partner's technique because of the feelings of being repeatedly deceived. The depressive's common response to prevent the manic partner's frequent attempted manipulation is to unconsciously reinact early childhood patterns by being resistant and withdrawn. The depressive becomes resistant and refuses to listen to nearly anything the partner says in order to avoid further manipulation and hurt. A destructive homeostasis is struck: the manic's nonsensical ramblings get crazier, and the depressive becomes more compulsive in order to prevent being vulnerable again. The couple's children will react either by running away, antisocial behaviors, poor school performance, or psychosomatic complaints.

Some readers will be uncertain as to whether they are manic or depressive because they see aspects of themselves in both types. The key lies in the initial, almost instinctive, response style to threat, fear, anxiety, and attack. Many manic types, especially those from the middle class who value educational, cultural, and intellectual activities, are able to control their manic dynamics by acquiring overintellectualized or obsessive-compulsive controls over their more instinctive impulses. Deep within, however, they remain manic types who are bright enough to maintain the facade for the outside world. The intellectualization and compulsivity of such manics are defenses, which sometimes break down at home when there is no one to impress. Under severe stress, these individuals do not pull in and become more constrictive as would a genuine depressive type; instead, they fly apart and become disorganized and conspicuously infantile.

There are also basic depressive types who force themselves to be what they are not by socially behaving in a manner similar to that of "typical" manic types. For example, many depressives work in occupations that require skills more indigenous to the manic. Because they must constantly strive to be more expressive and more socially involved than they really like to be, they are exhausted at the end of each workday. Rather than feeling restored because they have done something meaningful with their creative talents, they go home feeling that something has been taken from them.

It is easy to see how relational conflicts can emerge when the breadwinner comes home so drained each day that he or she is unable to give to the spouse and children. Most often, it is not possible to give emotionally to other family members when much of the available energy has been dissipated trying to prove to the self that one is not what he is. The reality of the human heart lies not in the way we wish we were, but in the way we are. Behind closed doors, when there is no one but spouse and children to impress, the real self tends to be exposed.

4 / The Effect of Yesterday on Today and Tomorrow

Despite the high incidence of marital disharmony and dissatisfaction, as well as divorce, few if any errors are made in the selection of a partner. At any given time in life, the individual's predominate psychological needs push him toward a person who will unconsciously cooperate in their fulfillment. The selection of a specific individual to the exclusion of all others is not motivated solely by unconscious needs, however, but in part by conscious desire. Such desire, however, is merely a derivation of the unconscious.

In a nutshell, pairing is governed by what can be obtained *from* the relationship, not by what can be given *to* it. Consequently, a person falling out of love (in this instance, a woman) might be more accurately regarded as one whose composite of needs have changed. They may have increased or decreased to such a degree that her partner cannot or will not cooperate in their fulfillment. The partner may have also changed and thus become unable to satisfy her once-met needs.

Relationships also deteriorate if someone or something outside the relationship holds more promise of need fulfillment than the partner. In some cases, an individual slowly discovers that the relationship is sufficiently destructive that he or she needs to get out to keep from "going crazy" or committing homicide or suicide. In such cases, the psychological needs related to intimacy are short-circuited and become irrelevant as emotional survival becomes the more dominant concern. As the relationship with the partner is severed and survival insured, basic psychological needs again surface for the selection of a subsequent partner.

Satisfactory fulfillment of one's need for intimacy is determined by the quality of the first love. The quality of relatedness is in-

118

fluenced by the mother's (or first love's) emotional responsiveness to her child, the amount of energy and knowledge available
to her about relationships, the enjoyment she derives from meeting the child's needs, her emotional commitment to the child, and
the intrinsic worth the child has for her (as opposed to extrinsic
or symbolic worth, or guilt or obligation). If the mother's relationship with her husband is unfulfilling, either she will be short
of tension-free affect and will respond to the child with agitation, or she will attempt to fulfill her emotional needs through
her relationship with the child. The fewer needs a child has had
met in the first relationship, the more demanding he will be in
the next intimacy. Needy and dissatisfied parents create needy and
dissatisfied children, who eventually expect to have their needs
met by a spouse. However, the spouse is usually too needy to genuinely cooperate. When the social climate is permissive, dissatisfied spouses go outside their marriages to attempt to meet those
needs, sure that "out there" a person exists who can "make them
happy."

During the second committed relationship, the unmet needs and
abuses of the first relationship are replayed and amplified. The
process of projecting the unmet needs, conflicts, unexpressed hostilities, and expectations of the first relationship onto the second
is called *transference*. This chapter details the nuances of parental
transference and presents examples in which one or both individuals in a relationship transfer unmet childhood needs and expectations for affection onto the other.

It is a common notion that when girls grow up, they symbolically marry their fathers; boys symbolically marry their mothers.
In my work, I have detected something considerably more complicated. Nevertheless, similar relational qualities and, to some
degree, opposite character traits still account for the initial affinity
in the selection of a partner. Therefore, if a boy's mother was a
manic type and his father a depressive, and if he identified with his
mother and became a manic type, he then would be more attracted
to someone with traits similar to his father's. If a daughter's first
love was her depressive mother and if she identified with her manic
father after the age of four or five, she would select a partner more
similar to her mother. Conversely, if she maintained her identity

with her depressive mother, she would select someone with character traits more similar to those of the manic father. The decisive factors are the complicated phenomenon known as *gender identification* and the degree to which the child was attached to, subsequently introjected, and consciously desired to emulate the ideals of the significant parent.

A few examples should clarify some of the common tendencies and conflicts in parental transference.

Betty, a woman in her early forties, was an extremely bright professional who had earned advanced degrees. Betty remembered her mother as unpleasant, rejecting, and overly critical of nearly everything she did. Her emotional attachment was to her father, whom she described as firm but more accepting. I asked Betty, "Who was your favorite parent?" She replied, "Dad, of course. You know my mother. No one could like her!"

Betty's husband, Bill, was a successful physician who unhesitatingly claimed his mother as his favorite. Bill had clearly overidentified with his mother and saw his father as ineffectual and distant. Unconsciously, Betty had been attracted to Bill because of his opposite character traits and his equally disturbed relational base. Her mother was a disturbed schizoid and her father an equally disturbed obsessive-compulsive. Bill's mother was also a disturbed schizoid, and his father was obsessive-compulsive. The primary difference in their character traits was that Betty had overidentified with her obsessive-compulsive father, while Bill overidentified with his schizoid mother. Unconsciously, Betty had chosen her critical, rejecting, and castrating mother all over again when she married Bill. And he got his cold, distant, ineffectual father, whom he despised.

Destructive transference phenomena were obvious throughout Bill and Betty's relationship. Bill was so psychologically and emotionally similar to Betty's mother that she began to respond to him *as if he were* her mother. Anything he did or said that remotely resembled the rejecting and humiliating injunctions of Betty's mother triggered the rage that she had felt toward her mother as a child, but was too frightened—and dependent—to verbalize. Bill also transferred his unresolved hostility toward and fear of his father directly onto Betty. When she did or said anything similar to that which his father had done or said, he felt rejected. For example, when Betty came home from work, showered, had a cocktail, and read the paper before dinner, Bill would accuse her of ignoring him and not caring about him. Such accusations enraged Betty because her mother had always accused her of being self-centered and inconsiderate. And so, they actively attempted to destroy one another. Intellectually, they knew that their hostility to each other's comments were grossly exaggerated. Emotionally, however, they could not stop the attack once they had been affectively aroused, for their need for vengeance went deeper than they knew. Their marriage ended in divorce.

Emotional disturbance always carries an undercurrent of hostility and resentment from the first unsatisfying relationship. It is impossible for disturbed children to express their pain directly to their parents. Instead, they tend to suppress their pain in order to get what little "good stuff" available. Almost uncontainable, the hurt from the insensitive parents remains inside, only to be later transferred onto those who resemble the first antagonist—or onto those who make enough noise so that the hurt cannot be successfully suppressed. The pain experienced in a disturbed first love must be directed somewhere. It will not just fade away. Thus, individuals who have rigid controls against expressing anger outwardly turn it inwardly upon themselves.

Emotionally disturbed individuals are almost always overloaded with unconscious conflicts, hurt feelings, and irrational attitudes, which they cannot help but transfer onto their partner. After a short period of marriage, disturbed individuals will be aghast at how similar their spouse is to their disturbed parent with whom they also could not get along too well. Those who pair in mid-adolescence—especially those who do so to get away from a rejecting, ineffective parent—invariably end up with someone similar to that parent. Even unsophisticated observers realize that it was too uncanny to be a coincidence.

The tendency for disturbed individuals to pair with their symbolic mothers involves their widespread insecurity. When they consciously wish to get away from the first relationship, anxiety forces them to immediately scramble for a psychological replacement. Since they have neither individuated nor separated, they are attracted only to those whose dynamics are similar to the parent's. They hope that the partner will be able to take better care of them and love them the way they want to be loved. During courtship, the partner may respond favorably. After the artificiality of the courtship subsides, however, the substitute "mother" returns. Although she had a new body and a new name, she is often very similar inside.

Healthy individuals also transfer many relational expectations onto the spouse. But the trust, openness, and desire for mutual interdependence from the first relationship are carried over to the new relationship. There, they provide substantial security and an operational base for compromise, empathy, new awareness, and behavioral and attitudinal adjustment. Any unreasonable demands, interactions, or insensitivities can be confronted by the couple and eventually corrected. Over the years, as enough "leftover" material is worked through, the couple realizes new levels of independence and maturity. The younger and more disturbed an individual is when he pairs, the more volatile and direct is the transference onto his partner. Three factors contribute to this. First, emotionally disturbed individuals often desire to pair earlier than do those less disturbed. Second, when adolescents pair, they are obviously still in a stage of psychosexual development. As mentioned in Chapter 1, childhood dynamics and emotional reserves are neither adequately challenged nor developed until one separates from the first love and the family by living independently. Therefore, significant changes usually occur in individuals when they are presented with adult responsibility. Finally, young people are generally more impulsive and unrealistic than mature adults.

Many disturbed adolescents have an unconscious need to have a child in order to obtain a person who will need them and love them the way the parents did not. It is never possible, however, for such adolescents to successfully parent because they are often as needy as the helpless child. The stresses of attempting to meet a child's needs are frequently more than a teenaged mother can endure, and she often returns home, hoping to get some of the nurturance her husband is unable to provide. The husband may turn to another woman, return home, or both. For such a couple, the separation from parents has not yet begun.

Even though one partner in such a couple may be a depressive type and the other a manic type, the distinction is sometimes unclear due to the impulsiveness of youth. Their mutual expressiveness, both physical and verbal, adds to the damage they inflict on one another. For, if they were to keep the pain to themselves, they would not directly damage each other. However, they are often overwhelmed by the responsibility, energy output, and delayed gratification required to make a satisfactory adjustment to adult living. Due to their inability to contain immediate impulse, many young married couples are hot-headed and sharp-tongued, thus causing great pain to each other, which forces them to build emotional barriers rather than bridges.

Even healthy adolescents who pair can bruise each other to such a degree that one or both will want out. When each has been hurt by the other, nearly anyone who is not as rejecting as the partner is considered more pleasant to be with. Moreover, in addition to the emotional damage, the responsibility of a child may hasten the decision of even healthy adolescent mates to divorce. "If we could only have met at another time," they often lament, "things might have been different."

Almost every unmarried person over the age of 25 has been involved in at least one serious relationship. If such a person has matured in the interim, he can usually look back on his earlier involvement with both curiosity and a sigh of relief. Clearly, he would not choose the same type of mate today. However, if the individual has not grown and is presently burdened in an unsatisfactory relationship, he may look back with envy, nostalgia, and melancholy. The "good old days" when living was less burdened, less responsible, and more fun is where he wishes to be. Nevertheless, life and responsibility go on.

The panacean love affair, which many married people believe will cure burdensome or monotonous living, is representative of a true adolescent regression. Involvement in a love affair can serve as a temporary time-out from responsible adult living. During those moments of eroticism, a pseudosense of youthfulness and enhanced self-esteem may lift depression and the burdens of adult living. Affairs also offer the person a temporary affirmation of personal worth, which the partner may have taken for granted or forgotten. Many people, even those who oppose infidelity, secretly entertain the idea of having an affair in order to once again be aroused and valued by, and be important to, someone who will not take them for granted.

Most often, love affairs are overloaded with idiosyncratic symbolism, which can offer pseudogratification and escape. Affairs cannot be honest, however, because the delusional aspects of the erotic fantasy, and the accompanying confusion prevent integrity. More often than not, they make living confusing and more complex. Affairs may offer an escape, but it is doubtful that they solve anything. *Being caught* in an affair by one's partner, as strange as it may seem, is more apt to lead to the resolution of marital problems than is the actual affair. (See Chapter 5.)

PARENTAL TRANSFERENCE

Many conflicts have been caused by one partner's comparing the other's way of doing things to the way his mother or father did them. One of the most memorable transference conflicts during the early years of my own marriage evolved around the proper use of the kitchen sink. In the house I grew up in, the back door entered a small hallway, which lead to the kitchen. After an afternoon's play, I would usually enter the back door, go directly to the kitchen, and wash my hands in the kitchen sink. My mother kept soap and plenty of towels close by. In my wife Ginny's childhood home, when someone's hands were dirty, he went to the bathroom to clean up. In her house, the kitchen sink was used exclusively for preparing food and washing dishes. It was *not* for dirty hands. So, in our own home, Ginny expected that no hands would be washed in the kitchen sink.

Now that I look back, the number of arguments we had over the kitchen sink seems absurd. At the time, however, our feelings of conflict were very real. Whenever I went into the house with dirty hands, I automatically went to the kitchen sink. Only when I felt piercing eyes behind me and heard Ginny's angry huff-and-puff did I realize that I was doing something inexcusable. My response was usually to attack her for being so uptight about something so insignificant. She would then accuse me of deliberately trying to annoy her. Fortunately, we soon moved from that house into one with a half-bathroom by the rear door. If we hadn't, we might still be fighting over the sink.

Another example of transference from our marriage is what I call the "garbage-in-the-refrigerator conflict." It still infuriates me during those moments when I take myself too seriously. My mother has excellent culinary skills and enjoys food, and so the refrigerator in my parents' home was always packed. For over 20 years, I went to that refrigerator and helped myself to nearly anything at nearly anytime. Now, Ginny is a professional, and her self-worth is not dependent upon being a good cook or homemaker. Our refrigerator is seldom full. Nevertheless, when I take something from it, I expect it to be edible. Many times during the first years of our marriage, I sipped cold milk out of a carton and gagged on it. It had been there too long and had spoiled. My first response was again automatic: I immediately wanted to blame Ginny for keeping inedible food in the refrigerator. However, she responded that it wasn't just her refrigerator and that I could have thrown out spoiled food just as easily as she. Even so, my unspoken thought was that my mother would never let food spoil in the refrigerator.

Over the years of working with married couples, I have seen tempers aroused over equally trivial issues. As conflicts were examined in counseling sessions, it was easy for me to see that each partner had transferred idiosyncrasies and expectations, *which had absolutely no significance to anyone else.* When these habits and expectations needed to be changed in order to provide greater harmony, fights often began. After all, if someone had been doing the same thing all his life, it must be right. So, the question of who is going to change what habit for whom can create havoc. If individual adjustment to habits becomes rooted in a power struggle, or evokes too much anger and rejection, a perennial conflict can emerge. In already disturbed relationships, molehills can easily become mountains. The issue changes from one of trying to adjust habits for greater marital harmony to one of defensiveness and maneuvers for power.

In some marriages, the man transfers a high number of expectations onto the role of the wife. For example, one husband I met became infuriated when his wife did not match and fold his socks properly. Another, accustomed to taking care of his socks himself, was equally upset when he opened his sock drawer to discover that his wife had folded and matched them. When one looks beneath such behaviors, however, the reasons why people seem able to fight over nothing begin to make sense. One fellow was angry when his wife would not wake up to make his breakfast at 6:30 every morning; another man got angry when his wife *did* get up to have breakfast with him. Before marriage, he had enjoyed being alone in the morning before going to work. Since he worked closely with people all day, he liked having a quiet house entirely to himself. Thus, his wife's presence was an irritating intrusion, and they fought during breakfast for years. When his wife awakened, she wanted to feel a sense of togetherness because that's the way it had been at home. She felt anxious and alone if she could not emotionally connect with him early in the day.

Taken at face value, the carryovers from one's first home and family, which become reenacted in the second home, may be interpreted as habit. Psychologically, however, those who are shackled into repeating the expectations and familiarity of the first family, and who become angry when that does not happen, are struggling with childhood dependency needs and the desire to regress to earlier years. Some people need to recapture the security of the first family so desperately that they panic when the spouse does not cooperate in the simulation. Those who are tenaciously gripping memories of years gone by tend to compare the experiences of today with what they think they remember from yesterday. Naturally, they always evaluate the past more favorably. Deep within, their dependency needs and insecurity prevent them from experiencing each day so that they can grow from it. Consequently, they do not emotionally mature from daily experience but instead remain fixated at about the same age that is prevalent in their fantasy.

When people wish to return to the "good old days," they most often mean adolescence or childhood. Whenever their emotional resources are insufficient for coping, they unconsciously desire to return to a time when they were being taken care of and when living was a little easier. When it is too painful to look back, some people look forward to the "brighter days" when life will be over.

The unconscious desire to regress and to be dependent again, this time upon a new "mother" whom one will have exclusively to oneself, is an important psychodynamic in pairing. Some of the antagonism inherent in all new relationships is attributable to the gradual discovery that the new mother is merely an insufficient substitute. The pressure that one partner places on the other to change increases the resentment of the spouse who frequently is made to feel not good enough. The message from the partner who is pressuring the other to change is, "I want you to love me more, or better, or the way mother [i.e., first love] did, or the way she should have." It is a fact that the greater the desire of one partner to change the other, the higher the probability of conflict, resentment, and irreversible damage to the relationship. It is also true that the partner who exerts the greatest effort to change the other may well be the more disturbed of the two. The intensity of such effort is merely an indication of one's self-dissatisfaction and relative absence of self-acceptance.

FATHER TRANSFERENCE

While conducting family therapy, I sometimes ask the children which one of them is their mother's favorite and which one is their father's favorite. I then ask who is mother's second most favorite, and so on. The parents become anxious during such direct questioning because they believe that they should love all of their children equally. They are amazed when the children are in perfect agreement about whom they think mother and father love the most.

If one child (for instance, a daughter) is mother's favorite and is more attached to her, she will more than likely transfer qualities of that relationship onto her eventual partner. If father remains the primary attachment figure for the child, she is likely to pair (unconsciously) with someone who resembles him and to transfer certain aspects of that early relationship onto the subsequent attachment.

It is important to understand that separation, individuation, and maturation following the loss of the first attachment tend to mitigate the powerful unconscious tendency to pair with an unconsciously familiar parental substitute. The greater the degree of emotional separation from parents and family, the less powerful are the effects of direct negative transference. Living alone while separating from major attachments will activate one's basic psychological reserves, which could eventually enhance psychological maturation. Seldom does that occur, however, as most young people who leave their family home date regularly, live with a roommate, or seek some emotional involvement in order to avoid the pain of separation anxiety and aloneness.

In order to predict with some confidence the type of person to which one will be attracted, it is necessary to be aware of one's childhood attachment shifts. The age that a child makes shifts in the attachment to parents is extremely important in the detection of transference relationships. For example, if an adult daughter feels that her attachment was to her father, it is important to know her age when that occurred. For, if it happened during late adolescence, there is a high probability she will transfer *mother* residuals onto her partner. If a daughter becomes "daddy's girl" during her first five years and she retains that attachment, there will be little doubt about the parental transference in her marital relationship. Similarly, if a son is dad's favorite child during his first five years and he retains that attachment, he will have an unconscious predilection toward women with dynamics similar to his father's.

In some disturbed families, the child's relationship with the mother is sufficiently negative that the child (in this instance, a son) becomes attached to the father only because he is present less often, and, by virtue of that, he is less punitive and less negative. Therefore, even though the boy's attachment to the father is generated by negative forces, it is still an attachment. In such cases, the son will be unconsciously attracted to someone like the father and simultaneously enraged by the same characteristics to which he was attracted. A double dose of hostility is likely to be directed at the eventual partner. In the confines of intimacy, the anger and hurt over being rejected by the mother and being considered a nuisance by the often-detached father will surely emerge. The son will have a strong propensity to people who are distant, detached, and emotionally unavailable, which he at first mistakes for strength. Under stress, however, he soon discovers that "there is no one there." The situation parallels his childhood when his attachment to father was established because his father was not available.

Several years ago, I worked with a family composed of the most attractive people I have ever seen. The father was exceptionally handsome and sincere. The mother, who had been a fashion model, was elegant. Their three teenaged daughters could be described as sensuous. In fact, the eldest, 16-year-old Sharon, who was the identified patient, was so attractive and photogenic that she was already being offered modeling jobs. As the parents tried to explain their problem, it became apparent that Sharon was in a great deal of pain. Her grades dropped from A's and B's to failures. Once "daddy's girl," she was now acting out with several boys, taking them to her bedroom while her parents were at home. These changes had occurred within the past year and were inconsistent with her previous behavior.

I asked to speak with Sharon alone. After her parents and sisters had left the room, I asked "What is it, really?" She began sobbing, "It's my dad. He hates me, and I don't know why. The last year or so he began hating me, and I didn't even do anything. As long as he's going to hate me, I'm going to give him a good reason." Each time she violated her own ideals and moral training, Sharon experienced increased guilt and alienation, as well as the desire to act out by repeating her "sins." Decoding her unconscious intentions was not too difficult. After a few more minutes with Sharon, I invited the parents in while the daughters waited outside the office. The father was crushed when I told him that his "favorite" daughter believed he hated her. Teary-eyed, he couldn't understand how she could say that, becaues of his genuine affection for her. The mother was a little surprised too, knowing how her husband valued the girl. When the moment was right, I shared my impressions upon first seeing Sharon. "You know," I said, "if I had a daughter as gorgeous as Sharon, I might start ignoring her because of fear of my own sexual impulses." "That's it!" he said, astonished. "Now that I think of it, about a year ago, I noticed that I began to feel sexually excited every time I hugged or kissed her. I thought I must be sick to be aroused by my own daughter, so I began to pull back from her, hoping I could drive her away from me." Smiling a little, I assured him his approach had indeed been successful.

Sharon's way of handling the separation and hurt of being abandoned was to act out sexually with older boys (symbolic fathers). She expressed her resentment toward her father by being so promiscuous. In essence, she was trying to make her father jealous, all the while hoping that he would chase her boyfriends away and reclaim her.

I worked with the parents for the next few months. Within a short time, Sharon quit acting out, and her report card showed nearly all A's. Father and daughter had to detach from each other more gradually.

Sometimes daughter–father transference onto subsequent relationships can be most destructive. In unhealthy families, for example, the father's real attachment can be to his daughter rather than to his wife. Almost always, the father's concern for the daughter is more prevalent than his concern for his wife. Naturally, the mother does not enjoy being replaced, and so she usually becomes extraordinarily rejecting toward her husband and daughter. Her daughter not only becomes confused and needy, but also a competitor who must be destroyed. In most of these cases, the daughter is usually attracted only to older men or to emotionally flattened, beaten men whom she believes to be mature. As one might guess, she does not get along too well with women of any age. Because father unconsciously mixes sexual feelings with his affection, she becomes overly eroticized and frequently seductive. Stable marriages and interpersonal relationships are seldom realized. Marriage cannot satisfy the needs of such a woman because she was already married to her father. For her, marriage is an unsatisfactory substitute, a psychological step backward. There is little to look forward to in a relationship with an "ordinary" man for a woman who was previously married to "God the Father."

Parental transference is a subtle, pervasive phenomenon, the effects of which creep into all intimate relationships. Most marital relationships contain an overload of residual feelings from the first relationship. Parental transference, however, can also be confused and reversed. In such relationships, some children, usually the daughters, are never allowed to be children; instead, they are responsible for raising their parents and siblings. Pathological and very needy parents often employ at least one daughter as a symbolic parent and force her to take care of them. Clearly, the parents need the child, usually the oldest, more than the child needs the parents. When that child matures, it often doesn't occur to her until her own marriage is in trouble that she has always felt like an overly responsible mother. The gnawing feelings of responsibility, guilt, and anger, which she realizes have always been there, serve as the first cue. "Ever since I can remember," she exclaims, "I have felt responsible for my parents, and my brothers and sisters."

The trauma in reversed child transference is that the daughter (or, in some cases, the son) is unconsciously always angry because no one ever really cared about her. Consequently, she is only attracted to weak, infantile individuals so that she can continue with what she does best, parenting. Not only has she unsuccessfully raised her own troublesome parents, but she will, after a short time, have equal difficulty raising her own spouse.

Due to the lopsided parental role in her marriage to an infantile partner, whom she must essentially re-raise, something all to familiar happens. When she feels insecure and in need of support and affection, there is no one there. Those few times when her husband tried to give, she panicked because, for her, receiving from others is impossible. During her early years, much was expected of and taken from her, but little or nothing was given in return. In addition to continuous feelings of resentment, it cannot "feel right" to such a woman to be in a position to receive. This type of affectional cul-de-sac is evidenced when the infantile husband awkwardly tries to give to his wife. Whenever she is in a position to receive, however, her unconscious forces her to ridicule his attempts at giving and she declares it worthless. Whenever her husband tries to give affection, it is never the right kind, nor even satisfactory. In response, she attacks with sarcasm and doubts about his sincerity. Her favorite retort is, "Where the hell were you when I needed you?"

When one is in a position to receive, it opens one up to the longings of the past. Thus, "victims" of reversed child transference cannot accept warmth, support, or affection. To do so would only trigger the repressed rage caused by the affectional deprivation of what they desperately wanted but never received.

SIBLING TRANSFERENCE

In some families, a child's primary attachment is not with the mother or father, but with an older sibling. When siblings become attached to each other and attempt to meet each other's needs, their subsequent intimacies are almost always overwhelmed with insecurity, lack of direction, and competition. For, when a child's attachment is to an older sibling who is neither capable of nor responsible for providing protection, caring, discipline, and consistency, insecurity always results.

Sometimes, a child is turned over to an older sibling because the parents cannot be bothered or cannot manage. The younger child becomes both a plaything—often being treated like a doll—and a displacement object for natural childhood recklessness and aggression. The child's needs cannot be met. To get anything, he must become self-sufficient. Unable to become comfortably dependent on the older sibling—who resents the younger one's intrusion on his own self-interest—the child becomes pseudoindependent and more or less raises himself. Continuously angry inside, however, he will be unable to enjoy a comfortable, secure, and mutual relationship because he has never had one.

When children raised by older siblings pair, they are unconsciously attracted to a "brother type" or a "sister type." Sometimes, these "sibling marriages" appear ideal to the casual observer because the couple seems to get along so well. However, a healthy attachment to one another is seldom present. What each partner needs emotionally must be gotten outside the relationship. Although they are living together, each has a life almost entirely separate from the other. Feelings of genuine love are often sought elsewhere, usually from someone who is more clearly a power figure, in order for each to unconsciously feel taken care of by someone more capable than the older sibling. Neither can quite understand why they are so easily turned on to authoritative, dominating people outside of their relationship. Behind closed doors, the security and interdependency that is ordinarily received from healthy parental transference is missing. After all, the couple are "brother and sister." Whether they are really the friends they pretend to be, is doubtful.

TYPES OF RELATIONSHIPS

Ideally, both pairing and marriage could be more productive and less destructive if people were aware of their real motives and needs and were reasonably mature. But most people are not particularly aware of who they are, nor are they especially mature when they pair. Consequently, most pairing is essentially random, illogical, and irrational. Couples hope their relationships work out, but they never work out quite the way they expected. The amount of suffering induced by each other and their children can never be contained or calculated after a relationship becomes unsatisfactory and destructive. In this section, frequently observed "types" of relationships will be described. In almost all of them, the individual's capacity for intimacy and the oppositional character traits discussed in Chapter 2 apply.

Land of the Lost

Not for a moment should the reader believe that through marriage a parent "has not lost a daughter, but has gained a son" or "has not lost a son, but gained a daughter." It has been shown in the previous chapters that a child's initial emotional attachment to the parent must be mutual. Unconsciously, there is an emotional symbiosis in all parental attachments that is never completely severed. Frequently, it takes the death of one or both parents for a person to come to grips with his feelings of belonging, aloneness, self-dependence, and existential roots. In fact, children who were abandoned by their parents and who desire to meet them, "just to know," will experience the insecurity and aloneness to which I refer.

The individual's attachment to the primary figure or parents has literally existed a lifetime prior to pairing, after which it is expected to be gradually left behind. Even if the first relationship was pathological, it supplied some semblance of security, support, guidance, and love. Therefore, to leave whatever there was behind for the sake of serious pairing is in essence to suffer a sense of loss. When the initial passion, youthful impulsivity, and erotic energy wear down after a relatively short time of marriage, boredom, loneliness, and depression almost always become manifest. Although there may be hundreds of assumed reasons for these feelings, most of it can be attributed to loss of the first love or family. Some couples experience this postmarital depression almost immediately, particularly when one or both has had to relocate. For others, it is masked in a variety of activities unconsciously designed to avoid coming to grips with feelings of depression and loss of parents.

In millions of American homes, there are married couples who can attest to how much more complicated and difficult life became after they were married. During courtship, both partners are convinced that their "love" can carry them through any differences of opinion or even a catastrophe. After a relatively short time, however, their abundance of "love" vanishes (this is detailed in Chapter 5). As mentioned previously, each slowly becomes aware of feeling depressed, lonely, bored, and isolated. Some couples keep these feelings to themselves because they are sure there is no logical reason for them. Others are absolutely convinced that the marriage is bad or that they don't "love" each other. They reason that, if they were more "in love"—or at least felt the way they did during courtship—then those painful feelings would not be there and they would be happier.

Sometimes, couples abandon perfectly healthy and potentially satisfying marriages because of the negative feelings experienced from the loss of the first relationship. Although neither partner may be directly contributing to the other's suffering, each blames the other and the marriage. After all, they never felt so depressed and alone before they were married. Thus, they assume that the marriage is bad, not realizing that it was the act of getting married, which cut off all hope of returning home, that actually depressed them. Feelings of loss and aloneness after marriage are sometimes observed in those individuals who could not stand to be home when they were adolescents, but who desire to return home once they marry and have children.

Psychological literature has long recognized the effects on the parents, especially the mother, when a favorite child leaves home to be married. In some families, the "loss" of a favorite child is so painful that the attached parent may have a "nervous breakdown" or go into a deep depression that is never quite resolved. Sometimes, such parents die. In other families, loss of a child to someone else may deal the final blow, pushing a marriage of many years into collapse. When a child leaves, some parents are forced to deal with each other for the first time in years. Some discover a new relationship with one another, whereas others divorce or do their own thing. Still others slowly give up the will to live and eventually die a few years after the child's marriage. Whatever happens, life will not be the same.

It is known that the birth of the first child sometimes solidifies a precarious relationship. What is virtually unknown is that, for parents, the birth of the child symbolically severs any hope of ever returning to the first love. For some fathers, the birth represents the loss of the first love *for the second time.* Such men see their wives as more involved with their child than with them.

Playing Doctor and Playing House

Playing Doctor and Playing House relationships are common among adolescents and emotionally immature adults. Neither individual in the relationship knows much about the self, the world, or the responsibility of their interactions. Nearly always, one or both individuals are still emotionally dependent upon the parents. If one individual playing the game is married, he or she is usually emotionally dependent upon the spouse. The security of this dependence offers a temporary buffer from reality, which allows them to become preoccupied with each other's genitals and also to simulate the fantasy of playing house.

Because of the couples' psychosocial immaturity, this adolescent-like relationship is similar to very early developmental phases when children simulate parental roles by playing house. (Most children also play doctor, which requires them to examine each other's genitalia.) Some adolescents use the relationship to simulate roles they learned somewhere else. One thing, for sure, is that breaking up and getting back together are very important. Unable to have mature feelings of affection due to their adolescent-level self-preoccupation, they cannot know what each means to the other when they are together. Thus, they measure their love by the degree of anxiety, anger, and jealousy experienced when they break up. Only after they break up might they be able to evaluate the importance of the partner. In addition, each calibrates his lovableness by the degree of anger and hurt the partner feels toward competitors. Clever adolescents will create artificial, exaggerated responses to looks and glances from the opposite sex in order to make the partner jealous and to make themselves appear to be worth something to someone. Overidentification with popular peers, movie stars, or someone great provides the adolescent with a pseudofeeling of being worthwhile and lovable. To delude himself about how much he means to the other is another way to temporarily elevate self-worth.

Being primarily a receiver in their first relationship, adolescents playing house often find it a shock when they must give. As reality and responsibility intrude upon their play, one or both partners often want out. Playing house and doctor are not much fun after each has thoroughly examined the other and the bills begin to come in, which have to be paid.

Frequently, adolescent couples who marry return to their parents for help so that they can continue the first relationship as it was before. When one or both partners are overly dependent upon the first love, usually for money, the relationship seldom has a chance to mature and stabilize. Economically, the new family may look alright; emotionally, however, there is a powerful pull to remain dependent upon the parents. The dependence is often more than economic—the overall effect is to keep the new family dependent and immature.

The negative factors the couple once used to calibrate "love" later become exposed for what they are. That is, jealousy and anger in their exaggerated forms are indicative of overdependency and insecurity rather than of mature affection. The more insightful individuals, upon realizing this, begin to seriously wonder if they have ever been "loved."

Not all Playing House and Playing Doctor relationships incur difficulty during the early years. Sometimes, it is not until their own children become adolescents that such couples come face to face with where they left off in their own development. Seeing their children free to come and go and free to play house and doctor stimulates their inner turmoil and desire for further growth. The responsibility of reality did not help them to develop but rather held their growth in abeyance. In some cases, they divorce and resume life at approximately the level of psychosocial maturity of their teenagers. They are once again free to play house. This time, however, the playmate may be different, and they are apt to be less eager to take it seriously.

Some couples, usually after much conflict and ambivalence, try to grow up with their adolescents: they lose weight, buy a new car, wear youthful clothes, become physical-fitness fanatics, and so on. They compete with their teenagers' friends, while presenting themselves as the most "mod," the "neatest," and the "coolest" parents in the neighborhood. Occasionally, they are appreciated more by their children's friends than by their chldren, who are embarrassed by their parents' behavior. And the couple seems able to relate to adolescents very well, as long as they're not their own.

Phallic Wife

Some men, usually those who are unable to genuinely relate to anyone, seek only the most beautiful, voluptuous, seductive, and relatively superficial women. Deep within, these men are insecure, inadequate, emotionally weak, and infantile; they feel worthless and impotent. These pervasive feelings began in an insufficient first relationship and are often carried throughout life. To compensate for their real feelings, such men are usually competitive and strive for positions of prestige and power in order to prove to themselves that they are nothing like the way they are inside. To them, it is necessary to have a glamorous wife to prove to others that they are secure, powerful, valued, and successful. Moreover, they only feel "right" when others are noticing their achievements and possessions. Naturally, their most valued possession is the Phallic Wife.

While I was supervising family and individual therapists in training, we facetiously coined the "small penis syndrome" to describe the behavior of men who try to evaluate others via subtle questioning: What kind of car do you have? What do you do for a living?—i.e., how much money do you earn? Where do you live?—i.e., how much is your house worth? All these questions are related symbolically to penis size and inevitably to feelings of power and status.

Middle-class males usually compare symbolic penis size by economic standards, while lower-class males do not have a broad educational, occupational, or professional stage upon which to display themselves. They stress the development of muscles and macho, and boast about the number of lovers they've had. Fast and loud cars, motorcycles, or anything motorized are compared. The lower-class male with the fastest, loudest, biggest, and best of anything usually feels as though he has the biggest and most enviable penis.

For some men, to show off the prized wife in the hope of making other men jealous is to symbolically show off the valuable phallus. Such a man is unable to see his wife as a human being with human needs. Instead, he sees her as a parcel of real estate, which he is sure everyone else wants. Because of his deep-seated inadequacy over penis size, he doesn't want others to see his wife when she is not at her best. He also doesn't want her exposed to anyone who might take her away. Consequently, he feels proud and potent when his wife looks great at a social event but panics if she looks at anyone else. If his wife dresses up or takes a shower before going shopping or out with woman friends, he suspects she is seeing another man. If she's a few minutes late getting home, he feels angry and threatened. To his chagrin, he discovers that his wife is not as easily controlled as his other possessions.

In order to protect themselves and to feel secure, some men "institutionalize" their wives by keeping them busy, pregnant, or both so that they are always safe from other males. Whenever his wife is not at home, however, such a man's first thoughts are usually not for her safety but rather that someone might be molesting his phallus. Some lower-class males physically beat their wives into staying at home. In extreme cases, a straying wife, her lover, or both are sometimes killed by an enraged husband. For him, to lose his phallus is to lose all feelings of power and importance.

Deep inside, the wife realizes that her husband was attracted to her looks and body. Although that may have satisfied her for awhile, her unfulfilled human needs will eventually come to the forefront. She will more than likely accuse her husband of wanting her only for her body and for sex, or she will complain of feeling like just another possession. Her husband, however, is apt to feel even more impotent because she may well be asking for what he cannot give, a sustained intimate relationship.

When the husband sees someone more attractive than his wife, he unconsciously desires to possess her too. The wife is usually aware of her husband's wandering desires, but is not too concerned because she knows he has enough trouble getting his penis up at home. What she does not realize is that her husband is truly potent only while he is in pursuit. It is only after he owns the pursued woman and she realizes his inadequacy that he cannot perform too well.

Vaginal Husband

Externally, the Vaginal Husband may appear to be similar to the Phallic Wife. However, a woman's motives for wanting such a husband are slightly different. Often, a guilty, inhibited, puritanical woman is attracted to a handsome, self-centered, attention-demanding, and "devious" man. She is often embarrassed by and feels guilty over her sexual impulses. As a child, she was taught that her vagina was more worthwhile and more desirable than she was—but also the dirtiest part of her. Her vagina was almost viewed as a separate entity by her parents.

From preadolescence on, her parents were more concerned with her vagina than with her. Whenever she was out of their sight, she was interrogated, "Where have you been so late?" or "Did you behave yourself?" The questions were a way of asking about her vagina. The young woman, however, knew how to decipher the code, and she resented it. Her vagina and its protection were more important to her parents than her feelings, needs, and concerns. Later, when the young woman paired, her parents let her know that the "only thing he wants is sex."

Now, when the realities of her marital relationship have become apparent, the woman is in a terrible bind. When Vaginal Husband attends to her in a loving manner, she believes it is only because he wants her vagina. Because amorous activity often leads to coitus, she becomes convinced her parents were indeed correct. However, when he becomes upset with her repetitious accusations ("You only want my vagina, not me as a person") and abstains from sex to prove it's not true, she wonders what's wrong with her vagina. To have that valuable part of her ignored, which has gotten almost constant recognition for as long as she can remember, is the final blow. She has little choice but to feel inadequate, resentful, and unloved.

As mentioned, such women are unconsciously attracted to men who are handsome and socially valuable, but also a little devious (bad). This description is very similar to those adjectives their parents once ascribed to the vagina. When married, they take care of their husbands in much the same way that they took care of the valuable but guilt-provoking organ. They seem most willing to help their husbands with their successes and interests, even at great expense to themselves. They take care of him, guide him, and ascribe much higher value to him than to themselves. They treat him as fragile, and they are simultaneously proud and guilty when he is on public display. Indeed, they feel too worthless or too guilt-ridden to have such a valuable "possession." Moreover, to think too much about their personal needs stimulates feelings of guilt, selfishness, and shame. They have learned well that their own needs and interests are not important. Their husbands let them know that, as did their parents.

In most cases, the Vaginal Husband is himself sexually confused. Because, deep within, he feels more female than male, he does not mind being "vagina" to his spouse. Such a relationship can be very satisfying as long as each partner is in the healthy-to-mildly-neurotic range of adjustment. Within the healthy range, the husband's mother will have had a fairly healthy relationship with her partner, but probably was overly anxious about parenting and invested too much of herself in her son. Within the healthy range, the Vaginal Husband is capable of appreciation, empathy, and appropriate guilt when his partner fusses over him too much. He is able to give and receive and is emotionally expressive and considerate, thus heightening his wife's ability to value him. In turn, this raises his desire to treat her the way she needs to be treated for her own growth.

The give-and-take that is natural in vaginal or phallus relationships will never approach equality. If it did, the wife would be most unhappy because she would be valued too much, and the husband would feel rejected, abandoned, and angry. Consciously, he believes that he is worth much more than she and that he should be treated in accordance with his higher value. Unconsciously, he cannot be genuinely attracted to someone who needs equal time, or to a woman who refuses to claim him as more important.

The Comforters

The Comforters are people who become attached to each other while one or both is in a crisis. Believing that they can thoroughly understand each other because they share certain life tragedies offers the Comforters a sense of support and emotional connectedness, which attenuates existential aloneness. (In other words, misery loves company!)

Two students away at college provide a good example. Psychodynamically, they may be worlds apart, but finding a person in a similar predicament tends to ease the pain of their aloneness and offer a feeling of mutality, which helps them feel less anxious. As long as they are together, they are sure it is "love." When they are apart however, they are riddled with uncertainty. Nevertheless, they offer each other enough comfort to convince themselves they should marry. After a short period of marriage, they begin wondering again.

Away from home many traveling salesmen, businessmen, and conventioneers find themselves flirting with women they usually would not have noticed in order to reduce massive separation anxiety. Even ordinarily faithful husbands surprise themselves with their urge to become involved with someone when they are in unfamiliar and possibly frightening surroundings. For the most part, women "on the road" do face these temptations, but to a lesser degree. Many of them seek out strangers for companionship's sake alone, whereas men more often use sexuality as a reason to be close.

Because of their psychopathology, some people are insecure, alone, anxious, and frightened nearly all of the time. When they meet someone equally disturbed, who also believes that the world is cruel and people are insensitive, an attachment is formed almost immediately. They are not aware that when people are in enough pain, nearly anyone will do.

The categories of people who are attracted to one another because of trauma, crisis, and overall pathology are endless. Juvenile delinquents, social outcasts, alcoholics, drug addicts, and juvenile runaways make up a large subculture of people who are attracted to each other for little reason other than that they are in the same boat. Given a later time, there might not be any attraction at all. People who have divorced, parents who have lost children, children who have lost parents, and people with similar defects (e.g., blindless), in similar institutions, with similar beliefs may be attracted to one another primarily because of their "underdog" identification. When a strange or traumatic set of circumstances becomes invested with excessive emotional energy, the probability is increased that two people with similar experiences will become attracted to each other for no reason other than that they can identify with each other and have suffered together.

A marriage with comfort as its primary basis may work out for awhile, but time has a way of healing the initial emotional bruises and emotional trauma. If it does, the attachment to and appreciation for the Comforter can be lost. When a person is trying to grow and move beyond personal tragedy and anguish, it is humiliating to be reminded of the days when living was traumatic—and very hard to forget when the Comforter lives in the same house.

Obligation and Guilt

For some couples, the basis for pairing is neither desire nor capacity for positive relatedness, nor healthy psychological adjustment; instead, the marital coagulent is obligation and guilt. In this type of relationship, one partner (in this instance, the husband) may have wanted out for as long as both can remember. When he finally musters up the courage to depart, the wife reminds him of what was "taken" or "lost" or "sacrificed" during their time together. Some wives, desperate over the prospect of being left alone, frantically try to convince him of the good times or draw upon almost any guilt-producing lever to keep him home. When the play on guilt does not keep the husband in line, the wife might employ psychological blackmail, threats, and promises of imminent evil. In such cases, the relationship is essentially destructive, and the about-to-be-abandoned wife is more concerned with the panic and humiliation of being left alone than with the actual relationship. The idealistic symbols of marriage and the individual interpretation of the value of "being married" carry more meaning to the guilt-and-obligation couple than the actual *process* of relating satisfactorily to each other. If they could satisfactorily relate, it wouldn't be necessary to use guilt and obligation to hold it together.

The bottom line in guilt-and-obligation marriages epitomizes the individual's attempt to manipulate the partner through a power play. It is indeed a fallacy that there is no strength or power in mental illness. Even an apparently helpless person has more power and control ("pathos power") over others than do most healthy individuals. A typical instance involves a spouse (in this example, the wife) who threatens to "go crazy"—which usually means "out of control"—if the partner leaves. The message to the husband is quite clear: "If you leave me, I am not sure what I will do." Of course, the husband really doesn't know what his wife means by such a threat, which is exactly what prevents definitive action. No matter what the wife should do, there would be no question as to whose "fault" it was. "If I only knew for sure what my wife would do, I would have the freedom to leave," is the secret thought of the husband.

In an obligation-and-guilt relationship, each partner knows full well the vulnerabilities of the other. The wife being abandoned, for example, is often so desperate that she becomes brilliant at manipulating her husband. Her uncertainty over what will happen to her if the husband leaves can cause such behaviors as psychogenic heart attacks, suicide, and, in extreme cases, the murder of the children. Messages of the less desperate include threats over nervous breakdowns, becoming an alcoholic, or quitting a financially necessary job. Most of the stakes of destruction are too high to be ignored.

Some reasonable amount of guilt and obligation is present in all successful relationships. The higher the level of emotional maturity, the more apt self-imposed guilt and obligation serve as important bonding agents, holding the commitment to each other firm. Moreover, emotional maturity inherently includes the capacity for positive relatedness, which provides the greater bonding function. In relatively healthy couples, the satisfaction derived from the relationship, and the desire to remain married are natural bonding agents. During times of doubt, conflict, resentment, and hardship, when one or both may entertain serious fantasies about getting out, memories of good times, along with a reasonable sense of obligation and guilt, prevent either partner from doing something that might hurt the other. Without the historic accumulation of joyful times and without the capacity for positive relatedness, obligation and guilt in a relationship would tend to be destructive.

It's About Time

It's About Time pairing is observed in individuals who wait longer than is typical or statistically normal before pairing. Some of these people are somewhat frightened of intimacy and are probably aware that they are incapable of a sustained relationship. Nevertheless, they are unconsciously programmed to pair before they reach a certain age or goal. As they approach that time, they convince themselves that they are ready to make the big step. After a short period of marriage, however, they begin to wonder about how ready they really were. That is, after more than an average number of years of living alone, marriage sometimes turns out to be more trouble than it is worth. Because the individual is convinced that he is supposed to know what he wants, and is supposed to be mature, the It's About Time individual tends to ignore marital problems and his contribution to them.

People sometimes overlook the need for emotional maturity before seriously seeking a partner. Those individuals who "must get married" or who are convinced that their lives will truly begin when they find the "right person," are frequently the most disillusioned. On the other hand, some individuals know within themselves that they are capable of intimacy, but prefer to postpone pairing until they are more mature. Such individuals demonstrate more maturity than is typical because they recognize that they *may* not be mature enough to handle the responsibilities of marriage.

When one or both partners feel compelled to pair by setting age limits, distortions in judgment and in misinterpretation of interpersonal and emotional cues are inevitable. Whenever someone pairs out of desperation, he or she loses touch with their real feelings about what is best for them. The panic, so to speak, can easily prevent the unconscious need for a partner with similar relational qualities and opposite character traits to occur. Without these naturally tested necessities, the relationship is doomed to fail.

Thirty is the age that many people consider as the ceiling for "normal" pairing. When people pair for the first time at age 30 or older, they often have difficulty adjusting to the responsibility involved in caring for two people. They have been accustomed to coming and going as they pleased, and so some tension may result until they reach a satisfactory balance. Moreover, when the wife is 30 or older, the couple may feel pressured to have children immediately. If they already feel restricted by marriage, a dependent baby will only heighten their feeling of constraint.

The most serious disadvantage to the It's About Time marriage is that, psychologically, it can be a "shotgun" wedding. When people feel that they "have to" get married, for whatever reason, their urgency causes them to project fantasies, wishes, and ideals onto each other. Usually, these are much more favorable than what really exists. When a person is needy or desperate, he experiences an exaggerated capacity for relatedness, which he attributes to the partner's ability to "love." Reality often does not intrude until too late. "I wanted to get married so badly," goes the familiar rationale, "that I didn't see what he was really like. I think I was blinded by a few good features that were important to me at the time."

The Atonement

There are some individuals who, because of a destructive, rejecting relationship with their first love, will never adequately resolve their hurt and resentment toward their parents. They unconsciously enter into destructive atonement relationships, which can result in undefinable emotional and physical suffering and, in some cases, death. The hurts of childhood and the subsequent attempt to heal them provide the predisposition for the eventual destruction. In an Atonement relationship, one individual believes that he is "bad" and should therefore suffer. In extreme cases, he unconsciously desires to destroy that "bad thing" (the self) just as his parents (unconsciously) wanted him destroyed. The individual's feelings of worthlessness are sufficiently prevalent that it is impossible for him to feel good about being alive. Thus, in order to feel valued at all, he unconsciously seeks a partner who is perfectly willing to continue in his emotional demise. In such relationships, the bad person needs to be punished and disparaged.

To be abused and rejected by the partner is not interpreted as destruction at all, but as love. It is after all, what the parents did "out of love." The parental line—"this hurts me more than it hurts you"—is eventually interpreted as "caring." If the child believes it, he learns to associate his value and personal worth by his ability to endure punishment. Consequently, when he feels anxious, alone, or depressed and in need of affection, he provokes the spouse into abusing him.

Masochistic individuals seldom feel complete without a sadistic partner, who too easily shows anger and hostility. From childhood onward, they damage or destroy things in order to release their anguish. As children, because they were frightened of their parents, they direct their aggressive outbursts at people smaller or weaker in order to protect themselves against retaliation. They destroyed objects, as well as anything less powerful, such as small animals and birds. To kill and destroy released psychological anguish and brought feelings of pleasure. To see someone suffer was to vicariously release hostility, which brought temporary relief from a continuous state of anxiety, confusion, fear, and rejection. It is not necessary for the damaged individual to be a criminal. The damage inflicted upon children by needy, insensitive parents is nondiscriminatory.

An individual's need to hurt and destroy another is frightening and offensive to people who have no such need. Nondestructive individuals feel very uncomfortable in the presence of a destructive person, whom they quickly evaluate as "sick." On the other hand, people who need to continue the destructive relatedness of the first love are unconsciously intrigued by and attracted to sadists who delight in inflicting pain. In short, masochists need sadists and sadists need masochists to carry out the patterns of love established by the first relationship.

Frequently, sadists feel guilt over their desire to harm the partner. They cannot stop, however, because the urge is generated by their unconscious feelings of needing to destroy someone just as they have been destroyed. That urge must be expressed toward the partner, who in some way reminds the sadist of the first love. Not until the second love dies, or abandons or divorces the sadist can he feel a sense of rest and reduced inner tension.

Several times over the years, I have observed Atonement relationships in action. When the sadist has adequately "cleared the slate" of childhood damage by destroying the partner, there is a notable change in the dynamics influencing subsequent partner choice. If the sadist can take at least a year to grieve over the loss of the partner and to do adequate psychological penance for what was done, the second choice is usually much healthier. If, on the other hand, the childhood damage was too severe, he will immediately search for another masochist to continue the symbolic destruction of the first love; the second relationship will be a duplication of the first. The exact number of sadistic scenes needed to provide catharsis is unknown. For instance, one pathological woman went through five husbands in less than 20 years; four died from heart attacks, and one divorced her.

Rebound

There is an extraordinarily high number of tumultuous, unsatisfactory relationships among those who paired while attempting to recover from the loss of a previous partner. When an individual has been abandoned, divorced, or widowed, he frequently begins immediately to seek a replacement. During the period of grief and emotional confusion, there is a tendency to transfer the positive qualities from the lost partner onto the replacement. In fact, some people consciously compare their subsequent dates to the lost partner, without realizing the implications of what they are doing. When one or two characteristics of the prospective partner remotely resemble those of the lost love, the grieving individual unconsciously completes the emotional portrait and, in doing so, erroneously assumes that the new partner is "exactly" like the one who was lost. The more thoroughly the individual can generalize and transfer characteristics from the previous partner onto the prospective mate, the greater is his capacity to deny the heartache from the loss of the previous partner.

Denial of loss, however, can only work for so long. When the individual gradually realizes what he has done, the remains of the grief and anger not experienced following the initial loss begin to surface. It is not at all uncommon for the individual to unconsciously attempt to drive the new spouse away because of the need to adequately grieve and to resolve the feeling of loss. If the relationship is relatively open and the communication honest, the second partner will confront the issues so that the situation can be either resolved satisfactorily or terminated. It takes a reasonably strong and articulate individual to confront the partner about the pressure to drive him away. Most people will respond to the rejection and leave or feel hurt for a long time.

The desperate desire to replace the lost partner usually forces the remaining partner (in this instance, the male) to actively and aggressively seek a substitute. Because of that aggressiveness and the tendency to transfer the characteristics of the lost love onto the new partner, the prospective partner is almost always swept off her feet. Amidst the desperation, each minute of the new relationship is experienced as days or weeks because things seem to happen so fast. Emotionally, each hour they are together can represent years. The confusion and hyperactivity used to combat the loss surrounds the entire relationship. Neither individual can be rational in such a highly charged emotional engulfment. The new partner is flattered that she could possibly be needed and "loved" so much, so deeply. Both are convinced that they have never felt this way before, so quickly, so intensely. Impulsively, they decide to marry. As long as they can keep running from themselves, neither will have to look back at the tracks they were trying to cover. Most people, however, eventually get tired of running. When they slow down, it becomes obvious why it all happened so fast.

Sometimes the one who has been abandoned is sufficiently hurt by the loss that he is *never* able to psychologically recover. The anger, depression, and bitterness is stored inside, for to let it go would mean to acknowledge that the partner is indeed gone. In such circumstances, the individual may pair with someone he could never really love. Instead, the new partner is often someone who is so emotionally detached that she evokes no feelings. To pair with someone who is a "nothing" serves as an excellent safeguard against ever again feeling love or loss, vulnerability or abandonment. Over time, however, the loss will either be worked through or repressed, and the person will want to live again. Unfortunately, he will still be married to a nobody. To help a nobody become a somebody within the confines of marriage is seldom possible. A favorite solution, if one chooses to stay in the marriage, is to have a child, thus giving the person on the rebound someone to love. Often, he feels the same way toward the child as he felt toward the lost lover.

Stepping Stone

Stepping-Stone marriages can be the most devious of all. The deviousness begins early in (or even prior to) courtship when one person (in this instance, the man) sets out to snare another. To net a good catch, he must psychologically seduce the woman by discovering her likes, dislikes, and emotional vulnerabilities. His next step is to become exactly like what he perceives the woman's "ideal" partner to be. It seldom occurs to the pursuer that, in order to manipulate the woman, he will have to become something he is not. Thus, he is being manipulated himself. Eventually, he discovers that what was initially construed as winning turns out to be losing. When one deliberately becomes what he is not in order to secure a partner, the day of reckoning will not be far ahead. To not have experienced the feelings and vitality of being in love and to pair with someone one does not love leaves life more than a little empty.

More often than not, Stepping-Stone marriages are generated by what the prospective partner has or represents—wealth, prestige, or social position—rather than by what he is as a person. For example, it is often those people who feel inadequate, unlovable, and worthless who seek to live in the best house in the best neighborhood, to drive the best car, and to make sure others know it. What they are really striving for is to compensate for their underlying feelings of nothingness. What they need in order to feel genuinely adequate and comfortable with themselves—the love of someone important—is exactly what neither can have. When they achieve their goal and start to rest, the pain from which they were running starts to surface. There nearly always comes a day of reckoning and thoughts of suicide.

Somewhat less devious than the individual who pursues a mate for wealth and status is the individual who is attracted to the partner's parents and siblings and their sense of family, as much as or more than he is attracted to the partner. This type of Stepping Stone is not calculated by external events such as wealth, social status, or physical beauty, but by the procurement of an affirmative human support system. To pair with an individual of one's choosing and to acquire an additional family can add to one's network of security and emotional stability. This is especially applicable when the future in-laws are mutually attracted to the future son- or daughter-in-law. When the Stepping Stone is toward a greater human support network, the individual commonly expresses that he finds it easier to relate to his partner's family than to his own. In such cases, the unconscious pull is not exclusively toward the in-laws, but the attachment to the spouse is hastened by such needs. In addition to the affection for the partner, the hope for inclusion in the spouse's family may well be the decisive factor in whether the relationship will result in marriage. When the attraction to relatives is too great, the spouse will probably feel used. Behind closed doors, there has been more than one marital fight over "You think more of my parents [or brother or sister] than you do of me!"

There are other Stepping-Stone motives that sneak out when couples are in conflict. The resentful, "You only married me for my _____," provides the first clue. Most couples have some difficulty deceiving one another after they have been together awhile. It is during these heated arguments that more truth slips out than people care to acknowledge. When rational controls give way to raw emotion, real feelings exude. Some of the more common Stepping Stones include the hope of eventually acquiring an estate or business, the partner's assistance in getting through college, the hope for inclusion in a higher socioeconomic class, and the status derived from pairing with an extremely attractive individual.

Dry-Wet Nurse

The most conspicuous of the destructive relationships is the alcoholic system motivated by the "nurse-patient principle." The nurse-patient dyad is comprised of a psychologically weak, distant, overly dependent, and infantile male alcoholic who pairs with an equally weak, distant, overly dependent, but somewhat more responsible, domineering, and castrating female. Psychologically, they deserve one another, despite what appears to be a lopsided and miserable relationship. Almost everyone who knows such a couple considers the wife a long-suffering saint who has done absolutely nothing to deserve her fate. Clearly, the husband is the obvious culprit—he must have a "dual personality." When he is sober, so the story goes, he is the nicest guy around, but when he is drunk a "brutal bastard" emerges. In some cases, well-meaning people help keep the situation alive by labeling alcoholism a disease. Therefore, when the husband is drunk and totally irresponsible, he is blameless.

While the husband is out on a binge, the wife remains at home, baffled and infuriated. Deep within, however, she needs a spouse who is psychologically inferior to herself. In fact, she derives gratification from knowing that her no-good husband is inflicting pain upon her, while she, a martyr, is holding the marriage and the family together. Each condemnation of her husband, whether inferred or direct, to relatives, friends, and children contains a pointed message about her goodness and his wickedness.

The Dry-Wet Nurse is frequently a struggling, conflicted, hostile, dependent individual who tries to deny these feelings by reversing her dependency needs. She desires someone who can take care of her, love her, obey her, and meet her every need. But because of her own incapacity for positive relatedness, she is frightened of equal-level adult intimacy. She can only relate with some degree of comfort to young children, who do not threaten or criticize her, and to infantile adults.

Unconsciously, the Dry-Wet Nurse is attracted to helpless, alcoholic males who often have the emotional maturity of an eight-year-old. Similar to children, the alcoholic is usually unable to maturely confront his "mother" (his wife) because she always needs to be right and powerful. If he does, she quickly puts him in his place. So frightened is he of his wife-mother that the only time he can be himself is when he is drunk. Moreover, conniving, lying, and subtle manipulation are the only ways he can relate to his wife. (The guilt from outside love affairs is exculpated by the common knowledge that many alcoholic men, because of the "disease," sooner or later become involved with other women.) More often than not, he will eventually return home to "mother." When he has been a good boy for awhile and has regained mommy's trust, he is ready for another binge.

The Dry-Wet Nurse was initially attracted to the defense mechanisms of the male alcoholic and was only partially aware that they masked his real personality. She sees a man who appears strong and tough, and she believes his stories of how powerful and fearless he is. She is sure he can use all his macho and strength to take care of her because he deliberately gives off an image of being totally independent and self-sufficient. In fact, he is always telling her how independent and stalwart he is. She also sees a man who is kind and generous, because he so often wants to buy drinks for his friends. She misses the reason why he is *so* generous: he only gives to be loved in return.

A Dry-Wet Nurse does not realize that her man is frightened, infantile, and overly dependent. She does realize that something is different about him, however, because she feels so comfortable and nonthreatened when around him. Something also tells her that he needs her desperately. To be badly needed is flattering and is usually consistent with her previous family identity in which she was instrumental in raising her inadequate parents, her siblings, or both. She has overidentified with the role of mother. Deep within, she wants to be mothered and valued, but to acknowledge it would make her too vulnerable. With minimal effort, she can usually remember that time during childhood when she promised herself she would never be in the scary position of ever needing anybody again. Consequently, she can only be attracted to weak, ineffectual, and passive-dependent males who pose little threat.

To see her man-child so weak and infantile, however, is to see that part of herself which she has tried to disown. She manages to maintain her ego integrity by destroying those aspects of her husband that are present in herself. The cycle becomes complete. She gets a chance to hate and destroy her husband who represents her own negative traits, along with the opportunity to vocalize the hate she feels for her own parents. He gets a castrating mother who continues to provide the damage that made him the boy he is.

More clearly evident here than in any of the other relationships discussed is that the destroyed alcoholic male unconsciously seeks a much-too-perfect mother substitute who can continue the denigration. All too often, the wife becomes a castrating, nagging mother surrogate who must care for, nurture, discipline, and support her boy. Despite the heartache that flourishes in the system, pathological needs are being fulfilled. Interestingly, it is not uncommon for recovering alcoholics and their spouses to divorce. If the male can get his dependency needs met elsewhere, either by peers who are recovered alcoholics, or religion, or both, his wife is apt to have little value to him. If he becomes stronger and less infantile, he may be too threatening for her. He then appears similar to all those other men who make her extremely anxious. In fact, he might say what he feels and then violently react against her need to disparage and dominate. Thus, for either to become healthier may ruin their relationship.

Everybody But We and Thee Is Sick

The Everybody But We and Thee Is Sick relationship is comprised of two individuals who have a major investment in the simulation of a "mod" or "socially aware" or "contemporary" identity. Influenced partially by the spirit of the times and partially by volumes on "how to get your head together in three easy steps," thousands of lost sheep delude themselves into believing that their psychopathology is proof of their specialness and complexity. After acquisition of some "with it" expressions, behaviors, and attitudes, they deceive themselves into believing that they know exactly who they are. Convinced that they themselves can deal with anything, they evaluate everybody, particularly the partner, for psychological symptoms and signs of inability to "deal with things." The symptoms detected in others are not bona fide clinical symptoms, but are merely behaviors and attitudes different from their own. Because they are frequently well-read, or college-educated, or have participated in group or individual psychotherapy, they believe that they represent the zenith of mental health, against which all others must be compared.

The American contemporary social climate is perfect for generating and perpetuating the Everybody But We relationship. Since one must be somewhat aware of national trends in order to simulate certain life-styles, the Everybody But We relationships are more common among the middle class and among those from large metropolitan areas that are the "place to be." This type of relationship commonly results as a reaction to the couple's developmentally repressed, overly dependent, and/or severely rejecting childhood. Their anger, hostility, and resentment, caused partly by feeling almost totally misunderstood, are suppressed. Pseudoaggression, which dissipates some of their pent-up feelings, is displayed freely toward people who are "sick" (i.e., conservative, establishment-oriented). Deep within, they are so severely repressed that they occasionally manufacture a token tantrum or display inappropriate aggression toward each other just to prove to themselves that they have no guilt over direct confrontations or displays of anger. Somewhere in their reading or in their therapy, they remember that "well people" are relatively uninhibited and are able to confront one another and exchange anger without devastation. Thus, they superficially adopt a mannerism of confrontation and directness in order to appear "real" and "self-actualized." While visiting friends, they go into their well-rehearsed act, "dealing with each other." Some people may be impressed, but their more attuned friends see through the act.

Another trademark of the Everybody But We relationship is the slowly acquired conviction that stable family relationships, marital fidelity, and mutual interdependency are rudiments of severe mental illness. In addition to the couple's display of pseudo-openness and pseudoaggression is their conviction that they are each totally self-sufficient and independent. If one listens carefully, however, their emphasis is not at all neutral and affect-free. The emphasis on independence and the energy required to directly act out that fantasy must come from somewhere. Only slightly beneath the surface lies the real motive: basically, the individuals are overly dependent, probably pathologically so, to the degree that one could never get the other to adequately take care of, value, love, support, or worship him. Due to the anger and frustration evoked by dependency needs that have never been satisfactorily met, they declare war on interdependence, long-term relationships, family, or anything else they unconsciously need but are not capable of getting.

Carol, an attractive, bright woman in her late thirties came to my office to get help for her preadolescent daughter. After we completed the girl's diagnostic work and developed an appropriate treatment plan, Carol was interviewed several times in order to elicit details about her daughter's conflicts and to discuss the treatment plan and possible alternatives to treatment. During the first session, it was obvious that Carol was extremely conflicted, defensive, and grossly out of touch with herself. She was in an Everybody But We marriage, which contained a liberal extramarital fringe. She told me about how she had grown over the years and had realized that total sexual liberation was the result of having worked through all her sexual hangups. She reported with some pride her weekend affairs and claimed she was having a great time "being free." Of special interest was that Carol volunteered this information. I had not asked her about any of this as it was not pertinent to our discussion. Carol needed to tell someone about her affairs to assuage her guilt and tension from deliberately defying her stringent childhood morality. Any astute observer of human motives would have easily detected that Carol's present life-style was totally opposite from who she really was. Although her "liberation" was consistent with the way her husband wanted it, she hated it, and she hated him for not being able to meet her basic needs. Each time she had aggressive intercourse with someone, she thought of how much she might be hurting her insensitive husband. In times of soul-searching, however, she wished they could return to the way it was before they got caught up in avant-garde behavior, yet she knew that could never again be. Such thoughts were painful because they evoked her basic sense of shame. One way to avoid that pain was to continue to run from herself (by compulsive sexual acting-out) and from the fact that she was in violation of her moral principles. Another way was to become even more convinced that she and her husband were well while everyone not living such a life-style had to be unenlightened and mentally ill. Carol's husband also secretly wished that everything could return to the way it was, when an evening at home together was pleasant. Too much had gone on, however, to ever return things to the way they were. Sadness came to each of them when they watched a stable couple or stable family interact on television. Although they never said so, each silently wished for the return of the time when a simple touch or sitting together in front of the fire on a brisk autumn's eve was all that really mattered. Each secretly wondered if following the impulses of their genitalia might not have been a mistake.

Most people have an amazing capacity for reinforcing and deriving pleasure from their own delusions, particularly those that in some way elevate one's worth in the eyes of social acquaintances.

Whether the delusions are carried out specifically to acquire social recognition or in the identification with the Everybody But We relationship, the bottom line is that one must continue to act out the fantasy in order to derive something from it. It seldom occurs to the couple that they get along better and are "happier" in the presence of friends and other social audiences than they are when alone together. Despite their attempt to portray themselves as open, free, uninhibited, and "together," nothing seems to go well when it really matters.

To be a charter member of the Everybody But We club, one must ascribe to the attitude that the genitals and sexuality are not private at all, but public. In some cases, both husband and wife engage in multitudinous extramarital relationships. If either exhibits concern or jealousy, it is interpreted as an indication of the severity of their psychopathology or as substantiation that they are sexually "hung up." The feelings of jealousy and anger, which should be present when a primary love object begins to pull away, are not allowed expression. Instead, they are suppressed, while the lack of emotional involvement and blatant inconsideration for each other, which are erroneously labeled as "freedom," become desirable ideals.

Such couples gauge personal growth by the number of extramarital affairs they can experience without guilt or obvious self-destruction. Most often, the husband begins outside relationships (for reasons to be discussed in Chapter 5), while the wife is hurt that he wants other women. Eventually, both out of retaliation against and encouragement from the husband (so as to exonerate his guilt), the wife too begins outside relationships. The gambit is set, and turning back is nearly impossible despite the frequent desire to do so. The excitement, irresponsibility, and sense of enhanced esteem surrounding each affair seem as though they should significantly alter the quality of the individual's life. The effects of developmental sexual repression and moral conservatism, however, are not easily resolved. Consequently, the penance required by the forces of guilt for violating one's real ideals is ever present. Sometimes, the guilt is reflected in an out-of-control obsession with sexuality and the compulsive seeking of serial affairs. Such obsessions help convince the self that one is not guilty or sexually "hung-up." For others, guilt is manifested by a compelling desire to run away and to be "free." Others unconsciously attempt to drive the spouse away in order to get the hurt they really deserve. Still others claim to "fall in love" with their outside lovers, and so they divorce the partner, in some cases abandoning their children, and begin anew. However, after a short time of involvement in the new relationship, usually after the mania has settled, the person comes to his senses to realize that there is no turning back. Those previous months and sometimes years of trying to convince himself that he is totally free turns out to be a disguised form of bondage.

Many individuals involved in an Everybody But We situation seem not to display much guilt over their extramarital involvement. These are usually people who already are so emotionally disturbed that the excitement and sense of affirmation they receive from outside encounters serve primarily as an escape from internal and external reality. Because they are already empty inside, taking advantage of, hurting, or using another for temporary satisfaction is mainly a continuation of what they have always done. They have little or no sensitivity to the feelings of others. Empathy for another is not possible when the desire to hurt or destroy is so close to the surface. Even when their emotional disturbance is sealed over by appropriate social mannerisms, their internal destruction is always transmitted to those who are in any way affiliated with them. The reception of destructive signals is always present when one disturbed person is living with another.

Some couples merely play at being sexually permissive, while beneath the surface they remain conservative, repressed, moralistic, and occasionally frigid or impotent. The playacting allows them a sense of belonging, and they receive feelings of security from identification with an avant-garde group, while simultaneously maintaining a reasonably secure, responsible, and trusting relationship with the spouse. They apparently derive sufficient gratification from their erotic fantasies and from their identification with the Everybody But We group to alleviate boredom while the trust in regard to fidelity need not be fractured. Their expressions of looseness and recklessness allow vicarious gratification while preserving their basic sense of morality. As long as their nuclear trust remains intact, they are relatively secure, spontaneous, and and free from debilitating guilt, depression, or other forms of self-destruction. When they approach the upper limits of flirtation and the preliminaries of seduction, they are able to pull back in order to preserve self-integrity and the integrity of the relationship.

Prince, Princess, and Pauper

A woman was stopped at an intersection waiting for the traffic light to change. Behind her, a car screeched to a halt, but not in enough time to avoid a collision. The woman's head hit the steering wheel, lacerating her forehead, which later required 17 stitches. In shock, she stepped out of the car and apologized to the arrogant man driving the other car.

"I'm sorry," she said, as blood poured down her face, "for causing this accident. Are you all right?"

"You're sorry! I should hope so! If you hadn't been there, I wouldn't have run into you!" the man yelled.

"I know," she said, "I'm sorry for making you smash your beautiful new car."

Over the years, while researching the types of marital relationships, I have noted that a peculiar attraction exists between the personality types described in the above anecdote. That is, a somewhat masochistic, overly responsible, sacrificing, and naive woman will often marry an arrogant, demanding, narcissistic, eroticized, irresponsible, and emotionally infantile man.

Psychodynamically, it is easy to see how perfectly these two deserve each other. On the one hand, the man desires to continue playing in marriage the role of the charming and valued Prince that he learned in his relationship with his first love, usually his mother. Meanwhile, his wife continues with her own thoroughly ingrained role: slave, mother, nurse, audience, psychologist. For her, marriage means complete dedication and servitude to her husband, the Prince. However, he feels no particular allegiance to his wife, the Pauper. After all, she is a symbolic nobody who can easily be replaced with any number of more beautiful and valuable servants who are out there ready to admire his brains, beauty, and talent. Deep inside, the wife feels like the nobody her husband believes she is. Nevertheless, a Pauper often feels fortunate to be paired with such a valuable person. Even though she knows that her Prince is dishonest, she can overlook his lies because she so desperately needs to be loved by "royalty," which proves to her that she is indeed lovable. At another level, however, she believes she is "shit," and her husband is all too eager to reinforce that belief.

Although Prince-and-Pauper situations are more common, grossly lopsided marriages are not exclusively male-dominated. Similar psychodynamics are observed in women who believe they are Princesses; they require a Pauper to worship, admire, and serve them. Like the Prince, the Princess can only be attracted to passive, subservient, masochistic, self-sacrificing men. For many reasons, this type of relationship is difficult to maintain successfully (see Chapter 5). The roles are as tenacious as the pain and anguish inherent in this type of arrangement.

Prince-and-Pauper relationships can proceed fairly smoothly as long as the couple remains blinded by the lust and primitive psychodynamic forces that initially propelled them toward one another. However, as soon as the relational balance changes, there will be significant hurt and hostility. Most often, the Prince becomes aware of what he always suspected: his wife is not quite enough for him. Moreover, it is demeaning to him to be faithful to only one woman. Even though he has diligently manipulated his wife into being the person he wants, she still doesn't satisfy him. It would be out of the question for him to acknowledge his pathological neediness. It is more reasonable for him to assume that the Pauper he married is doing something wrong. For example, he believes, she cannot make love properly; if she could, he wouldn't be interested in other women.

When the Pauper discovers that the Prince has been out with other women, they both agree that the fault is hers: she must not be able to satisfy him sexually. She remembers that, on the day after she came home from the hospital with their new baby, he wanted to make love. Of course, she refused him. If only she had given in then, she laments, he might not need other women now.

Princesses do things a little differently than Princes. A Princess often makes the common error of pairing with a "successful" man in order to elevate and maintain her royalty status. Most often, her man is really a Pauper. However, because of the time he spends on the job in order to remain successful, he cannot spend enough time worshipping the needy Princess. Even though he was a good subject during their courtship and is now a fair subject on weekends, there are five other days when no one is around to worship her. Without a Pauper around to provide adoration, what good is it to be a Princess? Sometimes, she handles her frustrations as the Prince does. She takes on a lover and becomes convinced it is "real love" because he treats her like a "queen." Even in her humble moments, she is not able to recognize her neediness. Instead, she verbally castrates her husband for not being more devoted.

To understand the dynamics of the Prince and Princess, one must examine the relationship of each with the parent of the opposite sex. Invariably, a Prince is created by a mother who cannot have a fulfilling relationship with her husband. Deep within, she is a self-destructive, insecure, overly dependent, and defensive woman who cannot handle a healthy adult relationship. Like her incipient Prince, she is an excellent blamer; she harbors great resentment toward her husband for not being able to meet her needs. She almost always has sexual problems and is confused about her own gender identity, preferring to be male. When that special son is born (usually the first or, if subsequently born, the most attractive), she invests too much of herself in him. Because of her sexual frustration, she transmits seductive messages. Because she is living for him and is overly invested in him, he unconsciously needs to be valued and the center of attention in his adult life. Consequently, he is motivated to achieve, frequently excels, and is usually a leader among his peers. Because the mother needs him for her own emotional survival, he has little choice but to return his dependency upon her, which she enjoys because she has a partner whom she created, for life. Outwardly, it would seem he should be extremely well adjusted because of the "affection" poured over him. Deep within, however, he introjected nearly all of his mother's pathology because he overidentified with her. Hostility accumulates toward her, which he cannot express because she has caused him to feel guilty over how much she has sacrificed for him. Later, when he pairs, that resentment sneaks out rather conspicuously. Guilt is also prevalent when he strays from his second love to have love affairs. Deep within, he is most unhappy, but he has no idea why.

An additional factor is seen in the development of the Prince and Princess. The Prince, for example, is inordinately competitive with other males, yet is uncomfortable around them. The causation is quite clear: he and the King (father) were competing for mother's love. Even though he doesn't remember, he won the competition because his father did not have a chance. Because his mother needed him so badly, she treated him like a Prince and became a servant to him. Despite his father's competition with him, there were times when father too showed him generous quantities of love. His mother, afraid she might lose the little Prince to her husband, poured out more "spoilage." The child became the prize in the parental game of "Who can love the Prince the most?"

Manifestations of these dynamics become obvious in marriage. The Prince's basic nurturing needs cannot be satisfied by anyone but mother. Realistically, however, that is not possible. The Prince is hostile toward his spouse as well as anyone else who does not recognize his "true worth." It does not occur to him that no one can ever be as singularly devoted as his mother. No one person can ever love him enough to satisfy his needs for affection. When he has one or two love affairs going, he receives almost enough love to get by. However, engaging in outside relationships engenders guilt because his mother has programmed him to be faithful to her. If he could only get his wife's permission to have an affair, he believes, all would be well. Some Princes and Princesses request approval from the spouse to take a lover, but the "inconsiderate low life" never seems to provide gracious understanding.

Not all Princes and Princesses engage in love affairs to enhance their divine right. Those who believe in fidelity usually sublimate their sexual impulses and are driven to positions of power, status, and social conspicuity. They then proceed to surround themselves with "low life" to worship and admire them. They perceive anyone approaching their level of power as a threat, and so they socially guillotine them. If they are in power at a social institution or any other program, incompetence tends to run rampant because they are threatened by the competence of others. Whether at work or at home, there cannot be more than one King in a castle.

When a Prince and Princess marry each other, they often know that it will probably not work because their courtship was stormy, competitive, and destructive. They see nothing peculiar in their primary motive for pairing: to capture someone who is also royal. However, once they have secured the valuable prize—each other—they are stuck with trying to live together. The power struggle begins as each tries to make the other over, in the image of the respective self-sacrificing parent. Neither is aware that abnegation of power is a humiliating, violent process, seldom accomplished without a destructive battle.

The original competition between the Prince's (or Princess') parents for their child's love sets in motion a complicated and permanent affectional style that often shackles the child for a lifetime. Unconsciously, the child tends to play the parents against each other in order to get emotional supplies from both of them. Later in life, when the Prince feels insecure, anxious, lonely, or in need of support, he often becomes involved in an outside relationship to recreate the childhood triangle. The third person represents one of his parents, whose role is to compete with his spouse (who represents the other parent) over who can love the Prince the most. Recreating the early childhood drama greatly enhances the Prince's self-esteem. In most cases, a Prince cannot simply have a clandestine love affair and then forget it. He must let others know; in fact, he unconsciously wishes to be caught by the spouse. Moreover, the drama would not be complete unless his partner found out. For, in addition to the unconscious need to have two people fighting over him, he needs to be simultaneously punished.

What's Up?

The What's-Up? interaction style is characterized by a conspicuous imbalance of equality regarding who dominates whom. The domination, however, is not straightforward and aboveboard, but instead is highly manipulative. In this type of relationship, the man is pathologically devious and severely disturbed, while the woman is overly dependent, overly trusting, and naive, although essentially much healthier. She is a person who has been "beaten" into a severely repressed, submissive posture. She hasn't the slightest idea that she is frightened of people, including her parents and her controlling husband. She has been taught long ago to behave and not to question authority.

The overtrusting, overly submissive woman often felt rejected by emotionally unavailable parents. Her parents did not have the emotional strength to lend a sense of presence or security to their child but instead rejected her when she was most needy. Therefore, she developed a heightened need for dependence, affection, security, and submission. She adapted to her parents' rejection and inconsistency through compliance and cooperation. She was aware at some level that her parents were incapable of meeting her needs, but that was too painful to believe. Instead, she tolerated the rejection by telling herself that her parents were just too busy, or had too many problems of their own, or that they just didn't know how to show their love. Those few times when her parents did show affection, she felt guilty about having believed they didn't care. The girl learned that if she could merely behave and mind her own business, she would make her parents' life a little less difficult. Moreover, she learned that to be seen and not heard, to speak only when spoken to, to be helpful and obedient, and to be "no problem at all" is what all good girls should be.

The husband in the What's-Up? relationship responded to parental rejection somewhat differently than did his wife. He was the child who learned to read the subtle cues of his parents. To avoid punishment and to win moderate approval, he had to lie and cheat. It was necessary for him to become an expert at manipulating others into caring about him. He was very good at putting things over on his mother, who at one level wanted to believe her son was a good boy. She didn't have the strength or concern to genuinely give, however, so when she tried to control his impulses or discipline him, he interpreted her "interference" as painful rejection. It eventually was easier for his parents to overlook his deviousness and dishonesty. It was also easier for them when their son gave up trying to manipulate them and began manipulating others, particularly women and friends.

The What's-Up males are so hypersensitive to the word "no" that they take every refusal and any attempt to control their impulses as personal rejection. To avoid the painful "no," they develop astute manipulative skills to seduce others into providing acceptance without criticism. Naturally, they are attracted to overly compliant, submissive women who *cannot say "no."* The What's-Up men are so in need of unmitigated acceptance that they actively avoid relationships where they are not in full control and where they cannot easily con others. Their words are glib, their moves smooth, and their motives devious. They will tell anyone nearly anything in order to avoid rejection and to get a compliment or a morsel of social recognition. Over the years, they have developed no real identity, other than as manipulators of others. Their lives are very painful from the lack of something, yet they have lied so much to themselves and everyone else that they cannot possibly know what is missing.

The What's-Up? couple is psychodynamically well paired. Neither is particularly capable of sustained positive relatedness. At first glance, it might seem that because the wife is so trusting, she must be capable; however, she doesn't usually trust with her emotions. Instead, she trusts because she has been taught to and because she becomes frightened when she doesn't believe in her manipulating husband. It is a false emotional trust rooted in overdependence and naivete.

In a What's-Up? relationship, the man gets a wife he can control and manipulate. Because the wife has learned not to ask too many questions, her husband's deviousness is seldom confronted. She usually hasn't the slightest idea about what is going on because he likes her ignorant and dumb. He covers up his incessant lies with more lies, and his deviousness with more deviousness. The wife, in order to keep from finding out any devastating truth, learns to play dumb very well. It all seems worth it because her husband is fairly generous when it comes to saying "I love you." She needs to hear those words so badly that if she did have any suspicions, they vanish. Her husband's talk is so convincing, and her need is so great, that she will remain quiet and obedient for a long time. After all, a good girl neither questions nor complains. Her job is to make her husband's life a little less difficult, which she does best by staying out of the way until she is needed. Her husband probably cares for her as much as he can care for anybody, which is not much.

If the manipulator is the wife, the husband has essentially the same characteristics as ascribed to the aforementioned wife. His naiveté and his desperate need for overt signs of affection make him very vulnerable. His wife may be out having serial love affairs, yet the "poor guy seems to be the last to know." When her deviousness is discovered, it is usually due to something so blatantly obvious that even a 9-year-old would have known about it long ago. Naturally, the husband is crushed. Due to his naiveté and inability to socially or emotionally discriminate appropriate cues in others, his only coping mechanism is to no longer trust anybody. Even if the threat is removed, he will continue to emotionally distrust.

When a naive wife has been hurt so much that she gives up playing dumb, it forces her husband (the needy manipulator) to try to get more of his needs met by others. Consequently, he becomes more devious in an attempt to make the spouse respond. When the devious husband is caught, whether for the first or tenth time, the spouse's emotional walls become thicker, forcing his deviousness to become more subtle. All the promises he made are shattered repeatedly. His naive wife's "last-time-or-else" threats are negated by her own feelings of not being able to live alone or to make a satisfactory life without him, which are erroneously labeled as feelings of love. If the wife should be strong enough or angry enough to chase the "lecher" out, her panic over living alone surfaces in full force. Of course, the husband will return. Why not? Things usually have gone the way he pleases. Besides, he knows that no one with much sense would put up with him.

It can be too frightening for a naive woman paired with a male psychopath to know the truth about what is going on. For, to know even a little about her devious partner is to catch him in myriad exaggerations, distortions, and outright lies. Perhaps her parents were right, she reasons, when they told her that good girls should never question. It is easier to be busy, and she is indeed "happier" just that way.

The Sacred Cow

In nearly all of the types of relationships heretofore described, each of the defined roles could have applied to either sex. However, the Sacred Cow role in a relationship is almost invariably

the woman's, although occasionally the man will play a somewhat similar role. An aura of holiness, goodness, and virginity surrounds the Sacred Cow. Often, she is not as pristine and virginal
as her husband wants her to be, but he nevertheless responds to
her as a consecrated entity who is essentially untouchable. Full
sexual satsifaction with a sanctified wife is not possible, nor is
creative sexual experimentation or erotic spontaneity. To enjoy
sexual expressiveness, the spouses of all Sacred Cows must look
elsewhere. Prostitutes were created for "that type of thing,"
whereas virtuous women were created for home, motherhood, and
glorification.

There is a tendency for some Catholics, Jews, born-again Chris-
tians, and Italians to create Sacred Cow relationships. That is,
in any home where the mother is elevated, identifies with the Vir-
gin Mary, or attempts to personify holiness and virginity, the stage
is set for the creation of sexually ashamed males. Such a mother
so outshines her husband that their adolescent son unconsciously
wishes to identify with her in order to be as good as she. On the
other hand, he prefers not to be like his conspicuously weaker,
less valuable father. A Sacred Cow usually fosters the sacred perception of herself in order to derive gratification from identifying
with perfection. A peek inside her psyche, however, would reveal
deep feelings of guilt over sexuality. Although a woman may
never have conducted herself in a way that would support her self-
deprecation, in her fantasies she has sinned grievously. Sometimes, a woman who acted out sexually in late adolescence has
tremendous guilt that forces her into a psychological convent—
i.e., being a Sacred Cow—where she can remain virginal while
living a secular life.

In view of the Sacred Cow's conflict, it is not difficult to understand her son's ambivalence. Unconsciously, the mother transmits
signals about her own heightened sexual interests to which he
responds with increased sexual excitability. Consciously, she reacts
to her own erotic impulses by being virginal. The message is quite
clear: sex is beneath her, and anyone who wants it is bad. Because
of her dynamics, her son is left with a quickened affinity for sexual
arousal but feels guilty about his sexuality and desire for intercourse. He unconsciously seeks a Sacred Cow for his wife, hoping

to find a virginal prostitute who will seem pious to everyone else, but who will be a nymphomaniac in the bedroom. Since that is almost impossible, his psychological compromise is to pair with a woman who is as sanctified as his mother tried to be. Thus, he gets a conscientious wife and a dedicated mother for their children, but neither a friend nor lover. For erotic love, he has to go outside their relationship. But when he has done so, he hates the woman and himself because of what they have done. Severely pathological men often beat or torture the lover, with no idea where the impulse originated.

Some clergymen and overly religious men of every faith typify the reversal of the Sacred Cow syndrome. These men have anointed themselves and their temples (bodies) against carnal impulses. Unconsciously, they need to have sinners around who "glorify the flesh" so that they can denounce them while preserving their own divinity. Their hostility toward sexuality and their almost continuous preoccupation with declining moral standards and sexual decadence provide a direct cue to their own sexual conflicts. Of course, they are not able to let themselves become aware of those particular psychodynamics. It is easier to vent at the less sanctified. Even when the wife of a male Sacred Cow has erred in her ways by seductive antics, sexual involvement, or both, he refuses to examine his contribution to the relationship. When his wife's erring is discovered, he wishes she could have been more like his pristine mother. He will never realize that she is very much like his mother, only more honest. She may in fact be acting out a part of herself that the Sacred Cow mother could not.

An interesting double bind becomes evident in Sacred Cow relationships. Because of the ambivalence surrounding sexuality, an attitude of purity or chastity holds in abeyance the unconscious desire to act out sexually. That which is supposed to be so unimportant, therefore, becomes all-important. Even though men and women paired with Sacred Cows are usually careful not to get caught in their outside relationships, they need to be discovered, and so their unconscious resentment eventually wins out. What better way could there be to hurt someone who has made normal sexual desire something abominable? What neither realizes is that some of the resentment and hostility are residuals from the messages of the first love. The world sometimes comes to an end for many female Sacred Cows when they discover that their spouses have gone elsewhere for something so special. They are frequently devastated when they learn that their husband's lover was nothing but "low life." "How dare he want to put his penis in *me* after it has been in that . . . in that *thing*!" she exclaims.

Suffering Together

Emotionally disturbed children gravitate toward each other. Most have little choice but to later become emotionally disturbed adults who eventually pair and create more disturbed children who become disturbed adults who. . . .

One of the most intriguing and disquieting aspects of psychopathology is that one's attitudes about oneself, others, and the way life is seem to have always been there. Because a child's parents and family are his first reality and because his family is all he experiences, the relationships that seem so destructive to the professional clinician are not considered unusual by family members. Destructive relationships are all they know, and pathological relatedness, in essence, is their reality. When a disturbed adolescent approaches an age when pairing becomes feasible, he usually becomes attached to someone who will provide him with an ongoing supply of pathological material that is similar to what was distributed at home. Any possibility he might have had for growth and psychological maturity is forever lost when, amidst his confusion and neediness, he pairs with another disturbed child. From his perspective, nondestructive relatedness—being happy, healthy, and responsible—is "sick." Sometimes, after years of continued heartache, a few such individuals are able to break free and slowly start on the road to a less destructive existence. In addition to the "miracle" that fostered their breaking away, is their amazement at having stuck with such a pathological situation as long as they did.

Suffering Together relationships are invariably comprised of two emotionally disturbed adolescents or equally immature adults. Because adolescent girls are usually more mature than boys of comparable age, the typical suffering relationship consists of a slightly more mature girl and an extremely weak, infantile, overly dependent boy who is totally unaware of his infantility. At one level, the boy realizes that his "woman" is a very good catch, not only because she may be beautiful to him, but because he feels that she can and will take care of him. In many respects, she is more dominant, as all good mothers are. In about the same proportion that the boy recognizes his need (feelings of love) for her, he also begins to respond to the threat of losing her. Moreover, deep within, he feels so badly about himself that he begins to hate her. "How could she be any good," goes his thinking, "if she is willing to have anything to do with someone as rotten as me?" The love-hate-possession interaction begins. Even though it is painful for the girl, it is also flattering for her frail ego because she desperately needs to be needed.

The classical Suffering Together situation is not engulfed in positive human relatedness at all, but is deeply rooted in pathological dependency, jealousy, control, guilt, and destructiveness. Nothing positive or healthy can evolve from such a state of affairs. It is a hectic, stormy drama, which unfolds quickly and worsens until the couple marries. After marriage, there is a short reprieve, and then the situation becomes even worse. Their lives become deluged with so many unresolved conflicts that it is never quite possible for them to slow down the destruction in any one area long enough to find an adequate resolution. Whenever they approach a quasi-reasonable solution to one major conflict, other problems command their attention. Because disturbed individuals can seldom break away from pathological anxiety and conflict from within, they cannot successfully resolve conflicts. In fact, most often their efforts to make things better make them worse.

Before marriage, the intrigue and fantasy regarding the sex organs serve as a catalyst to keep the Suffering Together relationship alive. Because sexual confusion is inherent in all psychopathology, the disturbed male needs a good mother to take care of him in a way his real mother could not. He also needs a vagina of his own to manipulate, "screw," and to do with as he pleases. His pathological dependency needs force him to overly invest in his wife and her vagina so that she wonders if her husband is not more interested in her vagina than he is in her. Some of the more vocal,

uninhibited women will say exactly that in their repeated arguments, but they have no reference as to how accurate that statement may be. Even when his pathological jealousy forces him to
attack her and to accuse her of "screwing everybody and anybody,"
she cannot allow herself to believe that he cannot see her as a
whole person. Because of his jealousy and sexual conflicts, the
man only sees the vagina being penetrated by a penis that does not
belong to him. His principal mode of retaliation is to try to destroy
the owner of his vagina. The process of literally beating her into
total submission begins and never quite ends. He doesn't care
much for her as a person, but he needs her vagina to remain ever-
present and available should he decide to make use of it.

Trust, autonomy, liberation, and even choice are totally out of
the question. Any effort the wife makes toward such ends is discouraged by the husband and is beaten out of her. Because the
husband's mother didn't care for him the way he wanted and because his infantile dependency needs are so great, he is out to make
sure his wife never gets away. It is not possible for him to believe
she genuinely cares for him because, deep within, he feels so badly
about himself that he is convinced that no one could ever really
care. After all, if mother didn't care, who else could? When she
threatens to leave, he threatens to either beat her, kill her, or commit suicide, and she panics. He has played successfully on her fear
and guilt, forcing her to believe that, if he dies, it is because he
loves her so much and she wouldn't have anything to do with
him. She is simultaneously stuck and entranced: "Surely, if he is
willing to die for me, he must love me," goes her delusional
thinking. She never quite realizes that he is an emotional corpse,
to whom all types of destruction come easily.

Pathological jealousy exudes from everywhere for those Suffering Together. If the wife looks at or talks to another man, homo-
cidal urges surface quickly in her husband. However, it never occurs to him that he hates her, even though he wants to kill her!
Moreover, when rational thought is impossible, the "other man"
can be anyone—even the wife's father, brothers, or female friends.
Not only might they take the husband's vagina away; they might
put the idea in her head to leave him for someone better. His turmoil is endless. Since he believes everyone is better than he, every-

one is thus a threat. Left to his own pathological desires, he would like a robot who can be locked in a closet and kept ready for his use. However, that too is insufficient, for the husband needs to display his wife before others so that they see that she is faithful to him alone. His esteem is almost completely tied up in her; if he lost her, he would feel the nothingness that has been there for as long as he can remember.

At home, there is insurmountable conflict. If the wife takes exceptional care of herself, the husband accuses her of dressing up for someone else. If she doesn't take care of herself, he accuses her of not caring for him. If she smiles too much, there must be another man making her happy. If she's depressed, he is angry that she doesn't have the energy to give to him. If she enjoys sex too much, she's a whore; if not enough, she's a bitch. To stop his anxiety over possible loss and powerlessness, he needs to hurt her. To see her suffer makes him feel better for awhile. Amidst the turmoil, he is unconsciously getting even with his mother for all that she did to him. Even if he feels guilty about hurting his wife, he cannot seem to stop himself when "that urge" comes over him.

The Suffering Together husband's desires are twofold. First, he must treat his wife like garbage, and, second, he must make sure she is socially institutionalized to the degree that his word is law. To feel any sense of security, he must think for her, control her, and own her *in toto*. Eventually, the wife may give in because of fear and because the opposition is too persistent. She may begin to believe that she is as worthless and ugly as her husband claimed. His work is complete when she actually believes that she is nothing and that she should honor and obey only him because he is so good to her. In addition, she should feel grateful to him for staying with her because she is nothing but trash. He has symbolically won out over his mother and has successfully reduced his second love to the hostile dependence, helplessness, and nothingness that he has always felt.

Almost always, emotional disturbed youngsters entertain bizarre, grandiose fantasies about how they might die for love or the loss of it. Some go so far as to plan their suicides should their partner ever be taken from them. Major physical messages such as beatings, suicide attempts, and death wishes are all mysteriously associated with love. Constructive communication, empathy, and legitimate caring for each other are fairly high-level emotional operations not available to the seriously disturbed adolescent.

Sugar Dads and Nipple Moms

Sugar Dads and Nipple Moms relationships are conspicuously interwoven in parental transference. One partner, at least 10 years older than the other, is clearly the "parent" to the other partner's "child." Most people recognize substitute-parent relationships for what they are, and there is a slight social taboo against them. Nevertheless, they do occur, although they seldom continue as smoothly as they began. Theoretically, it could be stated that if a person pairs with a perfectly symbolic parent and participates in vicarious incest, he has returned to basic emotional and psychological roots. Ideally, this should offer the "child" exactly what is needed for "happiness." Seldom does it work that way, however, because substitutes always seem to be substitutes.

Unconsciously, nearly all adults can admit to being attracted to older, attractive, and financially secure "parent substitutes." To acknowledge that fantasy, however, might cause them to be labeled "sick." In fact, almost universally, people are slightly aghast when they hear of a person pairing with someone much older.

To return to one's unconscious roots by marrying a Sugar Dad or Nipple Mom can quickly result in emotional holocaust. The motives for the child desiring the parent are quite clear. The motives of the parent for the child, however, are never quite pure nor are they free from psychopathology.

In the lower socioeconomic class, the woman pairing with an older man may be partially interested in his ability to protect and direct her, and partially interested in the economic security he offers. In addition, she also gets to be controlled and owned. She is usually an insecure, inadequate, disorganized, phobic individual who is unprepared to cope with her existing life situation and the "cold, cruel" adult world. Pairing with an older, more mature man, who is willing to tell her how to live, make decisions for her, and control both her spur-of-the-moment and destructive impulses, offers her a sense of well-being that she has not felt since early childhood. For a short time, she is enthused about her new daddy because he seems to know how to handle everything and make it right. After living together, however, she slowly discovers that his knowledge of everything and his willingness to control her are reaction formations against his deep-seated feelings of stupidity, doubt, and insignificance. Deep within, she didn't get a father at all but an emotional brother in disguise.

"Children" pairing with substitute "parents" seldom realize the pathological defensiveness and inadequacy in the partner. A woman is unaware that, when she pairs with a man like her dad, the man avoids psychological suffering by setting himself up as an infallible god. Children, after all, should love, honor, and obey their parents. And good children, who have been given so much, must never challenge the decisions or wishes of the omnipotent chief executive officer. Sugar Dad's economic power base can now go on without being challenged. No one will ever know how disturbed he is, because children, if they are dumb enough, do not know about such things.

Middle- and upper-class individuals enmeshed in Sugar Dad or Nipple Mom relationships are influenced by dynamics similar to those described previously. However, they must contend with two additional factors: exploitation of the wealth and social status of the "parent" by the "child," and the indirect sexual exploitation of the "child" by the "parent." Each partner is only partially aware of the *quid pro quo* obtained by such an arrangement. The "child" receives financial security, elevated social position, and release from the burdens of making a living alone. The "child" (in this case, a female) also gets to remain a child by having her new dad continue the parenting role. She sometimes moves into the husband's house and continues with her irresponsible childhood. In return for being taken care of, the "child" must show respect, obedience, and appreciation. It goes without saying that she must also be sexually available to her emotionally insecure husband, who deep within feels worthless, unappreciated, and somewhat ugly and unattractive. Due to his age, the husband may have secret fears of genital inferiority. To help allay these fears, he usually pairs with a much younger, attractive woman. If someone young and beautiful will make love with him, he can temporarily deny any feelings of antiquity and ugliness.

Sugar Dad and Nipple Mom relationships cannot be totally understood without considering superficiality and the inability for positive relatedness. Most often, these are "showpiece relationships," in which much of the gratification is derived when the "parent" is able to show off the lovely "child" and the "child" is able to show off the successful "parent." Both partners are far removed from genuine peace of mind because of their heavy reliance upon others to reinforce their delusions of worth. Little do they realize that most people are not particularly impressed by their ostentation, and those who do pay attention are more apt to be hostile, not envious. Exactly what the couple wants most from others is not available. So, in order for them to believe they are what they are not, they adopt an attitude of sophistication and snobbery. When the pretentious fanfare declines, however, the "child" surreptitiously studies the "parent" and wonders how it could have happened.

Pathological motives for Sugar Dad and Nipple Mom pairing always carry an overdose of emotional pain. The attractive "child" may receive financial security and borrowed status but has forsaken the irretrievables of youth, passion, "love," and life. Usually, the physically attractive "child" worked at being so. Therefore, physical beauty may be of utmost importance to the "child" pairing with a "parent." It does not take long for the "child" making love with an "old man" or "old lady" to become disgusted. The "antiquated" body of the partner may be offensive, and some "children" even become nauseated at the thought of their partner's body. They would much rather be with someone younger and more attractive.

A fairly hectic and increasingly more frequent Sugar Dad involvement has been observed between a middle-aged man and a much younger woman. Approximating what might be called a "midlife crisis," he escapes from responsibility and depression by leaving his wife to marry a younger, sexually overactive lover. During the erotic frenzy, he experiences what he considers "real love" for the first time. It is only after his reckless passion subsides that he realizes what he left behind by divorcing his wife and abandoning his children. He desperately needs his bride, whom he admires because she is vibrant and uninhibited in bed, and for awhile can help him forget his pain. At the same time, however, he hates her because if it weren't for their involvement, he would still be a father to his children, and he painfully wonders if his new life is a mistake. The couple has sex frequently. Even though sex eventually becomes less satisfying than masturbation, the husband clings to his wife, idolizing her for his awakened sexuality. To help him remain impassioned is the only way she can indeed "make" him forget the intruding thoughts of what he left behind.

SAINT AND SINNER

Every married person can recall trying to change the partner to some degree in order to alleviate discomfort and provide more pleasure. In short, in most relationships, the partners try to change each other into someone more pleasing. In a Saint-Sinner relationship, however, there is an abnormal emphasis on helping— or forcing—the "less desirable" partner to change into someone more desirable. One partner (in this instance, the husband) declares himself a "Saint," and considers his wife (the "Sinner") a malleable nobody, mere clay to be shaped by his skillful hands.

As the relationship progresses and the husband tries to remodel the wife's behavior and attitudes, it occurs to her that she is involved in something unhealthy. Her husband is usually a severely disturbed individual who was almost totally unaccepted during his own childhood. His wanting to change his wife is an extension of his relationship with his parents, who let him know in countless ways that he was not quite good enough. Regardless of how hard he tried to please them, they were unable to recognize him or his achievements as worthwhile. The child, aware that he was unable to measure up to parental standards, may have actually excelled. As an adult, he may be successful by all outward indicators; inside, however, he feels like a despicable nobody. He is angry both at himself for not having been able to satisfy his parents and at them because they could not accept him for himself. One way he could feel worthwhile was to pair with an equally "worthless" individual and then make her over. Deep-rooted feelings of rejection, hostility, and never amounting to anything, experienced by the teacher-husband, are transmitted to the student-spouse. She discovers that, regardless of her efforts to become what her husband wants, they will never be enough.

If the relationship endures for several years, an unexpected twist of fate frequently occurs. The wife's frustration, humiliation, self-examination, and achievements eventually cause genuine change and legitimate increases in her ego strength. By the time the husband is in a position to enjoy his creation, his thankless student has far surpassed him and frequently wants to leave. Meanwhile, her infantile husband remains the same. His only recourse is to hunt for someone else to "help." Helping or forcing another to change (as many professional people-helpers discover) is an excellent way to avoid facing one's own personal problems.

Most Sinners, however, do not recognize their increased strength because the righteous partners keep reminding them of how much more they must achieve. Sometimes, the Sinner leaves because of the constant criticism and rejection. Other times, awareness of how serious the Sinner is about leaving jolts the Saint into backing off. Or, quite accidentally, if the Sinner plays the game right, the Saint might possibly be open to her feelings and may realize the need to change some of his craziness. Professional help is a must if the couple wants to stay together. Without professional help, the original lopsided Saint-Sinner relationship may be quickly reestablished.

Strike Two–Strike Three

Patti and Jerry, a married couple in their early thirties, had each been married once before. They were referred to my office to get help for Patti's nine-year-old son, David. During a fight on the school playground. David had clobbered another boy with a baseball bat. Naturally, both his teacher and the school principal were concerned over his outburst, not only because of the possibility of injury, but because it was so unlike David to be abusive toward other children. Patti was extremely upset that her son, who had always been happy-go-lucky and a model student, had shown signs of anger and agitation over the past few months.

After evaluating the child, I met with the parents to discuss an appropriate treatment plan. Patti asked anxiously "Can you tell us what's making him act like this?" I tried to lessen her anxiety by asking her to slow down a little. Then I explained that I was going to take a roundabout way of helping them understand David's problems. They both settled down and seemed very receptive to what I was sharing with them. We concluded the session with the realization that David was not seriously disturbed and that most of his present anxiety was *not* due to inadequate parenting or the previous divorce, but to outside pressure in his present environment. Both parents were relieved, but were quite eager to know the nature of the outside pressure. Patti quietly asked, "It's us, isn't it?" I said, "It sure looks that way. But before I speculate about why, I want each of you to think about any conflicts between you that you have kept to yourselves or tried to ignore. I would like to see you again in a few days to see what you have come up with."

That evening, Patti called and said she needed to talk to me immediately about some of her conflicts with Jerry. She revealed that she had been furious with him for over two months and was so "goddamned angry she could kill him. I pointed out that frequently the most emotionally sensitive child in the family unconsciously acts out the unexpressed feelings of the parent to whom he is most attached. David's symbolic expression was a perfect example. What better way for him to act out his mother's anger than to hit another boy with a baseball bat? Patti seemed to understand and accept this explanation. When I asked why she and Jerry hadn't tried to resolve their marital conflicts, she said, "I'm afraid to let him know how angry I am. It might threaten our relationship, and I already have *one strike against me.*"

Because this marriage was the second for both of them, Patti felt it *had* to work. So, she decided to be the epitome of submission, patience, and long-suffering. In attempting to establish security in the new marriage, she chose to suppress her real feelings and promised herself she would never rock the boat. But Jerry had in fact been insensitive to her, and she had a right to be furious. She chose instead to suppress her hostility. When David absorbed it and acted it out at school, however, she and Jerry were forced to deal with each other.

In most Strike Two–Strike Three situations, both individuals have been previously married and divorced. (In some, only one partner has been married before.) Because of the hurt, shame, and anxiety, over the previous divorce, the partners must convince themselves that the new relationship *will* succeed. Surely the gods, or whoever is in charge of happiness, will bless the relationship. Besides, they often believe they are now more mature and experienced because they have been through at least one previous relationship and have learned from it. Most Strike people convince themselves that they married a good-for-nothing the first time. However, that rationalization becomes more difficult to maintain the second time around, and almost impossible by the third. Nevertheless, most people are experts at self-deception.

Many Strike relationships are defensive. They prevent growth because they are set up to protect the self from knowledge that would be painful if realized. Even though conscientious people may pay lip service to the notion that it requires two to make a relationship succeed, most often they don't really believe it. They may admit to having a few minor shortcomings but seldom to those that contributed to the dissolution of the prior marriage. Undoubtedly, the insensitive (and perhaps crazy) first partner was the reason the relationship broke up. If they remain convinced that it was all the previous partner's fault, they don't have to examine their own contributions or worry that the same thing will happen again.

When the primary goal of a relationship is to make it work, no matter what, the couple pursues the outward symbols of a "good marriage" in order to convince themselves that they were right for each other. To derive meaning, or pleasure, or intimacy is not always the point. The goal is narrow: to remain married and not even think of divorce. Psychosomatic illnesses, overwork at the office, and their hectic schedule of events all serve a utilitarian purpose: they keep the couple away from each other. Each secretly knows that if they were together too much, they would argue and possibly break up. They are not about to let that happen. Seldom is the desire to make the marriage work equally determined. In most Strike relationships, one partner usually believes it more necessary to preserve the marriage than does the other. This can be most destructive because, automatically, he is forced into a position of extreme lopsidedness in which it may be necessary to exert anywhere from 80% to 100% of the effort and energy to make sure it "works." Exactly how much and from what source one receives enough nurturance to persist in the almost continuous giving is a basic question in life. In many Strike relationships, the partner exerting most of the energy to keep the relationship working (like Patti in the previous example), must suppress his own desires and emotions. This causes a great deal of anger and resentment, which must also be suppressed. Even though the couple remains married, their relationship may be extremely destructive, and the children will almost always act directly on parental conflicts.

I Gotcha, Now What?

Despite the contemporary mental health idea that bondage is sick and freedom is healthy, serious relationships nevertheless contain more than a modicum of possession, propriety, and restriction. To belong to another, and to be faithful to the exclusion of all others, can add to one's basic sense of emotional security. To be important to another person and to have impact on his destiny and emotional comfort is, in fact, to reduce one's own feelings of insignificance, powerlessness, and inadequacy, which are universal psychological phenomena. To help a loved one acquire "happiness," personal growth, and new horizons of emotional maturity is one of the joys of living.

Emotional investment in another carries power and responsibility with it. Power is experienced because, when a person is emotionally involved, he has much to do with the feelings and emotional fluctuations of the partner. One's feelings of worth, because of power and control over another, can also be achieved through the emotional mutilation of another. Pathological individuals have little choice but to hurt each other, for hurt is what they feel inside. Consequently, emotionally disturbed people learn early that to let themselves go and become involved with another will only result in disappointment. Their natural solution is to remain distant and impenetrable. Some disturbed individuals can only feel "right" while they are in sexual pursuit but essentially uninvolved emotionally. These people are emotionally involved in the *process* of pursuit and conquest, not in the *object* of the pursuit.

Many people, especially males, feel valuable only during the conquest. The more disinterested a woman seems to be, the greater is a man's interest in conquering her. If he can seduce the difficult prey, he feels more important and powerful. During an especially difficult pursuit, he may feel that his penis is gigantic and lovable, and not as filthy as he unconsciously believes. His multitudinous unresolved conflicts are ignored while he pursues the valuable woman. All the pain he ordinarily feels can be redirected onto his penis and the possibility of conquest, thus creating a pseudofeeling of emotional well-being. To manipulate the potential partner into a vulnerable position, where he can hurt her whenever he wishes, is to temporarily deny his basic feelings of nothingness and impotence.

Invariably in the I Gotcha pattern, the individual initiating the relationship has deep gender conflict. For example, because of overidentification with his mother and fear of his father, a son remained unwaveringly attached to his mother. The mother helped too by communicating the idea that his father and males in general were worthless and dirty because of that thing hanging between their legs. Therefore, from early years onward, the young male was embarrassed and ashamed of his sexuality and his penis. When the biological changes of adolescence became conspicuous, he could no longer deny his sexuality. To conceal his mother-identification, he was forced to become very sensual and competitive while working hard to prove to himself that he was tough, masculine, and sexually potent.

The overidentification with mother left permanent scars. To compensate for his feelings of worthlessness and of having a small, dirty, and insignificant penis, he now must seduce as many women as possible. If he can cause hurt with his weapon, then women, for sure, will never forget he has one, possibly even a big one. Because the I Gotcha male feels conflict over his genitals, the vagina holds more than an average amount of curiosity for him. In fact, he is almost preoccupied with women, especially their genitalia. He feels an insatiable urge to penetrate every desirable women he sees. He can never seem to get enough, even though he secretly wishes his penis were a vagina, a fantasy that he cannot admit to anyone.

Conspicuously seductive women entrapped in the I Gotcha pattern are frequently propelled by similar forces. At one time, usually several years prior to adolescence, such a woman overiden-tified with her father (or other significant, dominant male) who was somewhat hostile and rejecting of women. The father made sure that his wife was rendered ineffective. Although he would not say so, he was overly involved with his daughter and more than moderately sexually interested in her. Because of his gender confusion, he wanted to believe he was responding to his daughter as though she were one of the "boys." A consequence of the father's messages was that the daughter preferred to be a boy. Because women were viewed as useless, she wanted no part of such humili-ation, and she secretly wished for a penis of her own. The I Gotcha females are noted by their aggressive, inappropriate hostility and competition for the approval and affection of males. It is not pos-sible for them to relate to males without being fully aware of their different genitalia.

I Gotcha women are frequently frigid and often fear their vagina is dirty or disfigured. Many secretly desire to become pregnant (and often do) to prove to themselves that they are indeed women, and that their genitals and womanhood are valuable. Some wish to have a brood of children to convince themselves that they are ir-refutably female. Others prefer to tease rather than follow through with coition. The purpose of the seduction, however, is the same: to expose the emotional jugular vein of the male. If the woman can manipulate a man into a vulnerable position, her worth and power are temporarily elevated. She likes knowing that she never has to be as helpless or out of control as the conquered male. She also receives assurance that her vagina cannot be as bad as she thinks, because a man wants it so much.

In cases of severe disturbance, the woman seduces the male and then proceeds to destroy him and his reputation, usually by gossip-ing. Some of her hostility comes from her initial frustration over not having a penis. The majority of it, however, comes from her conviction that all men are animals who only want to exploit women. She is totally unaware that she is living out the relation-ship that existed between her parents. Because her father declared her mother an inferior sex object, each time she has intercourse she is retaliating against her earlier childhood anguish. Her al-ready high level of anxiety is raised after a proud seduction be-cause of her hostility toward men as well as herself.

An important dynamic of the I Gotcha woman is her desire to seduce a "successful" man so that she can feel she is better than he. Her power over such a man is seldom positive or constructive because she wishes to destroy him in order to "make him pay" for what he has done. She is not aware that her real anger is toward her father (or other male) who once devalued her as a person while seeming much too interested in her vagina. She tends to feel "loved" only when she is involved in seductiveness, pursuit, and the power struggle over getting her man so aroused that he feels as powerless as she. After she gets her man, she, like the I Gotcha male, does not know what to do.

I Gotcha individuals have little choice but to be dissatisfied with a stable relationship or marriage. Without the manipulations, power struggles, and hostile expression, relationships seem boring and meaningless. Not only are these individuals uncomfortable in nonsexual interactions, they are extremely frightened of intimacy and even straightforward human communication. Whenever someone catches them off-guard and empathetically communicates with them, they are convinced the person is trying to control or seduce them. Clearly, the I Gotcha individuals see the world through sex-colored binoculars. A secure, stable, empathetic relationship is not possible. In sum, the I Gotcha individual knows gender confusion, insecurity, anxiety, hostility, competition, and unhappiness well.

The Nonrelated

Ordinarily, thoughts of marriage include love, romance, intimacy, sex, security, and companionship. As has been shown, however, many individuals are not capable of intimacy. Marriage for them implies sex and minimal security. Due to the damage done in their first relationship, these individuals are not motivated to pursue positive relatedness or healthy interpersonal involvement, but instead to avoid that which they perceive as negative and threatening. Such Nonrelated individuals are extremely defensive and self-destructive. They expend much effort constructing walls to keep out the enemy (i.e., people). Socially isolated, they are needy for human interaction yet convinced that "people are no damn good."

Their psychological compromise is to pair with someone whom they do not really care about, one who also has impenetrable walls. Their relationship is innocuous and might even appear "free" to casual observers, because neither seems to care about what the other does. In fact, nonrelated couples cleverly arrange their lives so that they avoid each other.

Out of their human need for social connectedness, they may intellectually discuss everything and anything, as long as it is not personal. Extensive discussions are merely another way to avoid emotional involvement. Some Nonrelateds believe that their communication is superb because they never argue about anything that really riles them. They choose their words carefully in order to exclude emotional content and intimacy.

Nonrelated marriages may work for a while, but sooner or later one partner becomes disgusted with the continuous game-playing and aloneness, and begins to strive for intimacy. When this happens, old feelings of vulnerability quickly surface in both partners. Anticipation of emotional involvement forces the psychological cavalry to shore up its barricades. To let down these walls would mean to open the self up to the possibility of unbearable hurt and humiliation. That must never be allowed to happen.

Over the years, I have learned that "one man's vulnerability is another man's naturalness." That is, exposure of one's real feelings is a natural part of living for people with a reasonable level of psychological adjustment. For others, however, even the most superficial self-revelation may make them feel vulnerable and emotionally naked. Due to terrible feelings about themselves, they are sure that if they revealed anything important and close to the heart, the other person would laugh at and reject them.

Pathologically defensive individuals feel threatened and psychologically transparent nearly all of the time. Anything that they believe in might serve as the essentia for ongoing battles with the spouse. If the partner is not in full agreement with their every idea and desire, they experience it as bitter rejection. Deep within, defensive individuals have an extremely frail, embryonic ego, which cannot tolerate the slightest personal frustration. As a result, they cannot relate to people very well, and so must be content with relating to objects or possibly to animals. To remain in control, they

pair with someone who is equally defensive and make an unspoken pact never to talk about anything personal or important.

Most often, individuals in a Nonrelated marriage carry distorted memories about how much they were in love years ago.
They can vividly recall a past relationship with a special person,
conveniently forgetting the pain and discontentment in that romance. For, reality doesn't matter to people who are alone and
suffering. Their lack of emotional investment in the present relationship forces them to aggrandize the past as proof that they are
capable of "true love." As each partner secretly gathers psychological militia to prove that they are capable of intimacy, the main
point is obscured. By the fact that each must gather substantial
proof of his capacity to "love" might well provide the first clue
that neither is. But the proof is indeed irrelevant. If either were
capable of sustained intimacy, they would have it; as long as
neither is, they cannot. Locating the culprit will not be of much
help.

THE POOR

Poverty is more than a money deficiency. Interactions between the
poor parent and his poor child, and between the poor child and
his reality are different than what is experienced and interpreted
by the not-so-poor. Living is hard for poor people because it is almost always hectic and burdensome. Lacking opportunities and
seeing life through the eyes of necessity, adds a dimension of fatal-
ism to their already high feelings of hopelessness and dependency.

Marital and family relationships among the poor are often
strained and unfulfilling. Children are often not a blessing, but a
burden that tends to make the parents' lives even more difficult.
When such children become adults, it is easy to understand why
they sometimes feel unwanted and unappreciated. However, they
seldom see their feelings that "no one gives a damn" in the context of their own development. Instead, they blame society and
the not-so-poor, whom they believe should give of their riches.

Many poor people develop an I-don't-care attitude in order to
better tolerate their feelings of despair. To take life too seriously
or to have much hope that living will get easier is not in accordance

with their culture, nor with their reality. It is better not to hope than to hope and then be disappointed. Many poor people cannot forget the effect of their failures, and few can remember the feelings of enhanced esteem that followed accomplishment and success. Most often, their lives are not geared toward acquiring something positive that might help their plight. Instead, they are motivated by avoidance of their reality and emotional pain by thoughtlessness and impulsivity.

Middle-class people who have encountered financial setbacks can understand some of the feelings persistent among the poor. To be financially distraught and out of work while others are employed and spending conspicuously heightens one's feelings of envy, anger, and destructiveness. Moreover, the economic demands of spouse, children, and relentless bill collectors multiply already high feelings of powerlessness and inadequacy. The good things flaunted on television, in newspaper ads, and in more opulent neighborhoods provide a steadfast reminder of what can never be. The conspicuous consumption of the upper-middle class contributes to the poor person's image of failure and nothingness. The anger that results from never having enough to ease the hardship must be dissipated somewhere. Most often, it is expressed in physical acting-out, such as rape, murder, vandalism, and other violence. There is also a high incidence of wife and child abuse among the poor.

Some lower-class individuals mimic the social behaviors and attitudes of the somewhat quiescent middle class by keeping a lid on their feelings and destructive impulses. They turn the pain inward and become physically ill. Accidents and other major crises are frequent, permitting them to express their destructive impulses in one catastrophe. In doing so, they derive relief from the omnipresent emotional suffering. To quietly destroy themselves rather than others is a major step toward "appropriate socialization."

Life is especially difficult for the conscientious poor male who must try to provide for his family. Despite his effort, most of his money must be spent to maintain his impoverished standard of living. When people have to give out more than they take in, they become caldrons of resentment and anger. If the husband decides to work at a second job to make ends meet, the emotional imbalance in the family system will raise havoc. His wife may protest because there will be no one to help with the children, who seem very needy and hyperactive. The husband fantasizes about the good old days before marriage when life was not so much of a burden. Even though he earned less money then, at least he could spend most of it on himself. Husbands dedicated to their families dismiss such thoughts rather quickly because they are scared by their temptations. Other husbands, in an attempt to recapture the dreams of yesterday, justify purchases of cars, motorcycles, guns, campers, and other such toys. Some openly seek love affairs, spending their dollars impressing the lover. Others burdened almost beyond their limits of coping, just take off. After all, what is there to lose?

I once heard an imprisoned criminal from a poor family say rather humbly, "I would kill someone for less than 50 dollars. What is there to lose? If I got caught, they would put me in prison, which is better than home. If they killed me, it would be better than living." Another poor couple proudly believed that they were beating the system when they giggled, "We don't care if we are in debt by overspending. The worse thing that could happen is that they will take away our camper. By then, it won't be worth nothing anyway." I felt sad for these people. They were so damaged that they had very little self-pride. They only felt united when they could combine the forces of their hostility against the establishment, people with money, or their neighbors. The remainder of the time, their hostility was directed toward each other or their children. The few times living went relatively smoothly, they wondered what was wrong.

Relationships among the poor cannot be understood until one becomes aware of their primary modes of expression and some of the inherent problems therein. Most people in the lower classes rely upon the more primitive expressions, which are predominately tactile or physical. An analogy can be drawn between the behaviors and coping skills of young children and those of many adults from the lower socioeconomic class. For example, children tend to use physical activity and repetitive verbal utterances to dissipate tension. Unless they are deliberately suppressed, young children who are threatened or angry will physically lash out at the antagonist and scream a barrage of disproportionate verbiage, which is primitive anger and hatred. The emotional theme of their outbursts seems to have little to do with their appropriateness. Observing children at play reveals frequent arguments over who is right, what belongs to whom, who has what when the other person wants it, or who is to blame for what. Stringent rules are necessary in order to establish order and social fairness. Dealing with each other out of empathy and concern is a high-level abstraction that is seldom as developed or refined among the poor as it tends to be among the upper classes.

In poor neighborhoods, there is a high level of anxiety, fear, panic, and raw expression of emotion. Disorganization, anger, and confusion are an integral part of family living. The noise from blaring radios and television sets, crying children, parents yelling, and so forth adds to the chaos. Thinking, contemplation, and cognitive controls over their uncontainable emotional impulses, are seldom in their coping repertory. Logic, orderliness, cognitive delay, and pursuit of knowledge and education to reduce the fears and unknowns of life are more representative of the middle class. Even the educated poor sometimes revert to a chaotic, physical method of dealing with stress and anger when frustrated. The emotional scars endured throughout childhood and adolescence resurge automatically when poor parents discipline their own children or when stress is severe. What one really is cannot be completely erased regardless of sincerity or effort.

Because life is chaotic for the poor, too much organization and quiescence tend to force them to think about their misery. To avoid this painful reality, crises are unconsciously created. The functional value of crisis is that it legitimizes full expression of pent-up hostility and anger, which otherwise need to be held in abeyance in order to live with some stability. During the early phase of the crisis cycle, when there has been sufficient shock and emotional catharsis, the relationship with the spouse can be most gentle, most tender, and even intimate. As the crisis is gradually forgotten, however, many of the old, familiar realities resurface. Aside from its release mechanism, crisis also provides a legitimate excuse to be weak and to receive from others. Many poor people, when they feel "strong," cannot let themselves be in a position to receive nurturance and caring from each other.

Because of their limited occupational, societal, intellectual, and emotional resources, the poor seldom realize the rewards of self-dependence or the elevated self-esteem and self-confidence that come from making it alone. Lower-class males are particularly overdependent, but they would never admit it. Neither their present competencies nor their value during adolescence are relevant in an adult world of acquisitiveness. As hourly wage earners who can be easily replaced, the poor seldom have a sense of pride in their identification with their occupation or in their ability to earn a substantial income. To feel worthwhile, they often seek the most obvious phallic symbols. That is, it becomes an obsession to have the fastest car, for example, or the sexiest woman. All too frequently, the only place they get any feeling of significance is in the home. But even there, it is not genuine or positive but forced and fearful. Equality is out of the question. The man must be king, or at least believe that he is, even though inside he probably knows his wife is in charge. At home, some of these men are partly satisfied by beating their wives and children into fearful submission. Home is the one place they can feel, if only for awhile, that they matter. If it takes the emotional annihilation of spouse and children, all the better, for emotional cadavers cannot threaten these men too much.

In many poor families, the pleasures in life are reduced to eating and sex. But as people become obese, their sexual energy is reduced. Due to the conspicuous double standard among the poor, a wife's obesity permits the "deprived" husband (even though he too is obese) to go elsewhere "to have his needs met." Aware of her husband's wanderings, the wife panics and tends to eat more. Symbolically, she is stuffing down her frustration and hurt. In doing so, another destructive cycle is established. It will not be easily broken.

When nearly every curve in the road of life is hazardous people naturally tend to become insensitive to their own feelings and those of their families. If they didn't, life would be almost unbearable. Consequently, under prolonged stress, the human adaptive system automatically protects itself against pain through avoidance, denial, and emotional blindness. Blindness to the self, reality, and others, along with a tendency to regress to the physical mode of operation, provide the emotional push toward an image of "toughness" and "crudity," which is seen in nearly all poor people. Due to their helplessness, inadequacy, and struggle, they go to great lengths to convince themselves that they are powerful, adequate, emotionally impervious, and fearless. Some of the poor become overly invested in their defenses and eventually find it impossible to be gentle, loving, or kind for too long, lest they be called stupid or immature. Most poor people, especially the men, are extremely sensitive to words like *dependent, childish, immature, weakling, mama's boy, tender,* and *effeminate.* Most will not seek professional help because they are sure that the therapist will discover what they unconsciously already fear. Since they cannot accept these attributes within themselves, they are sure no one else could either. Beyond a doubt, being poor is much more than lacking sufficient funds.

5 / Facts of Life and Love

The ability to remain positively connected to a significant human is the essence of marriage, and, in some respects, is the essence of the quality of human experience. When two people are emotionally connected, the experiences, feelings, conflicts, joys, and heartache of one directly influence the emotional life of the other. On the other hand, living can be anxious, relatively meaningless, and unquestionably lonely when it is void of at least one special person who cares and who might also help attenuate frustrations, anxieties, fears, and heartache or share in pleasures and achievements.

Most couples readily acknowledge that marriage does not guarantee caring, love, or even concern. In fact, quite the opposite is often the rule. The emotional climate of the world would be much different if more people were "happily married" and their children felt valued and loved. The truth is that many couples are not emotionally married at all. Some individuals, despite their desire to be otherwise, cannot manage to be empathetic, sympathetic, or even concerned with their partner's needs. In a good number of marriages, there are two lonely people who can barely tolerate each other. Despite the melodramatic idealism sometimes portrayed in novels and on television, successfully living together is one of the most difficult things for people to do.

In nearly a decade of study and clinical observation, I have seldom observed the so-called ideal marriage that some authors have manufactured—or claimed to have themselves—in order to sell books to the vulnerable public. Those authors who claim it possible to remain as "madly in love" throughout marriage as during the first six months are living in a fantasy world. I have occasionally observed a couple (or spouse) who were so grossly out of touch with their feelings that they had become emotionally inoculated against involvement with each other. Nevertheless, some of them claimed to have "perfect" marriages and advised that other couples merely "try harder" or "trust in God more."

In fact, the couples who claimed to have "perfect" marriages were most often psychologically weak, desperate people who feared even the thought of ever having to be honest with themselves. Deep within, they were overwhelmed with unresolved conflict and unexpressed anger, but were too frightened of these feelings to allow them conscious recognition. These couples cannot allow themselves to understand the marital difficulties of others, least of all those of their children, because they themselves have had such a "perfectly loving" relationship. Sometimes, their rose-colored glasses were shattered when their children, the products of their "perfect" relationship, got divorced or had severe psychological problems.

Nearly every couple planning to marry is certain their relationship will be happier than almost any other marriage. They are sure they will remain "in love" forever. As mentioned previously, even an extremely pathological relationship feels like "true love" to the couple involved. Caught up in the power of the attachment, the self-esteem from having unconscious needs met, the erotic fulfillment, and the stimulation of having mastered a new intimacy, both partners experience what is very similar to delusional thinking. While together, all seems to go well for them, and so they believe that they haven't any problems that cannot be worked out, which further reinforces their "love." Each is sure that the strength of their "love" will not only carry them through present conflicts, but future ones as well.

During courtship some couples unconsciously create problems for themselves in order to test their "love" by trying to mutually resolve them. Due to the blindness, naiveté, and distorted reality accompanying all passionate relationshps, the couple overlook how easy it is to apologize, forget, and forgive, and to overlook the partner's shortcomings in order to further reinforce the depth of their love. The problem with the idealism and mania of courtship is that most couples fail to realize that it is only a stage of relationship development. Instead, they consider it as a prototype of "true love" and then later resent each other when they lose what they believe they once had. Despite their attempts to recreate the harmony of courtship, it neither can nor will be the same.

In nearly all marriages, there is a fairly predictable deterioration process, which couples attempt to rectify in various ways. The first step in the deterioration is the *attrition of the facade,* which comes as the first crisis. Eventually, it occurs to each partner that what they perceived in each other during courtship is not the entire package. Each apparently constructed a facade to impress the other and to receive the other's "love." They forgot that, when they were together, it was because they wanted to be, and each deliberately tried to have a good time at nearly any cost. Each forgot that erotic energy made it easy to *want* to please the other in the way each wanted to be pleased. At the time, the reward was sufficient to force each into their best behavior. They also had no way of knowing (as discussed in Chapter 4) that it is not difficult to feel strong when one is partially emotionally dependent upon parents and has to be concerned only with the self. As the facade disappears, each begins to perceive the other more realistically. There is no guarantee that they will like what they see.

The maxim, "you don't really get to know someone until you have lived with them awhile" carries more than a modicum of truth. Even so, it might be more accurate to say, "you don't really get to know yourself until you've been attached to someone else for awhile." As the initial facade of courtship is relinquished, more of the real self becomes exposed. In the most heated arguments, when a couple lets down their controls, greater depths of truth are revealed. Couples seldom know about the mechanisms of the unconscious but are fully aware of what they can say or do to set the partner off and to excite threat, tears, or anger.

Theresa was an overintellectualized, repressed depressive. Her husband Paul was an immature, overly dependent manic, who had simultaneously been dominated and rejected by his mother. Consequently, when he was feeling insecure, threatened, and emotionally exhausted, he wanted to be dominated. The treatment plan for Theresa and Paul was for each of them to work individually with a therapist, and to meet for joint sessions twice a month.

Theresa could always get Paul into a rage when she attacked him for trying to mold her into his mother's image. One day in her individual session, she said, "Boy, did I screw things up last weekend. Me and my big mouth. One of these days I might learn to shut up." During the weekend in question, Theresa had become infuriated while they were making love. Paul was so ineffectual that she had had to stimulate and caress him, and eventually exert all the energy in their sexual encounter. Theresa resented Paul's regressive-passivity and disinterest. At the worst possible moment, when she was putting his penis into her, she said, "Am I doing this the way your mother would have?" Needless to say, there was just enough unconscious accuracy in her statement to enrage Paul. For two days, they didn't talk. Fortunately, his own therapist was able to help him work through the rage, and also to accept the part of his fantasies that he had preferred not to acknowledge.

When people are emotionally attached and live together for awhile, they not only expose their facade, but also their unconscious conflicts and needs. Relatively healthy couples with only minor psychological conflicts tend to accept themselves, each other, and their feelings easily. Naturally, the more accepting they are of themselves (a direct result of the degree of acceptance they received in their first relationship), the more accepting they are of their partner's problems, insensitivities, and unpredictability. On the other hand, individuals who have been criticized, rejected, and made to feel badly about themselves will have little choice but to treat their spouse in the same way. Manic types, of course, because they are unable to contain anxiety and stress, will often be more conspicuously castrating and blaming, while simultaneously directing confusing and pejorative messages to the partner in order to dissipate tension.

Everyone knows that superficiality exists in daily social and business interactions. Away from home, life must go on, and few people there wish to know about the feelings of others. So, most people adopt a social facade and idealized self-image. At home, however, this facade and self-image are seldom reinforced by spouse or children. It is not accidental that when the pressures of living become almost intolerable, many people run away from home toward anyone or anything capable of supporting their facade. To have another appreciate one's outward social demeanor and manipulations can temporarily restore self-esteem. When a spouse refuses to recognize the partner's "act," there is little choice but to go elsewhere to be appreciated. For others, home and the relationship with the spouse provide security, nurturance, acceptance, and understanding, which are the basis of emotional healing. For them, it's not necessary to go elsewhere to be appreciated, to feel special, or to feel loved. This is what satisfactory marriages are all about.

The second factor contributing to the depreciation of intimate relationships is the *imposition of reality*. Often, during courtship, or while living together, or during early marriage, one or both partners exclude others from their private social arena. Even those individuals wishing to show off their prize need time alone with the other person. As their attachment increases, they wish to nestle in their social-psychological "placenta" in order to reduce the possible loss of the person who has become so important. In their own way, they sever themselves from the mainstream of life, and to a degree they psychologically institutionalize themselves with thoughts of the other and the newness of "being in love." Friends, parents, and others previously important to their lives are slowly left behind. As the responsibilities of adult living intrude on the couple's privacy, they gradually awaken from their fantasy and realize they must invest energy away from each other and toward the more practical necessities of life. Depending upon a couple's psychological and financial reserves and their individual responsibilities, such reality takes its toll in varying degrees. Significant is the similarity with which couples report their feelings and behavior during courtship. Almost everyone, regardless of psychological strength, social position, wealth, intelligence, or physical appearance, reports nearly identical feelings during courtship, which could loosely be described as "being in love." As the illusions of courtship are slowly replaced by reality, however, intimate relationships often lose their vitality and become unpleasant.

Most couples remember their early years together as more pleasant than anything they experienced thereafter. During their courtship, they thought nothing of remaining awake most or all of the night just so they could be with each other. They recall working a little harder at doing things together because they wanted to share in each other's happiness. Later in the relationship, as energies were displaced elsewhere and realities made life more difficult, the couple could ride in the car for hours or sit at home for days, seldom exchanging a loving word or even touching each other. In badly deteriorated relationships, the thought of having fun together or making love becomes offensive.

Each partner secretly wishes to reverse time and revisit the days when living was more fun. Some think of having a love affair in order to simulate the feelings of courtship. Those who do have affairs, however, secretly realize that living has become even more complicated. Those not giving up on romance occasionally try to arouse each other as they did during courtship, but it cannot be the same. Much of the resentment between couples is generated out of the anger and disgust that follow their desperate attempts to make each other care more and better—the way they did when they were encapsulated in the fantasies of courtship.

The third factor contributing to the deterioration of the marital relationship is *erotic desensitization*. Looking at and making love to the same body year after year desensitizes individuals to the lust they once felt. Even the most physically attractive couples tire of each other's bodies after they have "mastered" each other, and desire to look elsewhere. Frequently in my work with couples, when one partner—for instance, the husband—learns of the other's outside love affair, he eventually wants to see the lover in order to compare his own attractiveness. If the lover is less attractive, his tension is momentarily reduced because threat is temporarily reduced. Within a short time, however, he castigates his wife, "I don't see how you could have gotten involved with him. I'm better than he is!" If the lover is more powerful and more desirable the anger quickly orchestrates: "I don't see how you could do this to me. I am working my ass off for you and the kids, and you're out chasing that stud!" The hurt is understandable, but to automatically assume that he is inferior or undesirable is very self-destructive. The point is, when someone has an outside affair that is predominately sexual, it rarely makes any difference who it is. Whether the intruder is more attractive is irrelevant. The new body, face, and experience provide excitement very similar to that which was experienced before the erotic desensitization.

As erotic desensitization erodes the passion between couples, they often force themselves to work at becoming, or to pretend they are, sexually turned on by the other. As stated previously, observing the same nude body day after day eventually does little or nothing for a person. On the other hand, a wink, a touch, a knee, a breast, a smile, or just being noticed by an attractive neighbor, friend, or even a stranger might energize the desire lost at home.

Erotic desensitization may have devastating consequences for those individuals who rely heavily upon their looks for their sense of esteem. For example, if an attractive woman receives her primary support and social recognition from being noticed and desired, it comes as a terrible blow when her husband doesn't seem to be nearly as aroused as everyone else. She has little choice but to feel betrayed, angry, desperate, and worthless, and she logically concludes that her husband no longer cares for her.

Due to the powerful passion that exists in the beginning of all relationships, both individuals feel sufficiently aroused that they have little difficulty containing other needs, interests, and desires in order to preserve the physical arousal and potential consummation. Sexual arousal and the anticipation of satisfaction provide a substantial, albeit temporary, elevation in ego strength, which can be observed as exaggerated self-denial in other areas of the relationship. As indicated throughout this volume, it is not difficult for people to be cooperative, submissive, and energetic when their basic psychological needs are met and they consequently feel good about living. As a couple gradually becomes desensitized, however, their correlative needs are also ignored, forcing the artifacts of pseudo–well-being to diminish. As ego strength returns to its original level, unsatisfied needs, desires, and unresolved conflicts surface. By all outward appearances, the couple enters the ranks of the "unhappily married."

The fourth factor contributing to the deterioration of intimate relationships is the *emotional and economic demands on the family system*. Most often, the husband is the first individual to divert energy away from the relationship. Frequently, he channels his energy into his career and comes home exhausted. He may well have little energy left to give to his wife and children. Depending upon the wife's neediness, she could very easily interpret his reduced emotional investment as a reduced quantity of love. Emotionally, of course, she is correct. Whenever an attachment figure who was once present and available begins to pull back, the other will nearly always feel rejected. For example, after a child is born, the wife is usually busy meeting the baby's needs, and some husbands feel left out. In addition, in many families an unconscious competition for the mother's attention exists between the father and the children. This is especially evident in disturbed couples who cannot relate positively to each other. The couple becomes emotionally separated or divorced while legally married. Loss is loss. And the loss of a significant other's attention and affection feels much like rejection regardless of how well one understands the logic or necessity of other needs.

Reasonably healthy individuals who have peace of mind, a modicum of unresolved conflict, and the capacity for intimacy will be extrasensitive to the partner's divestment of attachment energy and will be comfortable discussing the feeling of "loss" with the partner. The partner, because of temporary demands on time and energy, may not notice the attenuation of emotional investment. Eventually, however, the "loss" will become evident to his own well-being, and there will be a mutual desire to restore relational balance.

It is probably obvious at this juncture that successful relationships are fluid and dynamic, and require regular communication and behavioral adjustment from each individual. When there is an underlying capacity for intimacy and positive relatedness, rooted in both partners' ability to be trusting and trustworthy, open, close, and interdependent, then the couple can usually make adjustments and grow together. However, when people wish to settle their differences "once and for all," or "do not want to hear about them" because they are threatened by conflict, or are so severely disturbed that their anger is endless, then ongoing behavioral adjustments are not possible. Such a couple becomes stuck, and they usually know it. Each is aware that the partner's heart is not at home, but because of their inability to communicate openly, they cannot be sure what happened nor do they know how to repair the damaged system.

A successful relationship is characterized by two individuals who have the psychological strength and relational capacity to discuss the pressures and idiosyncracies pulling them apart, rather than blame each other for not caring. Successfully paired couples have fewer needs for attention and nurturance and are therefore relatively self-contained in comparison to those who are disturbed and needy. Because of the self-containment, they tend to handle more effectively the demands of financial reality, responsibility, and one another's additional emotional investments without feeling deprived or alone. As the couple begins to feel out of step with each other, they are able to discuss their needs while having the strength to adapt to the demands and pressures that initially altered the quality of their attachment. After each altercation and adjustment, they emerge knowing how very important they are to each other.

The capacity for positive relatedness carries with it an inherent healing process and an appropriate level of empathy and consideration. Because of the couple's positive relatedness, each confrontation that results in behavioral and attitudinal adjustments helps them to become stronger, more self-contained, and even less needy. Resentments, when present, can usually be worked out satisfactorily as the couple persists in their effort to do so, rather than refusing to discuss them. With each successfully resolved conflict, the couple becomes more confident that they can handle nearly any conflict that might arise.

When resentment, anger, criticism, and the desire to reject and harm each other pervade a couple's relationship, the last stage of decomposition has occurred. They will not be able to restore harmony by themselves. As their feelings of unity collapse, each individual becomes more needy, more angry, more vicious, more defensive, and less able to talk about anything in a civilized way. The couple's ability to make practical day-to-day decisions becomes nearly impossible for fear that one might be giving in to the "enemy." If the duration of psychological damage persists, both partners become unable to discuss even the most innocuous subject without trying to prove the other wrong or somehow demeaning him. Patience has succumbed to sharpness, kindness has been replaced by roughness, gentleness by abrasion, cooperation by resistance, openness by "get the other guy first," and peace of mind by embittered agitation and anxiety.

As their relationship reaches the last stage of deterioration, both partners construct and reinforce psychological walls in order to protect themselves from further invasion. The battle takes on a vicious, devious flank attack. Rather than hit the front line, well-camouflaged verbal snipers are employed to surprise the enemy at the weakest location. A couple at this stage of deterioration become ingenious strategists. They are capable of sneaking into microscopic ruptures in each other's defensive barricades, hitting with relentless force, and retreating with valor to their own fortress, where they gloat over their ability to cause damage without being wounded.

George and Maureen were professional therapists who came into family therapy because of the severe symptoms of their teenaged son. Like many people-helpers, they were embarrassed to seek help for themselves. It soon became obvious that their relationship was infested with anger, hurt, resentment, and overall unhappiness, and that their bright, sensitive son was acting out the hostilities of his parents. During the second session, Maureen heightened her relentless castigation of George, who seemed harmless because he was so tuned out from himself as well as everyone else. In fact, he sat impassively in my office, cleaning his fingernails with a penknife. Maureen, frustrated by her inability to reach him, yelled, "Goddam you, George! Will you listen to me? Let down those walls and hear me!" Realizing her hatred for him, I interrupted and asked if she really expected George to let down his walls when she was on the warpath. No longer able to contain herself, Maureen yelled, "I only want that son of a bitch to let down the walls for a minute so I can hurt him the way he hurt me!" George, tuned out as he was, kept picking at his fingernails. He didn't seem particularly alarmed by her outburst.

People do not construct barricades around themselves to retain happiness. They build them to prevent damage, threat, attack, and pain. Most relatively healthy people are able to let down their walls when they are not in danger. In fact, such people do not like walls and defenses because they foster anxiety and tension and deprive them of the fullness of experience. Consequently, fairly healthy couples are somewhat open with each other. Pathological couples have walls that were built in the first relationship, which cannot be easily removed. Overly defensive, guarded individuals seldom realize that, while their walls may keep out the enemy, they also keep out warmth, vitality, and positive influence of human relationships.

Humans—and for that matter, animals—can only accommodate so much pain before they detach from their emotional investment in the one who hurts them. As a couple's relationship collapses, they will psychologically detach from each other and relocate their attachment energy. It is not possible to predict where the "new love" will emerge, but, for sure, it will go somewhere. For example, in such families, the wife may overinvest her energy in the children. The husband may also overinvest in a child, but is more likely to turn his attention to his work, other women, drinking, or something inanimate. Exactly where the attachment energy goes is not important. What is significant is that when humans are emotionally damaged by a destructive relationship, they will begin to "love" someone or something else. Attachments and human dependencies are sufficiently unconscious and subtle that sometimes it is not possible for one to know where one's heart really is until whatever it is focused on is lost.

Nearly every couple in a deteriorating relationship tries in their own way to restore a harmonious balance to their marriage. Such efforts are usually unconscious. By far, the most common method used to hold on to what is left, or to regain what was lost, is to develop a mutual obsession. For example, such couples often attempt to prove their love and to make a new start by having a baby. Unconsciously, the intention is to keep the errant partner home and committed to the marriage. In family therapy, it is uncanny to see how many couples become aware of what they have done to prevent the demise of their relationship. In fact, many of them admit they they had a child after one of them was unfaithful and had been caught.

Whatever conflicts exist between them, the couple have to come together to create the new life. After the conception, they can channel their energy toward the birth of the child. The wife can pamper her body for nine months, and the husband will usually find it difficult to damage her when she is carrying a part of him. To damage her would in essence be to damage part of himself.

Of course, not all couples have a new baby to aid a deteriorating marriage. Some buy a house or other major item, or move to a new area. It really makes no difference what they do, as long as it is encompassing enough to keep their mutual agitation from consciousness. There is some truth to the adage that "ignorance is bliss." Unfortunately, when the couple's energy is freed from their obsession, the original conflicts surface in full force. To escape the panic and pain of their destructive impulses, they must get involved in another large project.

Over the years, while helping couples enhance the quality of their relationships, I have observed an intriguing phenomenon, which I have labeled "hostility shifts." Hostility shifts are not to be confused with the genuine working-through of accrued resentment and anger that is often seen in marital counseling or family therapy; instead, they are characterized by what seems to be a premature and inexplicable artificial harmony between couples. Most often, hostility shifts are detected in the more critical and verbal spouse. Frequently, the hostility is turned back upon the self, and, as quickly as the couple seem to "get along," physiological symptoms often emerge.

Mary Ann and Denny, a couple in their early twenties with a two-year-old child, had fought viciously throughout their relationship. Aside from being mismatched (both were manics), they could enter combat over anything, everything, and nothing. Within a few minutes of each battle, they had often forgotten what the fight was about; what mattered was who was going to win. Each was out to destroy the other at all cost, and each altercation generated more damage and more suffering.

Mary Ann and Denny were encouraged by their parents to see a marriage counselor. Accompanied by the usual apprehension, they went into therapy primarily to help the therapist identify the real culprit, once and for all. Thus, they were surprised to learn that the therapist was not a judge who would determine blame and penance. However, their rapport with the therapist was excellent, and he let them know that "when a relationship is in as much trouble as yours, both people are contributing, often in ways they are not aware of." Mary Ann and Denny accepted that and began looking inwardly for their contribution to their problems. Although their first two sessions were innocuous enough and each consciously tried not to attack the other, their anger seeped out.

Mary Ann and Denny showed up for the third session ready to terminate therapy because they felt they no longer needed it. Arm in arm and smiling, they seemed friendly and romantic. As the therapist began to discuss their interactions, their relative lack of hostility was obvious. When the couple related the events of the preceding week, the therapist learned that Mary Ann had been in bed for three days with excruciating lower back pain. However, she reported that after visiting a chiropractor, she not only felt better but also felt gentle and amiable toward her husband. For the remainder of the week, they had gotten along better than ever. Mary Ann's hostility had localized in her lumbar region, and she felt little conscious desire to attack her husband. Consequently, Denny felt little need to attack her. She quit fighting back and swallowed her pain, and thus established a new balance in their relationship. Denny was pleased because his wife was more submissive. She was pleased because they had quit fighting and could probably save their marriage.

The strange part of shifting hostility onto the self is that it can dissipate emotional conflict, thus creating a temporary feeling of psychological well-being. Mary Ann and Denny had shifted their hostilities away from each other, thereby creating a fairly congenial attitude. Against professional advice, they terminated two sessions later.

Neighbors, ex-lovers, society, foreign countries, minority groups, and nearly anyone or anything can serve as a focus for anger and hatred. This is illustrated by the following case history.

One very disturbed couple had been fighting for over two years before they came to me for help, not for them, but for their daughter, who had run away from home and had overdosed on drugs. In order to help the child, it was obvious the work had to begin with the collapsed marriage. The couple's hurt and anger were so deep, they fought relentlessly in my office. When I began to wish that the hour were over so that I could get some peace and quiet, it became obvious why their daughter had run away. Despite my efforts to slow down the attack, I could not. Each desired emotional plasma from the other and was out to get it. Facetiously, the schizoid wife told me after the second session that her next-door neighbor had asked her what the sessions were like and if they were helping. Too schizoid to control her thoughts, she had replied, "Hell no. We go to his plush office and fight like we do at home—maybe more, because he shuts the door and makes us stay there. The worse part is that the asshole therapist charges us a dollar a minute to do what we can do at home for nothing." Even though I laughed at her comments, inside I felt helpless, inadequate, and useless. Knowing that they were feeling the same way didn't help. I hesitantly assured them that therapy takes time and not to give up.

To my surprise, the couple came to the fourth session outwardly happy and considerate toward each other. Throughout the session, each was aware that they were not castrating each other, but was apprehensively waiting for the other to start. It was undoubtedly the first time in years that they were together for longer than four minutes without wanting to annihilate each other. Eventually, it became apparent that their hostility had shifted away from each other toward the husband's job, particularly toward his supervisor. Both were in full agreement about the "no good" supervisor, whom they psychologically slaughtered for nearly half an hour. As they vented freely, they experienced feelings of release and unity, which I was sure had not been there before. They had accidentally stumbled across an appropriate displacement object for the anger and hate they felt toward each other.

Hostility shifts are most often an unconscious and ambulant—but functional—part of satisfactory relationships. Those couples consciously wishing to avoid fights might have several displacement objects that serve as a catharsis when each is angry, upset, or intolerably anxious. Displacement objects can be noted in one's thoughts, fantasies, and talking to oneself. The best time to become aware of the hostility shift process in oneself, is after feelings have been hurt by spouse or children. In pathologically disturbed individuals, the anger can be generalized to everyone and everything. When a person is on the warpath, so to speak, anyone can serve as an object of hostility. As internal stress and anger approach intolerable proportions and one prefers not to cry as a release, the energy within mounts until the individual is a "bomb ready to go off." An internalizer, of course, will, at the most critical time, force the anger back on the self and develop somatic symptoms, which include headaches, gastrointestinal disorders, lower back pain, and diarrhea or constipation.

The concentration upon irrationally selected displacement objects has been of interest to social and forensic scientists for years. For example, criminals who mercilessly beat a child to death or kill a person they don't even know provide the most bizarre account. When tension mounts and the individual does not wish to destroy his partner or parent, the annihilation of a less powerful object or of an individual with little or no retaliative power is chosen first. If the object chosen has caused previous threat or harm, it makes it all the easier to justify irrational hostility. If not, it rarely matters. The destruction of another's property for the sole purpose of destroying something is another way to release pent-up anxiety. On a more socially acceptable level, criticizing and demeaning another person serves exactly the same purpose.

PROCESS OF SATISFACTORY RELATIONSHIPS

Although most intimate relationships (marriage, living together) gradually deteriorate to a disheartening state of toleration, some couples do adjust to the pressures and anxieties caused by themselves, their responsibilities, and reality. These couples are able to use experience and their relationship to grow individually, while developing a stable and contented life. Needless to say, remaining married, as opposed to finalizing a divorce, has little to do with a successful relationship. The majority of couples have difficulty tolerating each other, despite social pretense suggesting otherwise. Within some of these destructive relationships are individuals much too frightened of themselves and what the partner might do to even consider divorce. Yet others adopt a psychosomatic compromise. The underlying resentment is turned inward, and one or both partners develop various physical ailments.

Some mildly neurotic to healthy individuals, paired by "falling in love" rather than by one of the deviations cited in Chapter 4, may experience stages of relational and individual maturity as a result of their marriage. Erik Erikson, in *Childhood and Society*

(1964), described stages of human development that approximate the growth process found in successful marital relationships. Similar to Erikson's model, the process noted in successful marriages was also stage-dependent. That is, psychologically, people cannot be at one level of maturity unless they have mastered the psychological demands at a previous level. Clusters of behaviors, anxieties, and conflicts are inherent in each stage, and must be satisfactorily resolved before couples can proceed to the responsibilities, joys, and freedoms of the next stage. A higher stage of development cannot preclude an earlier stage, nor can a stage be haphazardly mastered, simulated, or eliminated. Fixation at one stage is fairly common if the individuals do not have the psychological strength, commitment to each other, and communication skills to satisfactorily resolve their differences. Fixations (i.e., being hopelessly stuck) always occur if the couple lacks the capacity for intimacy or if they are sufficiently disturbed that empathy for the spouse is not possible.

Sincerity vs. Exploitation

The first stage of intimacy is *Sincerity vs. Exploitation*, which is commonly known as courtship. In this stage, most of the couple's interactions are directly related to testing reactions and responses to a variety of fabrications. Some of the fabrications are meaningless, while others are endowed with idiosyncratic meaning to which the potential partner had better respond appropriately. If the partner responds to the scenario appropriately, it is concluded that he must be sincere and is not out to exploit or to harm. The fabrications cannot always do their job, as shown in the section on "What's-Up? relationships (p. 162), because some individuals who have been bitterly rejected and controlled by a manipulative parent can easily detect covert emotional manipulations. It fits their pathology perfectly, and they can pass any manipulative test *magna cum laude*.

Because no two relationships can be exactly alike, people usually have little logical basis for selecting a satisfactory marriage partner. To compensate for this lack of knowledge, the couple is nearly always acting out some type of drama learned from movies, television, or books, or from observing others believed to be "in love." Regardless of the act, this first stage is nearly always earmarked by provocative eroticism, romanticism, idealism, deviousness, caution, and caprice. If the individuals begin to care for each other at all, more games are employed in an attempt to distinguish between sincerity and exploitation. Everyone seems to know that genuine feelings of love, attachment, and dependency also make one vulnerable to hurt and loss. Consequently, during serious courtship, the rules of the game are easy: to get the other person to care more than you do and to become more vulnerable than you are. It is easier to break up if one never "lets go" entirely or if the partner invests more.

During this stage, it is interesting to observe emotionally immature adults. They behave like adolescents. After they have made a rudimentary attachment to each other, which provides minimal security, one or both keep one eye alert for someone better. "Better" typically means more attractive, more socially desirable, and in some way more valuable according to peer group standards. If they cannot be loved by anyone "better," they emotionally accept their situation and become more committed until their attachment and dependency bind them to the degree that it raises anxiety when they are away from each other. When they break up and experience the aloneness, separation anxiety, and tears that are part of any good love story it is not difficult to convince themselves of the depth of their love.

Tears are often considered a better indicator of sincerity than words. If one individual has sufficient impact to "make the other cry," they conclude the relationship is serious. A person who is unable to cry, for whatever reason, can become physically ill or "so upset" that he cannot continue with daily responsibilities. For one partner to miss work because of a breakup, or to convince the other of the misery caused, can sometimes represent the epitome of genuine sincerity. To become self-destructive because of the partner's wrath or emotional detachment signifies the depth of "real love" for some couples. However this "broken heart syndrome" is interpreted, it can be deviously endured by people who can cry at will and who have used tears as a manipulative tool since the first relationship. Nor do tears account for the pathologically self-destructive individuals who are nearly always looking for a justifiable exterior reason to break down and thus reduce inner tension.

If the relationshp proceeds toward a firm emotional attachment, a minimal security system is established that allows each partner to become more vulnerable and more real. At this point, the couple feels free to argue, make demands, or, if they choose, to become obnoxious in order to test the other's sincerity. During this stage and the next, nearly all fights somehow involve sincerity, commitment, and degree of love (i.e., who cares more? who doesn't care enough?). The woman is usually more concerned with the degree of the man's sincerity than he is with hers. Because men more frequently pursue partners for no other reason than sex, women naturally must be concerned with their sincerity.

If a couple expects nothing more than an evening out that concludes with a brief sexual encounter, sincerity and exploitation are not an issue. If, however, a person becomes aware of his need for genuine caring, commitment, and love, issues of sincerity or exploitation surface.

Due to game-playing, deviousness, the escapism inherent in courtship, and fear of removing one's armor, couples are seldom able to relate directly and honestly. Many couples believe that they are leveling with each other, but fail to realize that "controlled openness" is also a game. Some couples, for example, reveal just enough about themselves to convince the other that they are indeed open and honest. On important personal issues, however, they may be neither. Other couples establish unspoken rules in order to prevent themselves from becoming too honest or too personal. These couples have learned that "being in love" means that people do not disagree or fight; for those who are really "in love," agree completely on every possible issue. In order to prevent conflict, they deliberately decide never to discuss anything personal, controversial, or important. Such couples do not realize that people who do not care about each other also rarely fight. Nor do they realize that where hate runs deep, couples are also afraid to fight for fear of what might happen if they released their pent-up feelings.

If a couple does not make a commitment "for better or worse," their relationship cannot proceed to the next stage, nor can they make optional use of each other's opposite character traits for emotional maturity. Without a sincere commitment, the relationship essentially remains in the escapist and/or adolescent stage. Although escape, regression, and avoidance of adult responsibility may temporarily feel better than the frustrations of responsible living, a unique double bind is created. Without a sincere comitment, neither partner will become sufficiently emotionally involved for fear of being abandoned. Thus, the couple derives little more than an erotic convenience from the relationship, and they are suspended in an awkward state of apprehension. For their relationship to grow, they must emotionally invest in each other and commit themselves to the relationship. More than likely, each feels the emptiness but does not know how to derive more from the relationship. When attachment energy cannot go to one's partner, it will surely go elsewhere, thus making the relationship even more empty. It's usually not too hard to break up or to become emotionally uninvolved with someone else when a suspended relationship has not gone anywhere.

One rather bizzare couple, "married" for 18 years, came to my office for counseling. Their relationship was in such an embryonic stage that it was difficult to believe that they had lived that way for so long. It quickly became obvious that they weren't married at all, but were still struggling with the courtship issues of Sincerity vs. Exploitation. They were both surprised and angered when, after three sessions, I told them they would have to get married before I could help them. They assured me that they had been married by a priest 18 years earlier and had raised three children, and so they resented my inferring that they were living in sin. I apologized and commented that the only "sin" I saw was that they had been so unhappy for so many years and that they had raised three very disturbed children.

As they began to encounter each other, it was not difficult to detect their immediate tendency to emotionally "divorce" when under stress. As far back as they could remember, each had threatened to either leave or kick the other out of the house whenever a mild disagreement arose. When they became aware of what they were doing, they realized what I had meant about getting married. They had never made a sincere commitment to the relationship. It was sad to see middle-aged adolescents trying to survive in an adult world and attempting to raise healthy children.

Trust vs. Mistrust

Following a satisfactorily negotiated commitment, the relationship evolves to the second stage in which the majority of the conflicts are embodied in issues of *Trust vs. Mistrust*. Within this stage, there are three substratal levels of trust, which when adequately resolved allow the couple to proceed into the next stage (see Figure 4).

The first and most universal sublevel necessitating resolution is the guarantee of fidelity or exclusivity. Before each partner can let go of their guardedness and social facade, each must have reasonable assurance that the partner will always be there and will remain as much "in love" as they are at the time of their commitment. Otherwise, it is not possible for the couple to become appropriately vulnerable to each other or to be relaxed enough to give each other a feeling of security and well-being.

The first level of Trust vs. Mistrust infers an honesty, an integrity, and a reliability upon the partner, which, after a short time, render him predictable in his feelings and consistent in his behavior. After the couple exchanges sincere I-love-you's, a feeling of commitment and unity results. Each partner now "belongs" to the other, and each has become the central figure in the other's life. Even couples who have been burned in previous relation-

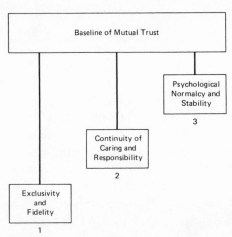

Fig. 4.   Three components of trust.

ships, and who consequently delude themselves into believing they do not own each other, deep within desire a feeling of exclusivity. People are capricious in their feelings, however, and consequently it is possible to feel something for someone one day and not feel the same way a short time later. If one individual cannot promise exclusivity, the relationship cannot get to the point where each partner can feel secure. Emotional and relational maturation cease as the couple becomes stagnant, anxious, and suspicious.

As shown in Chapter 2, a trusting dependency is a prerequisite for normal childhood development. Without the feeling of a secure, reliable, nuclear trust in a primary attachment figure, people become psychotic and are virtually unable to trust. If a relationship is grounded in the faith and trust of exclusivity for a sufficient time—possibly a year or two—and one member becomes involved with someone else, then the basic trust has been violated and will not be easily restored. The wronged spouse is wounded at the deepest and most primitive layer of human need and is overwhelmed by anger and desire for retaliation. When the nuclear trust in an invested attachment is fractured, there is little hope that it can ever be restored. It is not possible to go back, and, although counseling can help people move into new vistas of relatedness, many couples do not seek help.

When people are wounded at basic levels of human experience, they will be cautious about ever fully trusting again. Emotional spontaneity is lost, and jocularity is artificial and strained. The relationship begins its gradual demise as the couple prefers to handle the infraction of trust by themselves. After weeks, months, or years without substantial resolution of the violation of trust, the couple begins to wonder why they are in the relationship at all. Without the ability to be spontaneously close to the other and to reestablish the feelings of the initial attachment, couples have little choice but to affect each other negatively. The hurt begins to create doubts about previous joys and pleasures. The couple feels awkward and detached. Finally, it becomes more comfortable for the couple to be apart than to be together knowing that each feels the painful deluge of subsurface resentment and guilt.

The second level of Trust vs. Mistrust requiring satisfactory resolution is the continuity of caring and responsibility within the relationship. Couples begin their relationship more than eager to please each other, often by exaggerated self-denial and inhibition of emerging personal needs. As the relationship proceeds, in order to develop a trustworthy and harmonious system, it becomes necessary for each to rely on the promise of what the partner *says he will do.* Throughout the complexities of daily living, the sheer bulk of responsibility requires each not only to care about the well-being of the other but to care enough to follow through behaviorally with whatever needs to be done. In the marriages I've studied, 90 percent of the couples could not get beyond the struggle over who is doing more, who is doing less, who has it easier, who has it harder, and who is getting the better deal out of the marriage. The majority of conflicts emerged from broken promises over adjustments and corrections in behavior.

In most marriages, couples unconsciously tally the number of broken promises regarding household responsibilities. Regardless of how it is designed, there is seldom equity in the quantity of energy expended in maintaining the typical household. Some couples enter marriage unsure or unconcerned about who is supposed to do what when, but in a short time the division of labor is usually defined. What was earlier not important enough to discuss—because of their conviction that something as irrelevant as chores could never come between them—often becomes the focus of direct hostility. If a couple arrives at an equitable division of labor, and they genuinely appreciate one another for their contributions, few problems exist. However, when living becomes more difficult, either due to low ego strength or because neither can be trusted to offer empathetic caring to maintain their labor agreement, the anger and resentment cause another layer of trust to be shattered. As a result, it becomes burdensome to maintain family harmony.

Breaches of responsibility and trust are more complex than what might seem evident. As shown in Chapter 4, many couples are frightened of the other's potential for wrath, criticism, and rebuke. In pathological relationships where people cannot communicate their real feelings, behavior becomes the only mode of communication. Therefore, when one partner's behavior is not according to the other's specifications, it is concluded that he or she doesn't care. In such relationships, one partner's failure, for example, to take out the garbage or flush the toilet can excite feelings of mistrust and rejection in the other. The comment, "I don't feel like it right now" is interpreted as, "I don't love you enough to do it." When breaches of trust occur repeatedly, most couples back off from each other because of the hurt incurred when one believes and expects the partner to do what he says, but he does not follow through. In the strict sense of the word, "faith without works is dead." When faith in one another wanes and the problem cannot be resolved satisfactorily, the relationship also deteriorates.

As soon as a relationship reaches disparate proportions of inequity in the division of labor, the maturation process again becomes stuck. When such inequality exists, relationship growth is impossible because the one who believes he is being used will not tolerate idleness or independent activities from the partner. As mistrust replaces trust, the focus of the "wronged" partner becomes one of keeping the other under constant surveillance in order to insure a more equitable arrangement. Relaxation and rest cannot be enjoyed without guilt when one's partner is sagaciously maintaining the ledger of injustice. Fun, enjoyment, and spontaneity cannot be legitimately experienced because almost always there is "work to be done." In badly deteriorated relationships, pleasure and fun become negatively endowed. In a distorted way, suffering and hardship become the goals toward which the couple competes. On a regular basis, they squawk at one another about who works harder, who has given up more, and how miserable they are. If one can prove that he has indeed worked harder and suffered more, the argument is "won." He can go to bed that night righteously rejoicing because he is indeed more unhappy than the wretched spouse.

The trustworthiness of the spouse sometimes becomes suspect when one partner observes the other's conduct outside the relationship. If one deliberately lies or exaggerates to friends or relatives, his partner may question his integrity at home.

Closely related to the active deceit just suggested is the covert dishonesty observed in some couples. For example, some couples impress their peers with lies about their financial success or deceive them about how much in love they are. Of course, such behavior does little to help them develop their relationship or themselves as individuals. For instance, when a man knows that his wife is a hypocrite, he has little choice but to seriously doubt her word and intentions. In view of the numerous ways in which couples can deceive each other, it is not difficult to understand how easily couples detach from each other and why they can feel alone even while sharing the same bed. It is also not difficult to understand why there are so many unhappy, stuck relationships and unhappy, stuck people.

It takes a fairly high level of emotional strength for an individual (in this case, the husband) to be honest, open, and responsible with a spouse who in many ways has control over the fulfillment of his psychological needs. It takes even more strength for him to be honest enough with his wife to share his feelings and desires, which may be contrary, or even threatening, to her own feelings, convictions, and security. The healthier a couple is, the easier it is for them to consistently empathize with what each other might be feeling in order to eventually intercept each other's desires, and act on them appropriately. Emotionally disturbed individuals spend most of their energy attempting to heal psychological wounds from the first relationship or withdrawing from situations in the marriage that might hurt. When they are not trying to do so, most of their energy goes toward wants and activities that are in some way associated with compensation for their psychological neediness. When that much energy is consumed maintaining the self, it is unreasonable to expect empathy with the partner's efforts, especially when empathy may mean following through with their part in the division of labor.

The last substrate of trust that couples must resolve in order to proceed satisfactorily toward the next stage of relational maturity is confidence in each other's psychological and emotional stability. No one enjoys being around an unhappy, angry, resentful individual. Most people are already too busy fighting for their own psychological comfort (happiness) to emotionally invest in someone who is unstable, explosive, depressed, or complaining most of the time. Besides, one person's sadness and depression easily affect other individuals living in the same house. That is, these feelings tend to make others sad and depressed even if they had nothing to do with their onset.

Every relationship is unique in regard to the number of "bad" days allowed before the marriage begins to dissolve. Before all the substrates of Trust vs. Mistrust can come together to form an overall trusting relationship, the couple must have endured several years of relative security and faith in the partner's ability to remain consistently faithful, caring, responsible, and emotionally stable.

Repeated throughout this volume is that a deep and sincere emotional attachment to one's spouse is similar to a psychological symbiosis. The needs, conflicts, desires, and joys of one partner should directly affect the other. A sustained, secure, emotional attachment to the spouse is necessary to provide a foundation for emotional maturity. If one individual in a relationship, however, is emotionally damaged, then his unhappiness is also the unhappiness of the other. To feel for and with each other in a spirit of unity can buffer the pressures of living, especially when the unity is with someone who is a part of the self. The amount of heartache in a relationship has definite limits, however, before the more "stable" partner becomes fed up and detaches from the affective boundaries of the other. Similar to this is the partner who pulls away from the spouse's unhappiness. Being too unhappy for too long (even if the spouse had nothing to do with it) causes the partner to emotionally retreat from the front line. As the partner seeks psychological refuge, he becomes immune to the infectious emotional disease of the ill partner.

Undoubtedly, the most complicated aspect of trusting one's partner to be "normal" lies in the couple's ability to understand each other's irrational impulses and unresolved conflicts. Living is sufficiently difficult that frequently people do not understand their own motives and hostilities, let alone those of their partner. Somewhere in the midst of heated emotion, each individual must trust the partner not to deliberately or accidentally hurt him when he is down. (Disturbed individuals will, of course, look for the spouse's vulnerabilities and proceed to crucify him when he is defenseless and confused.) Couples with the most satisfactory relationships have developed an excellent communication system that allows for a trusting interdependency. They are also aware of what is troubling them in the early phases of emotional stress and feel free to check out their anxieties with one another. Seriously disturbed individuals tend not to check out emotions with the spouse. Not only are they unable to be open, but they have so many conflicts that they are always anxious or angry about something. Most often, their upheaval and anger is caused by something far deeper than the present situation.

In order to function efficiently in society, everyone needs to suppress anxiety, personal problems, and feelings of hurt. Thus, one result is that people become easily confused and disoriented under stress. The "safest" and best way to alleviate confusion and tension is by an anger outburst, which usually takes place at home. However, such outbursts frequently hurt those most loved. Rare is the couple who has learned to deal well with each other's anger. Those who satisfactorily resolve issues of trust are the same people who trust themselves, their feelings, each other, and the security of their marriage. Such individuals also know how to process their own feelings fairly accurately and to detect a cause and effect for their moods and irrationalities. Within this level of Trust vs. Mistrust, each individual must have more than a meager ability to analyze his own feelings and to share them with a spouse who is equally willing to listen and empathize.

An example of the expediency in which emotional processing can occur is provided from my own marriage. Ginny and I were gathered by our fireplace on one of those cold winter nights , enjoying good wine, soft music, and good conversation with four other couples. The mood of the group was jovial and spontaneous. As I began talking about some of our plans for our future, I found myself enthused over the sharing of myself with the group. Several times, Ginny questioned or corrected what I was saying as if she doubted my intentions—or at least that's the way it seemed. Finally, after the fourth or fifth interruption, I blew my stack, and yelled, "Dammit, will you get off me and let me finish!" She sniped back, "My, aren't we touchy tonight?"

I could see that our friends were getting a little tense. However, once Ginny and I get into a confrontation we feel the need to resolve it rather than carry resentment all evening. My outburst had drained off enough tension to allow me to check out what was really happening. I said, "Right, I might be touchy. Does it seem to you I'm being overly sensitive or were you being obnoxious?" Over the years, we had discovered that we can usually trust each other to own up to whatever is going on inside. She responded, "I'm not aware of being uptight today. In fact, I had a good day." As I thought about my own day, I realized it had been a bad one. I had felt hassled at work and a little beat up. In fact, I realized that I felt beat up to the same degree that I was boasting to my friends to try to restore my emotional bruises. Realizing it was my agitation that had caused the confrontation, I said to Ginny, "You're right, I had a bad day. I'm sorry for the attack." She concluded by saying, "I might have been a little obnoxious but you make me nervous when you talk about *our* plans and *our* future and I know nothing about them." We smiled and nodded. The agitation was over in less than a minute. Being freed of the hurts of the day made the rest of the evening more enjoyable than it might have been.

Almost everyday within the confines of an intimate relationship, there are feelings that need confrontation, discussion, and possibly some behavioral adjustment from one or both individuals. To just talk can be an excellent start, but most often words are deceptive and "cheap." When couples are living together in a vibrant relationship, each needs to feel important enough to have impact on the other. Each needs to be heard. The best way to feel that one is being heard is to know that when differences and hurt feelings arise, each will be willing to discuss the damage and aware enough to know who has violated the other, their "labor agreement," and their attained level of trust. Each also must know who is violating the stability of the relationship with his individual pathology. Lastly, each must have the desire and strength to make the necessary behavioral adjustments required to maintain a harmonious relationship. When living is extremely difficult and there is thus not enough strength for a couple to make these adjustments, their relationship cannot mature.

The interaction of the various substrata of trust in intimate relationships is an extremely complex phenomenon achieved in a small percentage of relationships. When one examines the stringent requirements of self-awareness, emotional maturity, capacity for intimacy, ability to communicate, and strength required for individual responsibility, it is no small wonder there are so many disrupted and unsatisfactory relationships. It's not entirely accidental that in over 300 relationships I've examined in the past decade, fewer than 5 percent appeared to have resolved the issues of trust sufficiently to move on to the next stage, Autonomy vs. Shame and Doubt.

Successful resolution of the indigenous issues in the stage of Trust vs. Mistrust is accomplished gradually as the couple establishes patterns of affective familiarity, confidence in the self and the partner, and mutuality of empathy and caring. The process takes time, not only to develop, but to be unquestionably proven over the trials and tribulations of time. It is not possible to suggest a "typical" duration for satisfactory attainment of this process, but it was not detected in couples paired fewer than five years. It was not noted at all in "living together" arrangements, even when the couple had been together over five years. A couple will usually know when they are approaching or have achieved successful resolutions of the issues in this stage because, prior to resolution, they will have spent hours talking and disagreeing over their interdependence upon each other, individual responsibility, fear over letting go, and the shame and doubt over being left to one's own sense of maturity and responsibility. The final resolution may take months or years to accomplish as individual fears resurge each time the partner seems to move too far away emotionally or physically. The resolution becomes a little easier if the basic trust discussed previously has never been shattered beyond a point easily restored.

Working through the issues in the couple's attempt at resolution represents a crisis in and of itself. It is similar to the fears, frustrations, and freedoms between an infant's sitting and his learning to walk unaided. Once the couple can successfully resolve the issues in this stage of development, independence, potential for individual growth, psychological comfort, and a new level of richness are added to the relationship.

Overly dependent and psychologically disturbed individuals will not be able to get over the hurdle, because of the threat of losing the partner. In addition, this degree of autonomy and responsibility will feel like rejection and total uninvolvement to those at a relatively low level of self-dependence. Being treated according to the "I do my thing, you do your thing" philosophy feels like rejection to those who have never been too self-reliant, and to those who feel mistrustful and overly dependent upon the spouse. To successfully resolve the conflicts of this stage, couples have to be unwaiveringly committed to each other and to the relationship. They must also have adequately resolved a sufficient number of prior crises to be convinced that they can conquer any hardship with their composite strength and positive relatedness. Each partner realizes that most of his needs can be satisfied by the other and that he is not likely to be as happy with anyone else. Each is sure of his value to the other and believes the partner to be an irreplaceable, valuable asset. Only after the couple resolves the conflicts inherent in this often dissident stage of Trust vs. Mistrust, with all its complexity and deviations, can they know the difference between bondage and freedom.

Autonomy vs. Shame and Doubt

Few relationships proceed beyond the stage of Trust vs. Mistrust into Autonomy vs. Shame and Doubt, the stage of genuine, mutual autonomy. Those couples who are equipped to usher in the final crisis of the previous stage seldom get beyond feeling shameful about what might be interpreted as leaving all the "work," whatever that may be, to the spouse. They also have feelings of anxiety and doubt about a higher level of freedom and their ability to handle the accompanying responsibility. Having been so dependent upon the other and upon their mutual commitment to each other and to their relationship during the previous stage, it is extremely difficult for each partner to become accustomed to what feels similar to detachment and, to some degree, isolation, which accompany the early stage of autonomy.

As each begins to enjoy greater autonomy, there is a relatively long and fluctuating period where both need to check out their doubts about whether or they can be "in love" and relatively autonomous at the same time. For example, the wife asks, "Are you *sure* it's alright if I go bowling with my friends tonight?" When the reply is affirmative, she has accompanying doubts and wonders whether her husband really means it because, when she presented the same request during the first two stages, it had never been quite alright. During the previous stages, however, the trust tests had not yet been successfully passed. Even when one spouse said a certain individual activity was "alright," abandonment, anger, and resentment were only slightly beneath the surface, in just enough quantities to ensure doubt and shame. Such doubt raised guilt and anxiety to the level where autonomous activity could never be fully enjoyed.

Doubtfulness and shamefulness are complicated phenomena, which can emerge entirely from within. They present the couple with another potential battleground for heightened anxiety and confusion. Not long ago, while attempting to help a couple work through the final crisis in Trust vs. Mistrust, a rather invidious interaction took place.

Jack, a successful professional in his early forties, raised his voice in exasperation, and said to his wife, "I don't know what it is, but I am damn frustrated by my feelings that it's not alright for me to go fishing with Bill next weekend. As much as I want to go, I feel it's not alright with you." June, his wife of 16 years, responded immediately, "Honey, I don't understand why you feel that way. We talked about it at home, and I am glad you are going. It is quite alright with me. I wish you could hear that." Their interaction seemed straightforward and emotionally concordant. Even so, there was something about the way June talked that made me nervous, and through the years I have learned to associate that nervousness with unconscious misrepresentation. "June," I interrupted, are you sure it's alright? Something in what you said doesn't seem right to me, but I can't put my finger on what it is." As we checked out all the possibilities, the real issue became clear. Although June at all levels of awareness believed it was alright for Jack to go fishing, she had a history suggesting otherwise.

Previously, whenever he had gone fishing for two days (which he did only once a year), June came down with a terrible headache, a cold, or influenza. When he returned, the kids were running amok and the house was disheveled, making June's nonverbal message obvious. Unconsciously, Jack associated a negative valence with weekends away from home. June was, of course, always glad to see him when he returned. The children were also glad that their father was back and wouldn't be going away for a long time.

As we analyzed June's real feelings about being alone for two days, it turned out Jack had the message right. Deep within, she resented being left with their children, even though Jack was such a good husband and father and deserved some time for himself. She was not aware of her ambivalent feelings; nevertheless, they greatly affected the amount of shame, anxiety, and guilt Jack experienced—just enough to ruin his weekend. June unconsciously felt better when he would return home saying he had had a miserable time and probably shouldn't have gone. Even when he had a good time, it was greatly reduced in its value because he was unable to share his joy with her.

June and Jack needed more time to work out their unspoken conflicts over the distribution of labor and June's dependency needs. Before they could enjoy the freedom and autonomy of this stage, they had to resolve June's feeling that she could not handle the children and the house alone for a few days at a time. Jack, on the other hand, needed to be *more* responsible when he was home in order for him to enjoy the freedom of mutual autonomy during subsequent fishing trips.

A similar type of subversive message was noted in the following case history.

Bonnie and Andy were a couple in their early thirties who had chosen to have one child and then to develop their careers. Their marriage was an exceptionally open and nonpossessive one, in which they assumed a "liberated" approach to child-rearing and family life. There were few problems in their relationship during the five years that Bonnie remained at home to care for their daughter. However, when their daughter started kindergarten and Bonnie resumed her career in real estate, they found themselves arguing over just about everything. They could seldom agree on everyday decisions, even those that previously had not even been considered decisions. So, they sought help because they knew something was happening that neither understood. They did not make the connection that possibly Bonnie's working had something to do with it, although both recognized that life had been a little more hectic since she resumed her career.

Because the couple was fairly healthy, their communication was also relatively straightforward and emotionally concordant, and, because they wanted help, their sessions were very productive. During our first interview, it was not difficult to see that Andy was threatened by Bonnie's job. As we got into the implications of her work, massive resistance and panic surrounded the issue to such a degree that it was best not to push the discussion.

I asked if I could see each of them alone for a few minutes. Andy was first. As soon as Bonnie left the office, I moved closer to Andy and said, "Some people are confused because they honestly don't know what's going on inside them. Others know exactly what is going on, but are either too embarrassed or too scared to say so. I want you to settle down a little, relax if you can, and talk to me. It's obvious that you know exactly what is going on inside you, but you don't want to say so." Tears of relief and joy rolled down his face when he realized that I knew but didn't think he was stupid. He said, "You are right! Having Bonnie working full-time scares the shit out of me, but I'd rather not tell her that because I thought—and she thought—that there was never any room for jealousy in our relationship. In fact, we used to almost brag to her friends about our honest and trusting relationship. After she began her job, I was embarrassed to tell her that I worry myself sick when she works nights while I am left home alone. Sometimes, she stops for a drink with her office friends, and I become furious with them and with her. Some of the men she works with are better looking than I am, and I know a lot of them screw around. I am afraid I'm going to lose her."

It was not necessary for me to see Bonnie alone. Most of the problem was Andy's. It was important for him to share his fear and anxiety about losing her. It was equally important and therapeutic for Bonnie to be able to gently accept his fears, even though deep within she knew it all along. She assured him that she would not leave him and promised that, when she did go out for a drink after work, she would try to be home at the time she'd said. They needed a few rules to help them allay anxiety. Primarily, they needed time in their new roles to further develop mutuality of trust so that they could indeed have the kind of freedom they wanted.

"Mutuality of trust" means just that. If one person is more trusting than the other, the issue is not satisfactorily resolved but merely held in abeyance until reality provides the test. Bonnie had trusted Andy throughout their seven-year relationship. Andy thought he trusted Bonnie—and he did—as long as she was locked up at home caring for their daughter. When Bonnie entered the real world, a different picture emerged. Put to the test, his trust in her was in the danger zone. He knew it, but wished he didn't. She knew it, but preferred not to believe it.

Emotionally there are no shortcuts to genuine autonomy. Even after seven very good years, Bonnie and Andy had to dispense with their illusions and work out their mutuality of trust. With their comfortable history behind them, however, it did not take them long to resolve their conflict.

Andy's fears about Bonnie finding other men more attractive provide the basis for the second level of doubt inhibiting the attainment of genuine autonomy: self-doubt. It makes no difference what people appear to be on the outside; inside the heart and inside the home are where most of the living and most of the damage are done. If an individual has pathologically low self-esteem, self-worth, self-confidence, and self-importance, then overwhelming fear, anxiety, and anger surface whenever the partner has too much freedom. If a person feels relatively worthless, he will always feel anxiety and threat when his primary attachment is around the opposite sex. ("After all, why shouldn't my partner want someone else? I am not much good.") Feelings of threat are especially prevalent in disturbed couples who spend a significant amount of time hurting each other. Despite their psychopathology and incapacity for positive relatedness, each is aware of hurting the other and each secretly wonders why the partner tolerates the abuse. That they do put up with it is interpreted, in some sick way, as proof of their love. Nevertheless, relationships cannot mature when an individual has high levels of doubt about his own worth. Such a person sees almost everyone else as a threat because he believes that nearly everyone else is better.

During a seminar on the dynamics of pairing, one obviously paranoid and disoriented woman made a special point to convince me that she and her husband had had complete autonomy from the beginning of their relationship. I said, "Are you sure about that? I've yet to see it; in fact, I've become convinced that it's not possible." Offended by my questioning her integrity, she became annoyed and said, "It's true. I have never cared what Frank did, and he doesn't care what I do." The audience became a little tense at her revelation. A long silence followed, and I hoped she would realize what she had said. But she didn't, so I responded, "Rather than talk to you individually, I'd like to sidestep the issue for now and talk to the group about people who unconsciously pair with someone they don't really care about so that they're never threatened by the possibility of loss." The woman listened attentively and somberly. If she were not so well defended, she probably would have shed a few tears when the topic hit close to her heart. As it was, I suspect she was sufficiently disturbed and probably unaware of her incapacity for positive relatedness. Nevertheless, she was proud that she was not involved enough with her husband to be in a position to be hurt.

Many people were so bitterly rejected by their first love that they were forced to become prematurely self-dependent so that they'd "never need anybody again." These unfortunate individuals cannot realize the difference between having one's early dependency needs met by a loving and giving parent, thereby gradually becoming independent, and detaching very early in life from rejecting parents in order to protect the self from further hurt. Those who became independent in order to protect themselves are left with deep, never-to-be-fulfilled dependency needs, which are too frightening to recognize. In later life, they pair with an equally detached individual who is incapable of human involvement. Their relationship may appear autonomous on the outside because neither rarely cares enough to get involved. Deep within, each secretly knows that if they should become involved, they might not be able to endure the rejection should the spouse ever leave or die. Secretly, they also believe that they are unlovable. If they were lovable, it seems to them, the first love would have taken better care of them.

The stage of genuine autonomy can only be achieved from experimentation, threat, and satisfactory resolution of issues involving holding on and letting go. The critical resolve is to maintain ongoing communication, attachment, and caring while the relationship endures the threat that the partner, because he is self-sufficient and mature, could indeed leave if he *wanted* to. In addition to the responsibility that accompanies the freedom to come and go, each individual needs to realize that the partner is in fact a desirable individual who might realistically be wanted by someone else. Sometimes, an illusion of autonomy is created when one individual is free to leave, but the other is too unattractive, overly dependent, or in some other way too undesirable to even impose a threat. In such cases, autonomy isn't reached at all. Instead, the undesirable partner becomes a caldron of anxiety, depression, and anger, all of which contribute to the undesirability.

It is probably obvious to the reader that only relatively strong, emotionally healthy couples manage to achieve autonomy in their relationship. These are the couples who have developed a *spirit* of positive relatedness and individual responsibility, rather than a complex system of regulations and punishment. There is security in an autonomous relationship that is based upon choice, rather than upon rules that *make* it fair. Without the evolution of autonomy and free choice in a marriage, the couple may become suspicious, feel overworked and gypped, and engage in manipulations over control and power. Most obvious is a system of repetitive, sterile, compulsive mandates, which insure bondage (faithfulness) and equality in the distribution of misery. Cruel restraint of the partner's desires and activities prevails over a gentle and loving encouragement for the partner to grow and to enjoy living. Discussions over ideas, personal growth, individual maturity, and self-fulfillment are not possible when each is desperately holding on, and restricting the freedom of the other. Neither is such communication possible when one partner is holding onto large quantities of resentment and anger because he feels the other has not assumed a fair share of the work load.

Undoubtedly, the most subtle and powerful hindrance to development of autonomy is that many people are not that capable of standing alone. In fact, they unconsciously want to be owned and controlled. During the initial stages of autonomy, some couples reported being frightened of their own freedom, impulses, and desires, and temporarily wanting to scramble back to the womb of Trust vs. Mistrust. At least when one feels owned, controlled, and overly involved with another, he can believe he is of utmost importance to the spouse. To feel totally alone is one of the worst experiences for most humans. But those who have matured beyond the early stages of relationship development do not feel especially alone or lonely when they are physically separated from the partner. They are able to take the feelings of affection with them and are confident that their spouses can manage their lives reasonably well without them.

When one considers how little opportunity most individuals

have for independent living, and decision making, it is not difficult to see how genuine autonomy might, at first, feel similar to abandonment and detachment. In childhood, one's parents and teachers handle most of the important decisions. In adolescence, the individual makes more decisions, but his life is still controlled by parents, teachers, peers, and social mores. Usually, the only independent and responsible decisions teenagers are involved in are those related to privileges and control over such issues as dating, curfews, and finances. For young adults, a high percentage of time is regulated by employers or college professors, who tell them what to do, how to do it, and when it should be done. The hours when young adults are not working and not in school offer the illusion of freedom and responsibility. Even then, however, some wish to get back into their daily routine of being controlled by something or someone other than themselves.

Thus, many couples are not able to arrive at a functional level of autonomy in marriage, primarily because of the powerful forces of their dependency needs and their relative inability to risk and be alone. For some individuals, it's much easier to blame frustrations, lost dreams, and unobtainable goals upon being married and responsible for children than to move forward. It's not at all accidental that many married couples report feeling "stuck." Often, they are not aware that it's their own fault.

Marriage and life in general, however, appear to move along more smoothly for couples who successfully resolve the inherent conflicts in the third stage. Because they have matured both individually and together, they are free to responsibly pursue personal interests while still enjoying a union with another human. There is an aura of happiness, confidence, and well-being about them. Many of each partner's emotional needs have been satisfied by the other, and they have in essence helped one other to become more of what they are capable of being. They are best friends and probably adept lovers. When demands of reality impose hardship on them, adaptive adjustments are made almost automatically without either one resenting the extra effort needed to succesfully accommodate the crisis. Seldom does the autonomous couple harbor resentment about "I have to do everything around here." The mutuality of their caring and their individual strength helps each to be ultrasensitive to the other's moods, feelings, and heartaches. Thus, when one individual is a little anxious, the other senses it almost immediately, has a good idea why, and quickly helps lighten the load. There is seldom any need for deviousness or threat in times of stress, because each is attuned to the other's needs and feelings and each has the desire and energy to help alleviate the hardship.

When one needs to ask, beg, or threaten the partner in order to receive love, attention, or extra consideration, something important is lost. It mitigates the meaning of giving. However, in low-strength relationships, the individuals are so self-occupied that there is no surplus strength left over for the partner or the children. Thus, if one did not threaten, plead with, or beg the partner to give, nothing would be received. In low-strength relationships, autonomy is not possible. As soon as each lets go of the other for any reason, they know they will get nothing.

Desperate and pathologically needy partners cannot let each other alone. Unless they are overly involved in each other's lives, they do not "feel right." As a result of inadequate caring in the first relationship, such individuals almost always feel that the partner doesn't love them enough. In severe levels of disturbance, the couple could hold each other for many hours each day and still feel alone. In such disturbed relationships, there is never enough love, and both parents and children feel the effects. Destructively needy individuals usually find clever ways to remain pathologically involved in each other's lives, for the thought of autonomy raises anxiety and feelings of aloneness into the panic zone. To the pathologically needy, being left alone is just another sign that they don't matter and are not worth being with—something they have always felt.

Initiative vs. Guilt

The last stage of relationship development, Initiative vs. Guilt, is not difficult to achieve for couples who have resolved the conflicts in the previous stage. Because such a couple has endured through time and has had the opportunity to fracture, if they so desired, their basic trust during the period of autonomy, they have become more unified and self-assured. Due to their years of successful living and communication, they have developed a complex network of efficient unity. They waste few moments attempting to resolve conflicts of the previous stages, and spend little time on depression, resentment, or anger. These are the alive people who seem to have few unmet needs and little to prove to each other or the world. The trust, security, autonomy, and freedom earned earlier paved the way for higher levels of individual expression, interests, creativity, and accomplishment. Initiative for personal accomplishment and productivity is often accelerated because one partner does not have to feel guilty about temporarily separating from the other when pursuing his own interests. When accompanied by maturity and responsibility, freedom begets greater freedom. Similarly, maturity, responsibility, love, and freedom beget vitality. In all, the couples arriving at the Initiative vs. Guilt stage are the people who have managed to master life, as much as that is possible.

In this stage, a peaceful and vital mood permeates the life of the couple. The security in their relationship stands out as does their integrity, vitality, empathy, acceptance, affection for each other, and stability. As the reader might guess, if the couple have children, the children show similar attributes. Relative to their age and experience, they show wisdom, initiative, responsibility, self-guidance, and self-correction far beyond what might be considered "normal." As adolescents, they find home is a good place to be.

Furthermore, when the majority of the parent's needs are legitimately satisfied, the parents' relationship with their children assumes a unique quality. They are not overly involved with nor are they dependent upon their children for their own unmet nurturing needs. Home life, family, and the development of their children are genuinely important to each partner. If one spouse chooses to remain home to care for the children full-time, the self-denial required is not viewed as sacrifice at all. Because the other is supportive, their life proceeds fairly smoothly.

During this stage of relationship development, there is no question about the couple's commitment, worth, and feelings for each other. Seldom are there conflicts over who has it easier or who loves whom the most. Because genuine autonomy and individual initiative are accompanied by mature responsibility and judgment, in this stage there is a relative absence of tension, anxiety, or agitation. Personal values have been clarified to the degree where they are functionally integrated into the couple's entire life-style. Most obviously, their values are in accordance with who they really are. They are practical values, slowly developed and "tested" over the years and void of the "ax to grind" quality observed in those trying to prove to others who they are because they are unsure themselves.

Almost all of life has become harmonized for couples reaching the stage of Initiative vs. Guilt. There is a casual reasonableness to their living, and love, work, passion, pleasure, and serenity are comfortably interwoven. Obsessions, compulsions, and enforced rules are relatively nonexistent. In fact, spiritless rules devised to keep the couple honest and committed were abandoned long ago, possibly when they resolved the issues of Trust vs. Mistrust.

Throughout this book, the word *love* has been used to loosely describe the feeling of affection between couples. Because many people can stop the progress of their relationship by superficially adopting behaviors indicative of a higher level of adjustment, I have deliberately avoided defining *love*. The emotional stuff that goes into the initial attachment between two people might be called *love*, but *need fulfillment, lust,* and *passion* are more accurate. When the lust, passion, and sexual curiosity are left behind, couples often believe they are no longer "in love." Perhaps. On the other hand, they are beginning the process of developing a more mature relationship. That process, and its inherent conflicts and necessary resolutions, are what comprise mature love. People can usually feel it happening when they successfully resolve stage-dependent issues. Some couples, convinced they know what love is, prefer not to discuss, argue, and resolve their differences because the process itself can be so tumultuous. Strangely enough, couples who don't care about each other seldom argue, discuss, or resolve anything either. It's too much bother.

Because of the quality of their first love, and particularly because they entered their relationship with the capacity for trust, openness, closeness, interdependency, and a deep commitment to each other, couples in the Initiative vs. Guilt stage have achieved a love close to that described in the New Testament:*

> This love I speak of is slow to lose patience, it looks for a way of being constructive. It is not possessive; it is neither anxious to impress nor does it cherish inflated ideas of its own importance.
>
> Love has good manners and does not pursue selfish advantage. It is not touchy. It does not keep account of evil or gloat over the wickedness of other people. On the contrary, it is glad with all good men when the proper spirit prevails.
>
> Love knows no limit of endurance, no end to its trust, no fading of its hope; it can outlast anything. It is, in fact, the one thing that still stands when all else has fallen. [1 Corinthians 13, 6–13]

Recently, I attended an art festival where I found an inscription burned into a small piece of weathered barn siding. It read, "If you love something, let it go. If it returns, it's yours; if it doesn't, it wasn't." Whoever wrote it must have known something about the process of human intimacy and the highest stage of relationship development.

*J. B. Phillips: *The New Testament in Modern English*, revised edition (© J. B. Phillips 1958, 1960, 1972). By permission of Macmillan, New York, and Collins Publishers, London.

6 / *Never Enough Love*

The ensuing discussion may be upsetting to readers because it hints that perhaps all is not well in the hearts of many humans. In addition, it infers a psychological determinism to marriage because each person's capacity for sustained intimacy is established long before he becomes interested in romance, pairing, and marriage. Some readers may feel that it's not fair that certain individuals are predestined to enjoy a relatively comfortable inner life, while others must suffer almost interminable anxiety, agitation, and conflict. Nevertheless, despite the tone of contemporary self-help books, which makes it sound as though people have full choice over their happiness, human experience shows that genuine change, resulting in genuine emotional maturity, does not come easily. The following section is in accordance with that viewpoint.

LEVELS OF PSYCHOLOGICAL ADJUSTMENT

Psychosis

Some people believe that "crazy" individuals reveal themselves through such social atrocities as murder, rape, spouse and child abuse, and alcoholism. Severely retarded people, who might be observed staring at nothing and drooling, are commonly considered crazy or mentally ill, as is anyone who has emotional outbursts in public. Conversely, intelligent, attractive, verbal, educated, financially successful individuals are sometimes considered supernormal, healthy, or well-adjusted, as are people who seem friendly, happy, and carefree. Although there may be some truth to these misconceptions, real psychopathology occurs inside, within the human heart and within the home. Even though volumes have been written on the subject of abnormal psychology, one cannot understand the real workings of the psyche until one considers the individual's capacity for sustained positive relatedness, and the intensity of the anxiety, anguish, aloneness, and neediness caused by the inability to emotionally connect with another human being.

Figure 5 shows the levels of psychological adjustment, the capacity for intimacy, and the typical conflicts related to sustained positive relatedness. Psychotic or borderline psychotic individuals basically do not have a capacity for intimacy. Because they did not receive adequate nurturance in the first relationship, they will always "feel" empty, compared with people of a higher level of adjustment. By either acting conspicuously crazy (schizophrenics) or silently crazy (depressive-psychotic), their relationships are detached and exploitive. Although they have the basic human need they will never be satisfied because they cannot let themselves get close enough to anyone to receive genuine caring. As long as they manipulate others, especially the partner, into a position of powerlessness (in order not to impose threat), they can manage to behave relatively normal on the outside. Nearly always, psychotics tend to treat other people much like the empty object they themselves are on the inside. When a psychotic's spouse is healthier and capable of a higher level of intimacy, the spouse commonly reports waiting for the psychotic partner to reveal himself or show some emotional substance. Some wait for him to "come around," never realizing that if he could, he would. Some fairly healthy individuals who have mistakenly married a psychotic often wait in vain for the psychotic partner to deepen the relationship and to become closer. Obviously, that cannot happen. While courting, some psychotics promise the healthier partner that they will fall more deeply in love once they are married. Whenever one pairs with a psychotic or a borderline psychotic, however, it is not possible to experience a personal relationship of any substance. When two psychotics pair, they see nothing unusual about each other's inability for sustained intimacy, and, at one level, they enjoy the distance. But deep inside, they hurt because they cannot experience affection.

Level of Adjustment	Capacity	Limitations
Mild neurosis	Excellent	Anxieties tend to center around too much self-denial and guilt because the individual is not able to live up to ideals, standards, and values associated with marriage, sex, intimacy, and child-rearing practices.
Severe neurosis	Good to fair	Despite good capacity, there is doubt about whether or not the individual is lovable. Doubt and guilt cause the individual to be overly punitive toward failure while becoming more repressed. Extreme difficulty expressing negative affects.
Personality disorder	Fair to poor	Overwhelming need to be close and intimate, but can only acquire pseudointimacy through manipulation, exploitation, and deviousness. Avoids genuine positive relatedness and is chronically anxious and agitated.
Psychosis	Poor to total incapacity	Positive relatedness and intimacy are not possible. Even if socially adequate outside, the individual cannot emotionally connect with anyone. Living is characterized by overwhelming feelings of emptiness and isolation.

Fig. 5. Levels of adjustment.

A psychotic initially feels psychologically "at home" with another psychotic because neither is capable of invading the other's emotional space. Neither has to worry about getting too close or revealing themselves too much because that cannot happen. With almost no capacity for genuine human attachment, each can feel fairly "safe" until one or both eventually try to get something emotional from the other. Even though they cannot be intimate, they still have the natural human desire for closeness and connection with another. It is that unquenchable need that creates severe conflict and misery for psychotics.

Undersocialized psychotics, whether manic or depressive, are unable to contain their destructive impulses. Thus, their relationships are nearly always blatantly hostile. In a marriage of two psychotics, each partner tends to project anger, fear, and hostility onto the other, keeping the entire family in a nearly continuous uproar. Threats of abandonment, homicide, or suicide are frequent because, deep inside, each needs something from the other that he can never have. One partner usually does not realize that the other does not have "extra" affection to give, but they do know that they feel unloved and miserable. In myriad ways, each attempts to get the partner to care or love more so that he can feel good. Neither realizes that no one could care enough to make him feel good.

In the undersocialized psychotic relationships, it is sometimes hard to identify which individual is the schizophrenic and which is the depressive. Time eventually takes its toll, however. The depressive and the schizophrenic are likely to become chronically ill or physically disabled. If an individual cannot get caring and intimacy legitimately, he will manufacture subversive ways to get it, and being physically ill is one of the best ways to force others to care.

Living with a schizophrenic is nearly impossible, even for another psychotic. The schizophrenic cannot let anything be. Nearly every emotionally arousing situation is overly charged, and the spouse or children get the brunt of the outburst. Nearly always, the schizophrenic's message to the spouse and/or the scapegoat child is conflicted and confused. There is hostility, and a double-bind message to love and hate at the same time. Psychological damage is always done to the spouse or to a scapegoat child if either gets too involved. It is not possible for a person to be close to or dependent upon a schizophrenic without being destroyed or feeling that he is going crazy. Schizophrenics are experts at setting up no-win guilt manipulations, which leave the respondent feeling as though he is stuck "between a rock and a hard place." In order to survive a marriage to a schizophrenic, the partner has to detach from almost every comment the schizophrenic makes. If these are not discounted, the respondent will begin to feel like the schizophrenic—panicky, disoriented, angry—and will want to hurt someone.

Although not clinically psychotic, Zahna was a borderline schizophrenic. Exceptionally bright, she held advanced degrees and was successful in her career. In order to remain in control and to protect herself against even the remotest possibility or rejection or criticism, she married Mel, a much younger, passive, overly dependent, compliant man. Although he too held advanced degrees, Mel was a construction laborer, and he liked his job. His work was not particularly challenging, but he didn't like a challenge. In fact, he didn't care to become too successful at anything. Mel was also fairly satisfied with his relationship with Zahna. She took care of nearly all his needs, provided an income that was nearly twice his own, and met all the responsibilities of running the household. However, Zahna was angry nearly all of the time because Mel seemed "irresponsible" and was enjoying the "hardships of living too much." As long as they were working and away from each other for most of the day, Zahna and Mel tolerated each other and had few confrontations. Weekends, however, were complete chaos. Zahna attacked Mel almost incessantly for being dumb, useless, passive, and "unsuccessful." She wanted him to make more money so she could feel that he was carrying his own weight.

Zahna and Mel came in for about six sessions in which I saw the most destructive double-bind messages I had noted in a long time. From the very first session, Zahna accused Mel of taking advantage of her and of being a child and a financial failure. She wanted him to look for a job that offered more money so that she wouldn't have to feel so responsible. Almost on the verge of tears, he said, "Oh, hell, alright, I'll look for another job . . . but the only reason I am going to do it is because I love you and want to please you." During the next month, Mel looked diligently while Zahna "supervised" his interviews. As luck would have it, he secured a job that paid nearly as much as hers and with an earning potential of more than twice Zahna's salary. The only inconvenience was that the job was in a city 50 miles away. The double bind was personified in the next session. Zahna was confused, angry, and more blatantly hostile than I had seen her, but she didn't know why. During the session, Zahna said, "I'm glad you got the new job, but something is wrong. I think you hate me for forcing you to take it." Mel replied, "At first I was mad, but now that I can earn so much I'm glad you got after me about it." Then the attack came. "God damn you, Mel, this has all been a plot! The only reason you took the new job was so that you could be away from me more." Mel jumped up and shouted, "The hell with you, woman! You make me crazy whenever I take you seriously. I'm damned if I do and damned if I don't. I'm keeping the job and that's that. I don't want any more of your shit."

The session settled down a little after that episode, but the point is clear. All manic types, regardless of the degree of disturbance, are experts at setting up irrational double binds. Why? Because they experienced these no-win situations repeatedly with their parents.

The reader can understand how incompatible the partners in a psychotic marriage are. The schizophrenic needs to keep everything upset and disorganized in order to feel psychologically "at home," while the depressive needs to keep everything rigidly organized and emotionally sterile. Each partner feels the other is trying to drive him crazy. Neither seems to realize that the real disturbance has been there for many years, and merely surfaces at home in the midst of insufficient intimacy. Too much order and solitude is emotionally threatening for the schizophrenic, while too much raw emotion and affective confusion threaten the stable social facade that the depressive partner works so diligently to maintain.

Schizophrenics must destroy those closest to them. For example, a wife dependent on a schizophrenic husband will have little choice but to feel his wrath. In his own way, he is similar to a young child attempting to function in an adult world: his dependency needs seep out everywhere. However, they are masked by his domination of his equally overdependent wife or children. Even though the schizophrenic husband is compelled to destroy something or someone, and cannot be close enough to his wife to enjoy a sustained positive relationship, the real pathos of his infantile dependency needs emerges when the depressive wife decides she has had enough. When she does leave, her husband's already high level of confusion, anxiety, and hostility come to the surface. Left alone, the schizophrenic has no one to tolerate and absorb his irrational hostility, or to act as a scapegoat. Much of his emotional anguish turns inward, and the underlying depression he has been trying to avoid mercilessly hits home.

The loss of the schizophrenic's partner can often be a major turning point if professional help is sought. About the only time in his life that the schizophrenic can be open to new input and can recognize his own contribution to his misery is when he is depressed and emotionally traumatized. Otherwise, he assiduously damages and depresses others in order to drain off his overwhelming anxiety. The death of a depressive spouse, for example, can initiate a period of genuine soul-searching and growth for some schizophrenics. To be alone in the house once occupied by the deceased partner and to realize, possibly for the first time, that the "no good" partner might have served a very important purpose, is often the first step on the long, difficult road to emotional growth. With no one to blame, castrate, or confuse, and no one to project anxiety, hostility, and guilt upon, the schizophrenic is forced to realize his contribution to his own misery. As any experienced psychotherapist will substantiate, helping the schizophrenic to realize this is a major therapeutic milestone. However, schizophrenics are often so weak that considering their own contribution to their unhappiness makes them angry because they do not have enough strength to absorb blame.

When they get too involved with someone, schizophrenics are virtually unable to control their destructive impulses. Theirs is not a passive form of destruction by any means, but a deliberate and demanding holocaust. However, their trail of destruction is not continuous; when they feel guilty or mildly depressed, they can be exceptionally acquiescent, gentle, and "loving." Because they cannot tolerate isolation and being ignored by spouse or symptom-bearing child, they sometimes appear to be most giving.

In order to establish some level of human connection, they cleverly manipulate the spouse into their control. When the spouse further detaches in order to avoid the holocaust, a long and painful battle between them begins.

When I was growing up, I had a neighbor whom I thought of as merely "crazy." Now, of course, I realize she was psychotic. This schizophrenic woman, whom I'll call Gloria, always puzzled me. Whenever I was in her presence, I could tell she liked me and enjoyed flirting with me. Fun-loving, Gloria was always laughing, joking, and acting generally crazy. However, when she was with her husband, George, she turned into a raving maniac, capable of cutting him up one side and down the other without apparent reason. George never fought back, but went away wounded. When he tried to heal his wounds with too much alcohol, Gloria would attack him all over again. She enjoyed doing this in front of an audience and derived pleasure from making George cry before others. George was harmless enough, perhaps too harmless, for he could not offer her the destruction she needed to feel "right." Throughout his life, he apparently could do nothing right and was considered an absolute good-for-nothing.

After George died, however, something quite astonishing happened: Gloria needed repeated hospitalization for chronic depression. She became an alcoholic, gained at least 100 pounds, and to my knowledge has remained almost catatonic. Although she lives in the same house, it is no longer a house. Instead, it is a mausoleum in which George is more influential than he was when alive. To hear Gloria talk, George was the most gracious and loving superhusband and superfather who ever lived. That "no good, rotten, son-of-a-bitch of an old man of mine," as she used to describe him, has become the patron saint of husbands and fathers. The last time I saw Gloria, I found myself wishing George could return for a year or two. Both of them might now be capable of a more satisfying relationship.

Depressive psychotics tend not to actively bother spouse, children, or anyone else. Because of their firmly established behavioral-social organization, they prefer to withdraw and to turn their agony inward, usually by focusing on a convenient bodily organ and becoming ill.

Their home life is geared toward maintaining order and quiet. Their children's natural spontaneity is stifled because depressive psychotics need quiet in order to intellectually shut out emotional pain and anxiety. Laughter, loud music, and joviality raise the depressives' anger and anxiety to the point of near rage. Moreover, depressives think that the noise made by spouse or children is what makes them angry. They do not realize that they are hostile all of the time, and that loud noise and uncontrolled emotion in the environment merely break up their withdrawal and intellectual processes to the point where their anxiety and anger cannot be contained. Depressives would obviously not want to believe that they could be that angry, because it's not socially acceptable to be hostile. It is easier to convince the self and spouse that they are indeed peace-loving and tranquil people who just happen to enjoy quiet activities. They claim to need a lot of rest and a lot of private time away from the family. Who can argue? When they do not get their proper rest (i.e., withdrawal), depressive psychotics become visibly agitated or seriously ill.

Observing a seriously disturbed couple's relationship quickly reveals how severe emotional disturbance can traverse generations. For example, as a disturbed depressive husband churns anxiety and conflict inside himself, he automatically has less energy available to meet the needs of his wife and children. Some of his children will become equally depressed because they learn that emotional expressions, affective responsiveness, enthusiasm, and emotional needs and problems are signs of badness or weakness. If the children make demands on him, they fear that they are upsetting their already tired and preoccupied father, and are causing him many problems. In fact, if they make too much noise or demand anything from him, they are led to believe that they will cause something terrible to happen to him. Naturally, the depressed parent is not at all blameless in the children's belief that they are worthless and responsible for all the bad things that happen in the family. The depressive's favorite reprimand is "if you'd only quit, everything would be fine"—that is, quit needing, laughing, crying, making noise, living. . . .

The withdrawal pattern of seriously disturbed depressives is all-encompassing. Because they are nearly always exhausted, their going out to social events requires a major effort. The only way they might have a good time is if the event is planned in advance and there is sufficient time to prepare for it. The mood, timing, and event must be right before the depressive can mobilize the energy necessary to try something new and unfamiliar, as well as to "rehearse" in order to look good socially. Superficial social events are in line with the psychotic's capacity for intimacy; the psychotic is incapable of greater intimacy.

Sheila and Phil were a terribly mismatched couple who had been involved with a variety of therapists over the years. They came to me for help with their daughter, who was acting out. At the first session, Sheila, who was healthier than her depressive husband, handed me a stack of photographs and said, "Here is the crap I have been living with for twenty years." The pictorial exhibit could have been labeled "Tuning Out." Most of the pictures were of Phil sleeping—in bed, on the couch, on the floor, in the family room, at the kitchen table, at the dining-room table, down the basement, outside under the trees, in the car, and in the garage.

Phil left for work very early in the morning and came home in time for dinner with the family. Afterward, he usually found a place to nap so that he could be fully rested when he went to bed. On Saturday mornings, he worked around the house for a few hours and then napped most of the afternoon. On Saturday evenings and on Sundays, he watched television, snacking and napping during the less exciting programs. He usually had a headache all day Saturday and Sunday. Early Sunday evenings, as his headache began to subside, he often showed some life, sometimes walking the dog, putting gas in the car, or even talking to his children. Mostly though, he began to think about getting to bed on time and arising for work on Monday.

About every 8 or 10 weeks, Sheila and Phil made love. Even though both were physically healthy, there wasn't much constructive energy available. Although Sheila played with him, caressed him, and told him all kinds of lies to get him excited, he could usually not get an erection. Many times, after engaging in foreplay to no avail, she would turn away, cry a little, and sink into a deep reverie, remembering the times other men had made passes at her but she refused them because she was married.

Personality Disorders

The primary deficiency of the psychotic—and to some degree the borderline psychotic—is in the initial inability of the child to establish a secure attachment to the mother. Oversimplified, personality-disordered individuals are those who, unlike psychotics, had an adequate initial attachment to their primary love object during their very early years, but who encountered considerable difficulty in the primary relationship somewhere between the ages of four and eight, which resulted in serious character deficiencies. Figure 5 shows that personality-disordered individuals initially have an adequate capacity for positive relatedness, but because of the disruption in their primary relationship with a nurturing and stable adult and the absence of a healthy parental-intimacy model, they are rendered incapable of subsequent, sustained, and satisfying intimate relationships.

There is no single reason for the disruption of a healthy parent-child attachment, as there is no single reason why a child and parent are unable to establish a positive and healthy attachment, the lack of which results in psychosis. There are three fairly common reasons, however, for the fracture in the primary relationship that results in severe personality disorders in a child. First, some mothers are excellent parents while their children are infants and toddlers. They respond adequately and reliably to infantile needs and, in fact, enjoy the dependency of a helpless child. These mothers may even foster an overdependency in the child so they can feel wanted, important, and valuable to somebody. When the child begins to assert his independence and makes his own wishes known, the needy mother finds she cannot handle what feels very much like rejection. Hurt by her child's emerging power and defiance, she begins to reject him with a "to hell with it" attitude: "As long as the little brat won't cooperate with me, I'll be damned if I'm going to do anything for him!" The child has no way of understanding why his mother pulled away from him emotionally; even if he did, it would make little difference. He experiences a pervasive feeling of insecurity, hostility, indifference, and rejection, which forces him into a premature self-dependence. Some mothers are so hurt by their child's striving for autonomy and their own loss of total control that they delight in the child's mistakes and are overly critical of normal childhood fears, feelings, and insecurities. Eventually, the child quits coming to the mother for solace, nurturance, protection, and security. As the low-strength mother detaches from the child, she may be heard to make such statements as, "Oh, sure you want me to hold you now but when I wanted to help you the other day, you didn't want my help. Unless you can be more considerate of me, I won't be considerate of you." Automatically the child withdraws attachment energy from the person who has traumatized him and redirects it to himself and his own achievements, attributes, values, desires, and impulses. The lack of an adult attachment during the latency years produces an almost overwhelming and chronic anxiety, aloneness, agitation. He develops a pathological hypersensitivity to criticism; if he is criticized, it negatively affects him for days or even weeks at a time. The child's personality development has been arrested, and serious character deficits begin to take their toll, which might not be apparent until adulthood. The personality-disordered individual will not let himself into the same emotionally vulnerable predicament again. To need someone who might eventually humiliate and reject him is too painful. Getting too involved with another human is more trouble than it's worth. Personality-disordered individuals are self-centered, self-occupied, narcissistic, and highly resistant to control from others: anyone attempting to control a personality-disordered individual will be met with the wrath of ages. Control feels too much like hatred and criticism, which the individual spends his life trying to avoid.

Some personality-disordered individuals prefer to believe that they were in charge of the premature separation from the primary figure and do not recall the mother as rejecting or emotionally unavailable. Most often, this belief is a first-line defense, which serves as an ego-protective mechanism throughout their lives. Personality-disordered people are so sensitive to criticism and rejection that they frequently reject those they are involved with before they can be rejected themselves. This pattern is especially obvious during the early courtship years when they reject prospective partners as soon as they sense the slightest possibility of being rejected or when they feel themselves caring too much. In therapy such an individual cannot eventually "forgive" his parents, the analysis is incomplete. No responsible therapist would release a patient who is still in the stage of working through the anger—although some irresponsible therapists do so to validate their own unresolved parental hostility.

A particularly destructive mechanism in many personality-dis-ordered individuals is pairing with someone they do not care about. That way, they are fairly safe, for to be criticized by an un-loved spouse does not hurt nearly as much as being criticized by someone one needs and "loves." Such pairing, however, is a pretty steep premium for insurance against being hurt if the partner leaves.

The personality-disordered individual who goes into therapy usually acquires sufficient strength to slowly resolve the fact that things did not go well during the first relationship. As he pro-gresses beyond the tears, the hurt, the anger, and is able to un-derstand and forgive, energy becomes available for a secure and responsible attachment to another human being. In the same pro-portion that he can let go of the anger, resolve the hurts, and slowly make up for his character deficiencies, he becomes less sensitive to criticism and more able to extend himself to others. The chronic tension he experienced for as long as he can remember slowly be-gins to subside.

The most frequent cause of severed attachments in personality-disordered individuals is "natural human disaster." This phe-nomenon occurs much more often with boys than girls. Some-time between the ages of four and nine, boys realize they are not female, but something quite different. Almost entirely by their own volition, they begin to separate from the influence of the mother and adopt behaviors, attitudes, and relational responses typical of what they view as "male." At this time, it is imperative that the father or another, devoted, significant male become more available as a primary attachment figure and role model. In high-strength families, where parents care about each other and have sufficient desire and energy to care for the children, the father is usually closely involved in the care of the children. In these fam-ilies, the shift in the son's attachment from mother to father is natural and almost uneventful. The healthy mother can usually see that her son wants to pull from her toward the father and gently en-courages it because of the love and respect she feels for her husband. Within her heart, she knows she would be proud if her son turned out as "good as his father."

In pathological families, a different transition occurs. If the mother considers the father the cause of all her unhappiness, then it is not possible for the male child to identify with him. In these cases, the male may remain attached to the mother and begin to hate his father, other males, and unconsciously the part of him that is most conspicuously male. Too much is given to chance in terms of the location of a significant male ego ideal. Sometimes, overwhelming peer pressure forces a boy to behave in a way that is inconsistent with the mother's values. If so, the male child will detach his primary investment in the mother with nowhere to go. When the mother has declared the father to be useless and fearsome or perhaps held him up as an example of a "mistake that must never happen again," it will be difficult for the son to identify with him. Even the father's positive attributes and his ability to provide some caring and guidance to his son are ignored, and his impact rendered relatively meaningless. When a father cannot provide a healthy model for his son, the child is cut off from a significant human attachment and is faced with becoming prematurely self-dependent, which has deleterious consequences in the son's ability to ever form close and significant attachments.

Being fatherless is a rather unique and complex character deficiency for many males. Most often, the fatherless boy will remain overly invested in his mother but will fabricate a supermasculine reaction formation to convince himself he is indeed male. Psychologically, an almost universal, "machismo" model is created in those fatherless homes where the mother transmits signals that men are no good. The creation of this type of male ideal is accomplished through the child's own process of reaction formation against his real feelings. Without an adequate male model, the boy logically observes that he is a man and mother is a woman; logically, *he* is the *opposite* of a woman. The gambit is then set for a complex denial and reaction-formation defensive pattern that will determine his emotional responsiveness for a lifetime. Believing men to be the opposite of women, the boy trains himself to feel and behave in ways he believes are opposite to women. Since the boy's primary identification has been with his mother and he has had the earlier years to observe, identify with, and behave like her, psychologically he believes he is a woman . . . rather that he is a human. But because he is human, the boy naturally will respond emotionally, much as his mother does; because he notes she is a woman, however, he will work to develop behaviors contrary to what he feels so he can convince himself that he is indeed the opposite of a woman. He is a man. Being alone and emotionally detached from a significant role model, he naturally feels vulnerable, anxious, and frightened. To protect himself from these feelings, he creates an external image and overidentifies with it to assuage anxiety. He tries to convince himself that he is not vulnerable but impenetrable, not weak but strong, not frightened but fearless, not impotent, but powerful and virile. In doing so, he loses touch with himself. When he feels like crying, he sometimes laughs; when he feels gentle, he becomes aggressive; when he feels threatened and insecure, he shows hostility and aggression. The personality-disordered male is so conflicted that he often seems to be a pathological liar. There is an inverse correlation between who he says he is and who he really is. Obviously, in the confines of intimacy, he cannot be trusted.

All personality-disordered individuals must live with chronic anxiety and agitation. Much of their suffering evolves from the severed attachment to the mother and the inability to form a subsequent intimate relationship. The remainder of the tension comes from their purposeless, transient, and empty ideals, goals, and values, which have little to do with the satisfaction of their basic emotional needs. The incongruity between the artificially contrived ideals and the real self render the individual perennially insecure, anxious, and doubtful. Manic-type personality-disordered individuals (schizoid personality) almost incessantly seek something that will *make* them less anxious and unhappy. When they think they have found it, they develop it into a fanatical obsession. For awhile, the obsession can consume the individual so that he does not notice the pain. The obsession is overly endowed with some of the early narcissistic attachment energy placed on the self, and an "intimate" relationship is established with the "new love." No one had better question or criticize the ideal at this point, because it is taken as a personal assault. As long as he remains in the presence of peers who admire a similar ideal, feelings of worth and well-being are temporarily enjoyed. As soon as the fanatical, obsessional focus declines, the chronic anxiety, aloneness, insecurity, and agitation again threaten his "happiness.' It is time to seek another obsession to assuage internal turmoil.

Void of a human intimacy model because of his parents' unhappy marriage, a personality-disordered individual finds sustained intimacy most difficult. He has no way of knowing what marriage and sustained intimacy are really like. Character-disordered individuals wishing to keep their marriage intact usually find it necessary to rigidly and fanatically adhere to a superimposed value system to keep them together. As long as a couple can adhere to a fabricated ideal, they can deny the underlying disturbance and keep their marriage together. (Almost always, such ideals are illusional—they have not been observed anywhere, but have been written about, or taught, or seen on television.) If the obsessional qualities of their ideal or purpose in life become shattered, the real self emerges, and the individual or couple is thrown into almost complete chaos.

A fairly common fanatical ideal in contemporary society is observed in the individual who carries on serial love affairs (this fits the psychodynamics of the personality-disordered individual perfectly). Not capable of sustained intimacy, he evaluates the obsession with love affairs in terms of the intensity of the orgasm and the lust for another. In short, sexuality, sexual performance, and reckless eroticism become the obsession by which the individual can deny all the underlying anxiety and aloneness. While an individual is obsessed with the physiognomy of the self and the partner, he hardly notices his underlying anxiety, conflict, and aloneness. Instead, these feelings are unconsciously channeled into deriving pleasure in the love affair, and in the attempt to elevate low self-esteem by the feeling of arousal and passion. After a short time, however, the obsession becomes nullified, and the basic aloneness and depression again emerge causing notable "unhappiness." At that time, another obsession must be sought in order to keep inner conflicts from the consciousness.

Obsessive-compulsives experience the same persistent anxiety, hypersensitivity to criticism, agitation, and aloneness as the schizoid, but they tend not to forsake their ideals and obsessions easily. When their fanaticism and obsessions begin to lose their ability to drown out psychological turmoil, they typically work harder and become more committed, more rigid, more structured, and, in essence, more compulsive. For example, if an obsessive-compulsive has adopted a religion as an ideal, he finds it necessary to become an expert. Fully engaged in his righteousness and intellectual processes, he studies intently and searches out references for his references. It is not possible for him to get enough information. Whether the obsession is religion, money, health food, sex, the women's movement, parenting, social justice, or crime, his every feeling and every behavior must be interpreted in accordance with his adopted ideals. He reads and rereads the basic book of rules of the obsession to be sure he doesn't overlook any truths or guidance. His basic tension, conflicts, and hostilities are so pervasive that when they come to the consciousness, the obsessive-compulsive is convinced he is unhappy because he is not doing something right.

The only requirement for a satisfactory ideal is that it must in some way hold promise of a better life or greater "happiness" for the personality-disordered individual. Inherent within the obsessional network is a guidance network and a conspicuously tangible report system so that the individual can evaluate his progress and self-worth. If one does this and then does that, happiness is sure to follow. Clearly, if one doesn't do it right, there will be no reward.

Many obsessions, because they serve as an ideal that was absent from the life of the individual, become a role model that can temporarily enhance self-esteem, but only if the ideals of the obsession are paraded before others who might ascribe to the same rules. In order to derive the full benefit from an obsession, it is nearly always necessary to join a group of believers. If the individual can espouse his beliefs before fellow believers, he can temporarily receive support and a sense of belonging and caring that he did not feel at home. Most often, personality-disordered individuals do not genuinely care as much about the ideal as they do about the identity, peer support, and pseudo–self-esteem derived from the obsession. And always when an obsession loses its compulsive quality, another must be quickly located to avoid inner turmoil.

In reasonably healthy families, functional values are absorbed into the child's psyche and provide him with a lasting sense of identity and continuity to his parents, family and society. During those times in adulthood when life becomes anxious, lonely, and hopeless, the relatively healthy individual has many pleasant memories of loving and caring times with one or both parents, which validates the self as worthwhile. When the pressures of living become too much, the realization that one has been valued, for no reason other than that he was alive, offers an encouraging optimism and confidence that is not present in the personality-disordered individual. It is the virtual absence of this intrinsic mattering that forces the personality-disordered individual to look toward extrinsic signs of value. However, when extrinsic signs and obsessions are shattered, lost, or changed, there is little inside but despair and emptiness. The tenaciously acquired but superficial value system of the personality-disordered individual can seldom offer tranquility or significant anxiety reduction. Perhaps the most ironic paradox among personality-disordered individuals is that most of them cannot tolerate being controlled. Yet, for them to function at all, they must fanatically adhere to all-encompassing obsessions, which psychologically control them to a greater degree than anyone else ever would have.

In the healthy family, there is a semblance of reasonableness. Moreover, human relationships and the well-being of the family members are most important to the parents. The parents are contented with themselves, each other, their roles, and the responsibilities of adult living. They have an empathetic interaction with each other and their children. These couples seem to "know" what to do with each other and their children, not because they have read books on child development or family dynamics, but because they have felt it throughout their lives. They are doing what comes naturally to them. The healthy to mildly neurotic couple doesn't have to prove that they are what they are not. Because many of their basic needs have been met, they are free to direct their energy toward accomplishing their goals. In the healthy family, there is a balance among work, love, play, responsibility, hardship, freedom, functional values, self-discipline, and self-guidance. It is not accidental that children growing up in healthy to mildly neurotic families become happy and contented adults, who will, without too much difficulty, raise reasonably contented children.

Personality-disordered individuals are unable to strike a harmonious balance in order to live a full life. Their inability to enjoy a sustained positive relatedness causes painfully high anxiety from childhood onward. The loss of touch with the self, along with the absence of a healthy attachment-identification figure, causes a substantial emotional vacancy, which they spend the remainder of their lives trying to fill. Their hypersensitivity to criticism and rejection evolves partly from feeling unloved by their parents and partly because they need love and acceptance from nearly everyone. Most character-disordered individuals are constantly searching for something they feel is missing. They are unable to put into words what it is they are looking for, but they do know that it is related to reducing their chronic anxiety and agitation. Some skirt the periphery of what is missing by seeking attention, power, control, wealth, or status—which are derivatives of wanting to be loved—but seldom find the real object of their search.

From the last two sections, it should be obvious that men generally suffer from personality disorders more frequently than women. Women are not naturally immune to personality disorders, but historically they have been more apt to be neurotic, which is a higher level of psychological development. The neuroses, by nature of the developmental onset and the parent-child dynamics forcing their origin, carry a relatively high capacity for sustained intimacy. Nearly any observer of family life and of the human condition in general has probably suspected—or has at least amassed subjective evidence that—women generally have a higher capacity for intimacy than men. Overall, men tend not to be as socially oriented as women, nor are they as comfortable as women are in talking about their real feelings or about intimate and personal relationships. More men than women are able to carry out superficial one-night stands without apparent guilt. In fact, some men are "on the prowl" for a woman who can assist in their orgasm without any intention of establishing emotional involvement. Over the years, I have seen many men who only want a woman for what she can offer sexually. Intimacy, a relationship, tenderness, or, in some cases, even knowing her name is irrelevant. I have heard many women claim that they were treated as little more than convenient slaves, sex objects, or social showpieces, who were "placed on earth solely for their husband's sexual convenience" and to care for home and children. One rather astute woman summarized the feelings of many women while describing her frustration with her husband: "If he could convince himself that doing it with a statue would give him the same goodies as doing it with me, I think he'd buy one. That way he could take it off the shelf, dust it off about two or three times a week, have sex with it, and put it back on the shelf for later convenience. He wouldn't have to talk, nor would the statue insist on some intimacy or express other human needs. The statue would also always be there so he wouldn't have to come home to an empty house."

Surprisingly, few people can honestly report that their own fathers had much to do with their nurturing and emotional needs while they were growing up. Instead, when people attempt to recall their relationship with their fathers, more often they report such memories as: he seemed to be busy all the time, he wasn't interested much in us children, he always seemed to have other things on his mind, almost everything else was more important than we were, he was able to tune us out very well, once in a while he would do something with us but most of the time he had other things to do, or about all I remember about him was getting scolded or spanked by him when we were too noisy or in the way. When women of a higher psychological development pair with a personality-disordered male for any of the reasons cited in Chapter 4, they frequently believe that he must be deliberately forcing himself to be preoccupied, detached, distant, and emotionally unavailable. Some women come to believe that something is wrong with them because their husbands do not seem to need an intimate relationship with them. It is often a little surprising when they discover that their husbands, regardless of how badly they may want and need a healthy intimate relationship, are not capable of sustained intimacy. Despite the wife's pleading, crying, threats, and cajoling, such tactics will not change a personality-disordered husband. Such a personality-disordered individual's capacity for sustained positive relatedness was nullified years before the partner came into his life.

Some personality-disordered adults, especially if they consciously decide to be devoted, family-oriented parents, are often excellent parents, particularly for the first child. They can be giving, involved, devoted, and emotionally attached to the child, but usually only until he reaches approximately the same age that they themselves became prematurely self-dependent. Because premature self-dependence begins sometime between the ages of four and a half and seven and a half, a high incidence of family stress and marital deterioration occurs with personality-disordered adults when their children force them to be emotionally involved in their lives while simultaneously requiring firmness, control, discipline, understanding, and affection. This is exactly what they cannot do, primarily because it was not handled well with them. At this age, children, especially boys, begin to push away from the mother and reject her in their attempt to separate. Most often she cannot handle the rejection, and she either rejects him in return or pleas with the father to control him. The father, if personality-disordered, will more than likely be unable to handle the same upheaval in the child's struggle with separation, controls, discipline, guidance, and affection. The natural tendency is for the parents to emotionally detach, causing all discipline and control to be ambivalent and/or rejecting. Without a sense of the parents' devotion and genuine attachment to him, the child will tend to interpret all discipline and control as deprivation and rejection.

The Neuroses

One of the most heated marriage-counseling sessions I can recall was with a personality-disordered male and his neurotic wife. They were mismatched for a variety of reasons, but they most closely resembled the What's-Up? aberration presented in Chapter 4.

Janet and Tom had had severe marital problems for years and had been to numerous counselors who, although they couldn't help much, managed to keep them together. Tom had aspirations to become a millionaire by the time he was 50, and Janet seldom knew what was happening. He was initially attracted to her exceptional beauty and gracefulness, and he believed she would "look good" for him as he strove to be a successful executive. He was a manic-type schizoid, and she was a depressive-type neurotic who was healthy enough to hold her own during his blaming attacks.

During one session, he lost control and yelled, "God dammit, you bitch! You are always on my ass about communication. Communicate, communicate, communicate! That's all I hear. We *do* communicate; you just don't like what I'm saying. For 10 years, I've been trying to tell you I hate your goddamn guts, and you won't listen. Will you get the shit out of your ears and hear me? I hate you! So get off my ass about this communication bullshit."

The room was thick with hostility and fear, and then embarrassment. Both were silent for a long time. I asked Tom where all his anger came from. Remorseful, he became teary-eyed and said, "To be quite honest, I don't think I'm capable of loving anybody. If I could, Janet would be the person, but for some reason I don't think I have it in me. For years, I've felt this way, but I didn't know what to do. It's really hard for me to love Janet the way she wants to be loved. And when I try, it only lasts for a few days. I can tell she needs more of me, but somehow I'm not capable. I think something is wrong with me—that's where the anger came from." Tom looked at Janet and said, "I'm sorry honey, I don't really hate you. I hate me for not being able to love you like you need to be loved."

Unlike this couple, most personality-disordered individuals are not open enough to recognize their incapacity for intimacy. Nor are they aware of their own psychological operations. The previous counseling Tom and Janet had received had made Tom partially aware of his real feelings, but his underlying disturbance remained. Although he was a little more open and possibly a little more trusting, he made little progress in his ability to be close or interdependent. He knew communication wasn't their real problem, but he had no idea how to change what was really wrong. Furthermore, he did not have the psychological strength to meet the responsibilities of work and family, and still have something left for himself.

Both of these individuals were unhappy in their marriage. Because Janet had a good capacity for intimacy and experienced it in her first significant relationship, she knew something was wrong in her marriage. Whatever their relationship entailed, it certainly didn't feel like love. Tom knew Janet wasn't satisfied with what he could offer, but it was all he had. She felt the void between her own capacity for intimacy and his incapacity, but believed he could change. There were short periods when all went well between them, but for that to happen he had to exert painstaking effort, which did not come naturally and could not be maintained for more than a few days. Left to his own dynamics, he would detach and become more interested in business or other inanimate objects. "Since I was about six," he recalled during one session, "It has been easier for me to relate to animals, money, and machines than to people." When he tried to remain connected to his wife and family, he became exhausted and depressed because he felt as though he were losing something. Because of his incapacity, there was literally nothing inside of himself to give. When he did, he felt deprived and weak.

If an individual has been accustomed to a reasonably high level of positive relatedness and pairs with someone who is less capable, the relationship will soon be perceived to be similar to rejection and indifference. For example, a husband who is capable of less will tend to view his wife as insecure and overly romantic. He will not understand why the wife seems to need so much attention, affection, and caring and, in some cases, may believe she is mentally ill. Because there are more personality-disordered men than women, there will always be unconscious "mismatches" in the couple's capacity for intimacy—which forces many neurotic-level women to feel unloved by their husbands. Statistically, many women must pair with personality-disordered men who are not capable of sustained positive relatedness. Consequently, they spend much of their lives complaining about feeling rejected and unloved. Some women, aware of their frustration, anger, and resentment, erroneously assume that their husbands do not want to be more emotionally involved with them or their children. They do not understand that he *cannot* relate positively for more than short periods of time.

Some psychologists and social theorists do not appreciate the finding that men and boys are more disturbed than women and girls. Males especially dislike this because it can easily be misinterpreted as an indictment against masculinity. Society would in fact function much more smoothly if it were not so, but it is. If proof should be needed, one might cite the higher incidence of childhood disorders among boys, such as learning disabilities and acting out at home and in school. Moreover, there are many more juvenile institutions, prisons, and mental hospitals occupied by males than by females.

Statistically, women live longer than men. There are undoubtedly many complex reasons for this, but it is well known that emotionally healthy individuals tend to be physically ill less often than the severely disturbed, and that emotional well-being and longevity are positively correlated. Charles Darwin's treatise on the survival of the fittest also applies to the longevity of and higher level of psychological adjustment in women. Before the readers attempt to diagnose themselves and their marriages, hoping to identify who is healthy and who is disturbed, a cautionary note is needed. For example, some neurotic men, who are indeed capable of positive relatedness, may at times appear to be personality-disordered because of their preoccupation with work or financial responsibilities. As long as they are in the neurotic range, however, the imbalance should be short-lived and corrected because of their genuine feelings of responsibility toward wife and children. On the other hand, true personality-disordered individuals are seldom able to establish a balance between emotional investment in people and other things; they prefer "other things." Almost everything is more important to them than spouse and children.

It is important that the reader understand that the full impact of emotional disturbance does not become apparent until a child leaves his parents to attempt his own fully "independent" style of living. Until that time, the child has been protected, guided, praised, and punished by parents and other authority figures. Although basic psychological resources operate throughout childhood and adolescence, they are not put to the test until one is required to "stand alone." Then, the real person evolves because he must support himself and be responsible for his own decisions. Frequently, the most ill-equipped adult will report that he was happier as an adolescent or child than he is as an adult. As a result of the final separation of adolescent dependency upon parents, living seems to become significantly more difficult for many people after they marry and have children. Erroneously, some people assume that it is marriage, in and of itself, that is the culprit rather than the accrued responsibility and effort required to be emotionally involved with spouse and children.

Neurosis is characterized by excessive inhibition, guilt, self-doubt, and episodic anxiety over the inability to live up to one's own stringent values, morals, and overly developed sense of responsibility. Clinically, neurosis is seen in the individual with a punitive superego, which forces him to feel excessive guilt over his inability to live up to what might be magnanimous and overly rigidified ideals. Along with the predisposition to guilt, however, is a good initial capacity for trust, openness, closeness, and interdependence. The major reason neurotics tend to be overly responsive to guilt is that they have remained open to parents and parental influence. The longer an individual remains emotionally attached to the primary love object, the greater is his tendency to overly introject parental values, morals, and ideals. Even if the family attitudes are reasonable and healthy, the young child will tend to overidentify with them. Later, he will feel considerable pressure to conform to them by punishing himself through guilt whenever he strays from the straight and narrow path.

If a child hangs on too long, it is usually because the parents are afraid to let go due to their own fears and dependency needs. Thus, the child tends to border on the precipice of becoming overprotected and overdependent, a tendency that is reenacted in the marital relationship. Most often, the overprotected and overdependent child will be bitterly frustrated when he expects the spouse to take care of him the way his mother or father did. The same individual may have difficulty expressing his needs to his spouse or to authority figures because he feels selfish if he demands too much from anybody.

Female children do not have to switch their attachments from mother to father or anyone else during their early development. Most often, a girl remains attached to the mother, seldom breaking the tie until she pairs. Since girls do not often cut themselves off from the influence of their primary attachment—unless of course the mother is too punitive and/or rejecting—they remain *open* and *vulnerable* to the first love, and equally *open* and receptive to the incorporation of the mother's values. However, the tendency toward openness and vulnerability may later give a woman great heartache, should she pair with a man less capable of intimacy and positive relatedness. If she pairs with a severely neurotic or personality-disordered individual, she will be sadly disappointed. Her disturbed husband cannot be open and vulnerable, but instead must deviously manipulate others, especially those who are open and vulnerable.

It is not difficult to see why a personality-disordered male would be attracted to a neurotic woman. In the same proportion that he is self-centered, self-serving, and weak, she is giving, submissive, and overly responsible. When their marriage evolves beyond eroticism and he pulls away to serve himself, she is left home to be responsible for their children and her childlike spouse. When things do not go well, the husband tries to talk his way out of his family responsibilities by playing on her openness, vulnerability, and guilt. If he is unhappy, it must be her fault. The personality-disordered husband is too weak to give anything emotionally and too defensive and out of touch with himself to realize his contribution to her misery. Meanwhile, the guilt-susceptible wife has little reason to believe her husband would lie when he says she is not doing her part. If he says everything is her fault, it must indeed be. She simply must work harder and be more "loving." When she becomes overloaded with responsibility and guilt, she might have a "nervous collapse," which often requires professional help. The husband is very reluctant to become involved. He knows he has been manipulating her and has had much to do with her "nervous condition." He fears that his wife's doctor will catch his lies and expose what he has been doing to her all those years. He knows the doctor will want to help them change and he fears his life will become more complicated.

Wives of personality-disordered business executives and other professionals sometimes present an enigma to the responsible therapist. When such a wife believes her marital unhappiness is her own fault, and her husband reinforces that delusion, they agree that she needs help. After all, she wants something from him that he cannot give, and she is unhappy because she cannot get it. The husband declares her neurotic, which her analyst confirms. Individual treatment is recommended. And so, for the next five to ten years, the wife shifts her attachment to the analyst and toward her neurosis. She is not as lonely and needy as before, which confirms the initial belief that she was ill and proves that the treatment is working. The husband, who doesn't wish to become involved in her treatment, remains attached to his career. Later, when he enters a midlife depression, he no longer has the energy to be away from home so much, and he now seems to need his wife. She terminates her analysis and is usually so confused by then that even her husband looks good to her. Terminating the relationship with her analyst generates a massive separation anxiety. She then shifts this energy to her husband, and, even though he is still not capable of sustained intimacy, he stays home more, which is what she wanted all along. The only practical problem is that their children grew up without a father, and the wife grew up without the help of her husband. The husband will probably not grow up, but will slowly become more and more depressed.

When one examines the human psyche, those dynamics that are capable of offering the greatest happiness are also capable, when one is emotionally threatened, of generating insurmountable conflict. The neurotic couple, for example, has a good capacity for intimacy—they are relatively trusting, open, and have the potential for closeness and interdependency. They also have stringent ideals, morals, and standards for human relationships, whether they be marital or parent-child interactions. But, neurotics are highly susceptible to the guilt caused by their inability to live up to the realities of their ideals. Their overabundance of "shoulds" and "should-nots" supply the neurotic couple with a fairly regimented arsenal of devaluation, which they can use at will against the self.

In addition to the anxiety and conflict over guilt in the neurotic marriage, the surreptitious influence of emotional repression and suppression is ever-present. Because of their high ideals, the neurotic couple must suppress some basic human impulses in order to live up to their standards of a good marriage. Nearly always, they suppress feelings that might suggest unhappiness, anger, or resentment, for they have learned that the happy marriage is relatively free of anger, resentment, jealousy, or even complaints about each other's shortcomings. Even though neurotic couples can usually handle disappointment constructively if they begin communicating early in their relationship, after a few years of suppression, it becomes nearly impossible for them to deal with each other honestly and directly. They live as though they never heard of anger or resentment. Consequently, each rigidifies the tendency toward repression, becoming emotionally deadened to the self and the partner. The couple may be perfectly capable of performing routine social behaviors reminiscent of a "good marriage" but inside the emotional satisfaction has been lost. Each secretly knows something is wrong, but refuses to think about it. Some neurotic couples eventually realize their mistake and either get help or try to work it out by themselves. Others become more convinced that whatever is wrong has nothing to do with the marriage, and attribute their problems to something else. Over and over, they tell each other how happily married they are, thus declaring their relationship off limits for discussion and remediation.

Nearly all neurotic couples are aware of their fear of confronting their real feelings. They tend to view differences of opinion and derivatives of anger as signs of a troubled marriage. Their real feelings sneak out, however, usually in the subtleties of subsurface and masked aggression, agitation, or somatic complaints (e.g., migraines, backaches, stomach problems, inability to eat, or obesity). If such repression becomes too severe, excessive phobias, paranoia, exhaustion, hyperactivity in the children, feelings of not being able to get organized, and depression often result. When people repress too many emotions, there is a rather bizzare consequence: they become deadened to vitality and pleasure as well as to pain. In about the same proportion as they block out feelings from consciousness, they begin to suppress feelings of pleasure and spontaneity.

Married for six years, Nancy came to my office virtually unable to contain her tears. In fact, she found herself crying a few hours each day for no apparent reason. And, although she had become increasingly unhappy over the years, she had no conscious idea why. Nancy was exceptionally bright and held a master's degree in education. She felt good about her own academic achievements and her husband's financial success. All in all, she believed she should have been happy. But something was wrong. Because of her high ideals, however, she was embarrassed to ask for professional help. In a month's time, she arranged three appointments and then cancelled each. The fourth appointment, she kept. She spent at least half of the session crying. "Please don't mind me," Nancy said. "I'm a Pisces, and all Pisces cry a lot." When I asked what all the tears were about, she said, "If I knew that, I wouldn't be here."

Because of her severe repression of emotion, Nancy was unable to bring into consciousness her real feelings about the great amount of time her husband spent at work or her resentment over trying to raise their children alone. Because of her values and ideals about a good marriage, she believed she had no right to complain. When she came to my office, she could no longer contain her emotions. Her tears were her only release from inside tension.

After a few sessions, Nancy settled down and began to talk more. She was obviously protecting her husband, Tom, because she refused to discuss their relationship, for she would not say anything even mildly negative. Obviously, she feared that what was really troubling her might shatter her ideal of their "perfect" marriage. Toward the end of our sixth session, I said, "Well, it's about time I meet with your husband to discuss your progress, and to allay any anxiety he might have. I am sure he is concerned about you, and he needs to be told you're going to be alright." She responded defensively, "He has nothing to do with my problems. Besides, he works real hard and can't take time off to come *here*." I played a clinical hunch: "I think I've got the picture. Your husband is an insensitive bum. Before I can be of any further help to you, I am urging that you file for divorce immediately. And by tomorrow, I want you out of the house." Nancy immediately broke down. "He doesn't even know I'm coming here. I am so embarrassed to tell him that I am unhappy. When I tried to tell him before, he felt guilty and thought it was his fault. It's not; it's mine." The repressive barrier lifted, Nancy began to speak adroitly about their relationship and how she thought that if she tried harder, everything would get better.

The following week Tom came in. He was anxious at first but open to discussing the marriage and the natural deterioration that had occurred over the years. Although he was aware that something was not right, he could not believe it had anything to do with their "perfect marriage." He was eager to tell me, as was Nancy, that they never fought, argued, or even disagreed. I assured him that, as our work began, things would seem worse for the first few sessions but would eventually get better. Because each was ready for change and neither had accumulated intractable resentment, they made optimal use of their joint sessions. They were soon able to integrate anger with affection.

Nancy and Tom are now aware that anger and love are not opposites, but part of living and intimacy. They, like so many couples, had an unrealistic idea of what a good marriage should be and thought they had to suppress their real feelings to simulate that ideal. In their zest to insure themselves marital joy, they began to become enemies. Neither wanted it that way, but they didn't know how to stop it. One thing they agreed upon, however, was that they never wanted to argue "like all those people who don't love each other." Neither realized that discussing differences of opinion was not arguing. They interpreted disappointment and anger as hate, which, if expressed, could easily lead to divorce. After a half dozen joint sessions, they began to spend hours at home talking about the craziness of having repressed all their feelings. In the vernacular, they had to become "crazy" before they could get better. To them, "crazy" meant discussing feelings: disappointment, anger, their frustration with each other. "Crazy" also meant seeking professional help. They tried both, and slowly began to feel "uncrazy." During their last session, they joked about how much sanity there is in craziness and how much craziness there is in sanity.

Not every couple entering marriage counseling or family therapy respond as readily as did Nancy and Tom. Some couples have so damaged each other that it is hardly possible to get them to talk about themselves or their relationship without doing even more damage. Most couples in the neurotic range of adjustment, however, are able to work through their hurts, misgivings, anger, and resentment until each can at least partially empathize with the other's frustrations and unhappiness. When couples are in the personality-disordered range, however, another situation exists. Even though each is convinced his anger, anxiety conflicts, and unhappiness have been caused by the other, nothing could be further from the truth. Clinically, the anger, agitation, hostility, and chronic anxiety have been there all along. It merely took a significant attachment and adult responsibility to bring it to the surface. Skilled therapists are usually able to distinguish between situational and appropriate levels of anger and anxiety that have evolved from the relationship, and primitive-archaic levels of anger and anxiety that have been there since childhood. When there is evidence of personality disorder, the partners should receive individual treatment before marriage counseling and relationship building or rebuilding can proceed satisfactorily. Prior to discussing changing the capacity for intimacy, however, it is necessary to examine the effects of anger and resentment on a marriage.

ANGER, RESENTMENT, AND "SPLITTING"

Most people are not as psychologically strong as they would like to believe. Frequently, a criticism, devaluation, frustration, broken promise, or even a statement of confrontation can upset a person's precarious psychological balance to the point where an entire day, or even an entire week, can be ruined. Surely, such hypersensitivity attests to limited psychological strength, self-confidence, and self-esteem. Since mere criticism affects most people so negatively, it is not difficult to understand why people have such difficulty in both expressing and responding constructively to outbursts of anger, which in its purest sense is meant to destroy. Whether people wish to acknowledge it, anger is a basic human emotion. It surfaces all too easily for some (manics) and almost never for others (depressives). And, it is one of the most difficult emotions to channel constructively within the confines of marriage and family life.

The origin of expressing and inhibiting angry and aggressive impulses is found in early infancy. I doubt there are any small children who, while in a fit of anger or frustration, have not struck out physically against their parents. By either pinching, hitting, biting, or kicking, while crying and yelling, small children easily express their anger. The parents, out of the command for self-respect, or anxiety over proper socialization skills, usually need to suppress or punish the child's expression of anger. Some parents are not only frightened of such anger; they commonly overreact to it because when the child gets *that* angry and loses control, someone may get hurt. Partially out of parental responsibility to socialize children and partially out of necessity to avoid emotional and physical destructiveness, anger is the first major emotion suppressed and channeled inward. But it always sneaks out. If not allowed a reasonable mode of expression, children will destroy their own toys or those of other children, write on walls, or physically aggress against siblings. When direct channels of expression are suppressed, anger will take on a subtle and passive form of expression. Passive forms of aggression in children include: negativism, contrariness, resistance, overcompliance to adult demands, excessive stubbornness, failure in school, restlessness, obesity, enuresis, encopresis, constipation, isolation, pouting, whining, lack of cooperation, and forgetfulness. If children do not learn appropriate ways to express and absorb anger in their first attachment, they are not likely to constructively handle those feelings with their second love. If a child's expressions of anger are overly controlled, prohibited, and suppressed during the first relationship, while the parent simultaneously directs anger at the child, much of the repressed anger will probably surface during the second relationship.

From adolescence to early adulthood, Carol was one of those sticky sweet, overly compliant, highly romanticized individuals. Direct expression of anger was impossible as was any awareness that her "great love for people" was a reaction formation against her underlying hostility. During courtship and the early years of marriage, she and her husband, Daryl, were forever holding each other, touching, and kissing, even in front of others. Clearly, they were committed to showing the world the depths of their love. Within a year after their marriage, as adult responsibilities accrued, there was not enough genuine psychological strength within their system to accommodate anything but exaggerated feelings of "love." After two years, they were at each other's throats. She became frigid; he was impotent. She became obese; he was depressed. She became castrating; he became an alcoholic. Neither wanted counseling, but thought they would give it a perfunctory effort to assure themselves they had tried everything before they divorced.

There was neither enough strength nor integrity in either of them to profit from marriage counseling, so each received individual treatment. During Carol's therapy, it was discovered that her parents had also been unable to handle anger constructively. She recalled that there had been years when her mother hated her father and "loved" one of the children. When the mother devoted herself to one child, she had found it necessary to hate the others. Carol's own parents represented the epitome of "splitting": when they allowed feelings of love to surface toward one person, they simultaneously began to show anger and hatred for someone else. She recalled that both of her parents always seemed angry at someone or something. For instance, when they were at peace with each other, they were at war with the kids.

Carol, like so many people, learned early in life that love and anger cannot coexist. Throughout her life, she recalled, that whenever she liked someone, she *really* liked them. She tended to overevaluate nearly everyone she liked and was unable to objectify her feelings or the relationship. If she disliked someone, she hated everything about them. She was unable to combine love and anger as her parents had. Naturally, her therapy sessions were inundated with fear, compliance, anger, and ambivalence. Eventually, however, Carol was able to consolidate feelings of love and anger. When she did get angry at her husband or children, it was over and forgotten in a few minutes. When they got angry with her, she was no longer devastated, but could recover and forget almost immediately.

When unexpressed or unresolved anger and resentment accumulate within a relationship, each partner emotionally separates from the other; eventually, they may divorce emotionally even if they remain legally married. Anger and resentment, even if undetected by friends and acquaintances, will be unconsciously experienced and registered behind the closed doors of home. As long as couples remain emotionally attached, they remain vulnerable to the negative as well as the positive feelings of the other whether or not they want to. The depth of their emotional attachment and the accompanying vulnerability make the reception of anger and negative feelings painful. In order to protect themselves against each other's anger and resentment, couples automatically separate and sever their emotional vulnerability to each other. While separate, they inoculate themselves from the pain of the other's negative feelings. In that emotional separation, however, they also sever the effect of the affection and other positive feelings that may also exist.

Figure 6 shows the evolution of emotional separation. The first set of concentric circles represents a substantial area of vulnerability and feelings of emotional connectedness. Satisfactorily paired couples have invariably worked out effective ways to express anger. When anger and hurt can be expressed and responded to appropriately with the necessary changes or adjustments from the partner, there is little likelihood of resentment reaching destructive proportions. Consequently, such couples are capable of remaining vulnerable and attached to each other. Because of their vulnerability and relative absence of anger and resentment, they continue to benefit from the attachment and enjoy feelings of security, togetherness, and confidence.

The next set of circles in Figure 6 shows the beginning of the emotional separation. The area of vulnerability shared by the couple begins to narrow, while feelings of emotional connectedness and security also decrease. Nearly always, unexpressed and

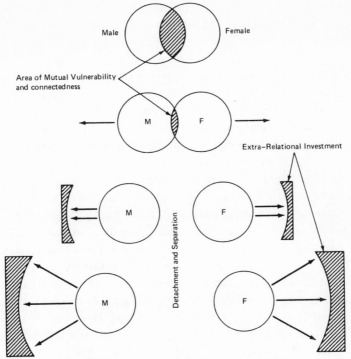

Area of Mutual Vulnerability and connectedness

Extra–Relational Investment

Detachment and Separation

Fig. 6. Process of detachment and separation.

unresolved anger provide the initial impetus for the detachment. During this step, the couple realizes something is wrong because they begin to feel less empathy, concern, and affection for each other, but are not sure what to do. During the earlier interactions of this phase, the couple will try to settle their differences if they are conscious of them and if they can communicate openly. The most well-adjusted couples will try to get back what they feel they are losing. However, if they are unaccustomed to dealing directly with hurt and anger, they will eventually feel that talking to each other only makes them more upset. As the intensity and duration of unresolved anger and resentment continue, their emotional connectedness and vulnerability break down and are replaced by defensiveness, distance, and mild indifference. When these feelings persist, the strength that the system once had to heal itself and the people in it, breaks down.

When empathy and caring are diminished, the couple becomes insensitive to each other and begins to disagree about nearly everything. They can no longer really listen to each other or let themselves be vulnerable to each other, nor can they receive each other's caring should it be available. If one partner were to let his guard down, the other might hurt him. Both feel defensive and more angry than ever before. As the duration and intenity of the anger increases, even a healthy couple who once could express and resolve anger, become frightened of what might happen if the lid is ever lifted. Each partner becomes frightened of himself and his own pent-up anger, as well as of the partner's wrath. Their emotional compromise is to keep it buried and to drain off small parcels of hate by criticizing each other, by being negative and resistant, and by arguing over the most insignificant matters.

It is during this phase of emotional separation that couples should seek help from a certified therapist or family/marriage counselor. Waiting for things to get better may be critical because, when a couple begins to lose their ability to heal themselves and restore vulnerability and connectedness, they are in more trouble than they realize. Almost always, the couple needs the strength and insight a therapist can offer to recreate a functional healing network. Even after the destructive aspects of the system are healed and the couple's vulnerability and attachment to each other reestablished, the relationship cannot be considered functional until the couple can utilize their own resources to deal with each other and heal themselves.

Toward the end of this phase and the beginning of the next, should the couple remain unable to heal themselves, the emotional detachment reaches a point where the marital system is almost irreversibly destroyed.

Lisa and Bill were an overly intellectualized couple who had read all the available how-to books on marriage and personal growth. Rather than empathize with or relate to each other, they analyzed each other instead, which only made them more defensive and less vulnerable. Despite my pleas for them to stop analyzing, they found it necessary to prove how bright they were. Nevertheless, many times throughout the sessions, I was able to help them feel something akin to empathy and caring for each other. At such moments, I quickly asked, "What are you feeling right now?" After a delay just long enough to allow genuine feelings of caring to subside, one partner would study the other for a moment and answer, "Nothing, really." After three sessions of not being able to break through their emotional separation, I asked to see Bill alone for a few minutes. When alone, I said, "Bill, what in hell are you doing? Lisa has worked through enough of her anger in her individual sessions, and she is not going to attack you if you show her a positive response. That's a promise." He anxiously replied, "You're probably right, but if I let go, it feels like I'm putting my cock and balls on the chopping block, and Lisa has the axe." I said, "Well, promise me that, next time, if the timing is right, you'll think about hanging your balls out. Unless you do, you'll never know whether she would have kissed them or chopped them." Bill got the message, and I later told both of them that each might have to risk a little more in order to get the "good stuff" from their relationship.

It is during the next phase of the emotional separation process that the duration and intensity of unresolved anger reaches the level where it can "break the camel's back." During this stage, couples cannot know how they really feel about each other. Outwardly, many are convinced that they don't care at all. There has been so much hurt and damage that each will shy away from the relationship and become attached to someone or something else, which is represented in the absence of emotional overlap by the circles on Figure 6. Love affairs are common during this phase of separation and are rationalized vehemently because "at least I am getting something positive from someone." Nearly always, having an affair is an unconscious retaliation against, and an indirect (albeit subversive) expression of hostility toward the spouse. In addition, the first affair of a previously faithful partner is often an unconscious attempt to reestablish the attachment in the marital relationship. If the straying partner gets caught, one or both partners almost always ask why, and the couple is then forced to deal directly with all the resentments, differences, and hurts they had laid aside. In fact, some couples are able to communicate more effectively after one has an affair. It is in the sharing of the whys that certain adjustments can be made that could not be resolved previously.

The feelings of indifference and emotional confusion prevalent in this phase persist in the final phase of separation. During both phases, the couple may seek a legal separation or a divorce. In the last phase, however, the couple detaches completely: "Why should we get a divorce?" becomes "Why shouldn't we?" Those preferring to remain married for economic, social, or religious reasons make it known to each other that they are as good as divorced. Every so often, they make love, primarily to release tension and to satisfy primitive animal impulse. When they do make love, it is usually lousy enough that each is secretly convinced he did the right thing by emotionally separating from the partner.

THERAPEUTIC SEPARATION

It may come as a surprise to those recently divorced, considering divorce, or wishing they were divorced, but divorced couples are seldom totally divorced. Many legally divorced and remarried individuals are, in fact, still emotionally paired to one degree or another to the first spouse. Similar to the schizophrenic woman who had enshrined her dead husband (p. 237), many divorced individuals become "more married" after their divorce than before it. Much as one's first love determines the quality of subsequent attachments, the effects of a first marriage, regardless of why it dissolved, leaves scars and memories not easily forgotten. The first marriage is often a scenario of youth: the first I-love-you's, the first embrace, the first dance, the first trip together, the first apartment, the first house, the first child, and so on all contribute to emotional associations that are impossible to forget. Although the experiences are gone, the memories remain and tend to sneak out unexpectedly.

Some of my most emotionally moving therapy sessions have been with divorced parents, especially fathers, as illustrated in the following case history.

> Brian had been married for 13 years before he and his wife were divorced. His wife got custody of their two children. During one of our first sessions, I could tell that he was avoiding his deepest feelings. Realizing that only 15 minutes remained in the session, I said, "It seems you should be talking about something else today. Imagine for a moment that this session is over and you are driving home. Something is

bothering you that you should have told me but didn't. What is it?" Immediately, Brian's lips quivered, and he began to cry without control. When he regained his composure, he said, "Oh, Jesus. It's my kids. I haven't seen them for so long, and I miss them." I asked, "What is it about them you miss?" Thoughtfully, he answered, "Their presence. I miss all the things I once thought I hated. I miss seeing them in their pajamas ready for bed. I miss reading them nursery rhymes. I miss holding them and talking to them about their feelings when they were injured or angry. I miss hugging and kissing them after their bath, and the smell of baby powder. I even miss stumbling over the toys they left all over the house. I miss watching them grow up and their excitement over things I never learned to be excited about. I miss their loud laughing voices and the times they sat on my lap while I read the newspaper."

Although Brian made some progress in the resolution of those feelings, from that day onward, seeing other people's children automatically stimulated tears of sorrow. For the remainder of his life, he will probably be tormented by doubts about his first marriage, as long as he remains honest. He will never be sure he did everything to resolve what seemed like insurmountable conflicts with his wife. Even though it seemed like the thing to do at the time, when he is honest with himself he realizes that he was irrational, hurt, angry, confused, and vengeful when they divorced. Sometimes, he is awakened in the middle of the night by his nagging conscience. Brian is honest enough to realize that he is still emotionally involved with his first wife, wise enough to know he cannot go back, and stubborn enough to not want to try. In his original quest to be free, he left his wife and children; alas, he is now more encaged than before.

When anger, hurt, and resentment mount to the level where one or both partners want to separate or divorce, care and caution should be exercised. While deciding whether to separate, most individuals seek information from those who might validate their reasons and rationalizations. Nearly everyone seems to want to help the couple make their decision. Seldom do these self-acclaimed experts really understand the psychological contribution of each partner to the failure of the relationship, nor are they qualified to understand individual motives, needs, and desires. Once the resentment toward the spouse surfaces, however, and the individual has a sympathetic audience, the inexperienced adviser and even the inexperienced counselor usually want to take sides. In badly deteriorated relationships, one or both partners almost always gather allies to heal the self and to crucify the bad guy. Unless the counselor is experienced in marriage dynamics, it is easy for couples to leave a session believing that the counselor has fully validated what each has believed for a long time: that the partner is to blame. In periods of crisis, people have an uncanny ability to hear what they need to hear.

An underlying psychological operation prevalent in nearly all faltering attachments is the mobilization of resentment, anger, and guilt into a massive push against the partner. This, as well as the almost equally strong pull toward someone or something else, causes many divorces to be far more messy and complicated than they would ordinarily need to be. While in the throes of emotional separation, people tend to become depressed, angry, and confused, thus increasing the tendency toward irrational decisions. During this period, people can be expected to show extremely poor judgment and self-destructive tendencies. When they find someone or something to alleviate the loss of the partner, they frequently load the substitute with illusional qualities, which aid in implementing a facade of self-assurance. Statements such as "This is exactly what I should have done years ago." "Marriage is for the birds—you should get a divorce too." "Wow! I must have been crazy to have stayed with him/her so long" are frequently defensive attempts to assuage guilt and heal wounded self-esteem. While such comments are prevalent, the underlying guilt, anger, and anxiety are nearly always strong enough to produce pathological delusions about the self, the new partner, and the future.

Maggie, a woman in her early thirties, was referred to me by her employer because she was not functioning well at work—she was lethargic, agitated, teary, and forgetful. During the first session, I asked Maggie if anything traumatic had occurred to cause her to be so inefficient at her job. She assured me that her life had been going quite well and noted that she resented having to come to a "shrink" just because she was making mistakes at work. Later, I said, "It may seem odd to you that I am going to make a brief interpretation of the problem based on such little information, but I detect a rather continuous theme of loss and depression. I have no idea what you may have lost, but are you sure you haven't suffered the emotional loss of someone or something important to you?" Maggie hesitated and then gave an emphatic "No." I said, "Well, the theme is still there, so whatever is causing your anxiety has something to do with feelings of loss and loneliness. Your boss said your job performance first became erratic about three months ago. Do you recall losing anything important about that time?" She twitched a little and replied, "Well, my husband and I separated about then, but I assure you that doesn't have anything to do with it." "You're sure?" I asked. "Positive! It was my idea that I move out, and I've never been happier."

She was beginning to panic, so I sat closer, softened my voice, and said, "Maggie, I know a little about happiness and suffering. I hate to break it to you, but you don't seem especially happy." My comment hit home. Maggie opened up and talked freely about having had an affair with a coworker named Dean, which motivated her to separate from Michael, her husband of nine years. After they had separated, she realized she had made a mistake, but felt too guilty and humiliated to ask him if she could come back.

When I later interviewed Michael, he freely vented his hurt and hostility over his wife's taking off with another man. He was still bruised by her affair and could hardly stand to look at her. Nevertheless, he still wanted her, but he was afraid to say so because it would only hurt more if she didn't want him. Neither really wanted a divorce, but they tried to convince themselves that they did. Each was too hurt and scared to try to get back what had been lost. They were waiting for fate and their lawyers to determine their future, even though they wanted to be married.

At his next session, Michael appeared more organized, less angry, and more open. Halfway through, he began to feel guilty about previously condemning Maggie, because she was really a "good woman." I asked if he would ever consider getting back together with her. He said, "God, that's exactly what I want, but she's going out with Dean. "No she's not," I replied. "Maggie has been living by herself and has had nothing to do with Dean for two months." She has had plenty of time to search her own heart, and guess what? She realizes she's made a terrible mistake. She wants to try again, but she's afraid you'll reject her. In fact, she believes you should divorce her to punish her." Michael sank into the chair and relaxed for the first time in months. After a long pause and a slight smile, he said, "It sure is worth a try. Do you think there's any hope for us?"

Maggie and Michael met the following week for their first joint session. Even though it was strained, they began to clear the air, hear each other, and reestablish an emotional connection. They were able to profit from their short separation. They also responded well to treatment and eventually terminated therapy with their relationship similar to what each wanted but thought they could never have.

In their individual sessions, it was not difficult to see that the couple had a good capacity for intimacy and that the opposite character dynamics were present. After enough confusion and resentment were expressed and each could become honest, they merely needed a professional catalyst to help locate their real feelings and to guide their interactions. Left to their own hurts and resentments, they could have made a terrible mistake. The ability to live life without making major irreversible errors can greatly add to what might be called "maturity" and "happiness." When a separated couple can receive competent professional help it is possible that their relationship will never be the same. Each partner might realize that they were holding on to nothing. Others begin to see themselves, their problems, their contribution to failures in the relationship, and the parameters of their needs and those of the partner more clearly than ever before. With their new knowledge and new skills, it is possible for them to form a better relationship.

Many couples who decide to separate or divorce do not receive professional help. Others stumble upon untrained professionals, who might be unfamiliar with marital dynamics and blind to their own unconscious. Couples who attempt a self-regulated separation are seldom able to profit from it. Amidst their anger, resentment, confusion, and the desire to be apart, many couples while separated begin to do things that may temporarily relieve their confusion, but do nothing constructive for themselves or the relationship. Time and again, when people separate there is usually a lover or the illusion of a lover lurking in the background. Eager to ease aloneness and separation anxiety or to accumulate vengeance against the spouse, one or both partners engage in an aggressive love affair, which convinces them that the marriage was indeed "dead" and for sure "lacking." The affair may stimulate adrenalin (which reduces the depression), artificially bolster inept self-esteem, and, most destructively, serve as an unconscious "splitting" mechanism. The lover, who unquestionably "understands me more than my spouse ever did," becomes endowed with positive affects while the no-good spouse becomes a focus of anger. With a fairly definitive and functional splitting phenomenon available, the person reports feeling more complete and more in love than ever. Of course, he does not argue much with the lover. Of course, the relationship with the spouse becomes more strained and more agitated; that is the emotional purpose of splitting.

The unconscious needs of the therapist are a significant factor in helping couples grow either separately or together. If the therapist is unhappily married and is unresolved in his anger toward his partner (or previous partners), he may unconsciously tend to "split up" the couple coming for help. If the therapist, for example, works with a couple whose problems are similar to what is happening in his own marriage, there is a likelihood that he may use the couple vicariously to solve personal conflicts. Therapy is off to a destructive start when the therapist's own needs and blind spots prevent him from seeing what he is doing to the patients. In addition, some inexperienced therapists obsess over a few key words, constructs, or methods and run everyone through their "magical program."

One rather schizoid female therapist was so attuned to male abuse (because of unresolved conflicts with her father) that she detected male chauvinism and male abuse even when there wasn't any. Her unconscious solution was to pair with an effeminate and submissive male whom she could dominate entirely, thereby reducing the possibility that he would ever hurt her. He also provided her with daily proof that men weren't worth much. As a therapist, she believed herself to be particularly effective with women who felt unloved in their marriages. Somehow, it did not occur to her that nearly everyone feels unloved in their marriages. Her sessions were little more than vigilant meetings where she would wait for the woman to complain about her husband's insensitivity and chauvinism. Because of her unconscious hostility toward her father, she felt compelled to mobilize the anger and hate in her female patients, and she felt good when they consciously turned it against their husbands. In fact, she encouraged the women to obtain financially rewarding divorces. She considered the therapy successful only after her patient had divorced and joined a radical feminist group.

Equally destructive is the authoritarian male therapist who believes that all women should remain at home to care for children, house, and husband. In his conviction that a woman's place is at home, one might locate a perfect reaction formation against unresolved conflicts with and hostility toward his mother. Because the mother may not have loved him properly, he unconsciously attempts to rectify the archaic damage by counseling his female patients to stay home and care for the helpless, unloved children of the world. The complex nature of a couple's personality dynamics—needs, desires, goals, and the husband's contribution to a faltering relationship—makes no difference to the therapist; he cannot see beyond his conviction that women belong at home, even if they feel unfulfilled there.

A rather unique but delicate situation presents itself in the pastoral counselor who has taken a course or two on marriage and as a result feels quite competent to counsel. Of course, some pastoral counselors are extremely competent, while others are theoretically, clinically, and emotionally impoverished and rigid. Such counselors will not permit their clients to even think about separation or divorce. Cloaking themselves with righteousness—with its inferred rejection—which makes nearly everyone nervous, they proceed to show their clients what God has to say about marriage, divorce, sexual practices, women's role, men's role, and how children should be disciplined. Within their limited framework, happiness, satisfaction, pleasure, and emotional well-being are not related to successful counseling. As "God's representative," they believe that successful counseling is convincing the couple to remain together even if they are mismatched or hate each other and are creating emotionally disturbed children as a result. Even if one partner should be hospitalized for psychiatric care because of the way they destroy one another, divorce must never be considered. Some of the more rigid pastoral counselors imply that if a couple should separate or divorce, they can no longer receive the emotional support and nurturance of the congregation and must sever their membership. At exactly the point in their lives when a couple might need the most understanding, support, caring, and acceptance, some pastoral counselors are forced to recite the rules of the church, which almost insures the couple of emotional, social, and spiritual exile—all in the name of God, of course.

Some pastoral counselors assure members of their flock that this life is no place for happiness anyway. Instead, life is likened to an endurance test so that God can select those people who pass for life in the hereafter. Some individuals, keeping the test in mind, construct their own salvation ratio: the more one suffers on earth, the more happiness he will receive in heaven. For believers, high levels of conflict, depression, unhappiness, emotional turmoil, self-denial, and suffering serve as assurance that their reward will be bountiful.

Family therapists who are starting out—and those trying to understand family dynamics—must remember that most couples who seek counseling have previously tried their best to make their relationship more satisfying. It is not unusual for such couples to have already tried nearly all of the recommendations that the therapist might eventually make. Some may even have tried a separation, which they set up themselves. When people are bruised, however, they are usually resistant to trying again some of the things they tried before, especially when they didn't get anywhere. Most couples know nothing about emotional readiness or the timing involved in planned therapeutic change. Instead, left to their own needs, they often try methods or techniques that often make things worse, or at best add to their feeling of hopelessness. While working with couples who are so bruised that both are defensive, hostile, frightened, and unable to discuss anything without attacking, the therapist should first make an astute clinical diagnosis to ascertain individual level of adjustment, opposite character traits, and extent of the damage. Because the therapist cannot always detect a couple's level of adjustment and capacity for intimacy in one or two joint sessions, each might need to be seen individually for a few sessions. When alone, each partner frequently will say what he is afraid to say when the other is present. In addition, it is important for the therapist and patient to note how much differently the interaction proceeds *without* the partner. This "differential responsiveness" helps the therapist understand fear, control, dominance, and the mood of the relationship.

If a couple is mismatched in terms of level of adjustment, but their character opposites are obvious, they need to know why there never seems to be enough "love" in the system, and why one partner doesn't seem to have sufficient strength to give much to the relationship, and why the individual capable of greater intimacy feels gypped and angry or depressed much of the time. It is always necessary to consider a couple's educational level, socioeconomic status, and intellectual ability when discussing their differential capacity for sustained intimacy. The couple should know some of the reasons why they haven't been able to change the system by themselves. They should also know that when people are bruised and at low-strength, they always become defensive, resistant, and resentful, which make it nearly impossible for them to heal themselves. When a couple knows that the therapist understands each of them as individuals, is not taking sides, and feels professionally responsible to help them grow as individuals *and* as a couple, then the hope, openness, integrity, and caring of the therapist are sometimes enough to help the couple change. Almost always, there is security in knowledge, especially if the therapist's interpretations help the couple to understand what they have never been able to previously comprehend. In that knowledge, if properly enmeshed in empathy and caring for *each* of them, comes the basis of trust in the therapist, which can help couples mitigate anxiety and defensiveness. Confidence in the therapist's skills and his personal genuineness can generate strength in the depleted system and thus facilitate the healing.

When a mismatch in levels of adjustment is present, the therapist, sometimes against his own unconscious desire to be liked, should work with the most hostile, frustrated, and accusatory partner first. Draining off some of that individual's hostility will relax the system to the extent that the more internalized spouse might feel less pressure and in fact become more demonstrative. Depending upon the level of hostility and crisis in the system, it is often prudent to work frequently with the more expressive partner in order to dissipate his anger.

Caution must be exercised by the therapist to avoid accidentally facilitating "splitting." Sometimes, the externalizing patient (here, the husband) misinterprets permission to vent as the therapist's alliance against the wife. It is best to interpret his hostility and catharsis in terms such as "needing to get out all those hurts that have been there a long time." Not until a secure rapport is established should the therapist let the patient know that by "a long time" is meant years *prior* to marriage. Despite the patient's resistance to the possibility that he was angry and hostile long before marriage, it is important for him to know how deep the hurt runs from the first relationship. If he is capable of accepting the interpretation, the more expressive individual might be able to hold the lid on displaced anger, thereby alleviating the pressure from the spouse who more than likely tends to withdraw under attack and who, while withdrawn, invariably gives less of what is wanted and needed, which only increases the attack.

While the externalizer's anger is being dissipated, the internalized wife should be seen by the therapist and helped to recognize signs of improvement—especially less anger—from the expressive partner. Even if she does nothing but pay attention to the husband, it is probably more than he received from her in months or years. As a result, the more impulsive-expressive husband may begin to feel more satisfied and less angry. Understanding each of the individuals and keeping abreast of exactly where they are at, along with an attitude of flexibility and caring, are critical therapeutic responsibilities. If the therapist misses what is really going on in the hearts of each partner, their resistance can easily be mobilized against the partner, their relationship, and treatment. After all, to be misunderstood and manipulated by a demanding, insensitive therapist is similar to what they have been doing to each other at home. Regardless of how disturbed each might be, without the therapist's caring, understanding competence, and responsibility to help them become more contented individually and as a couple, the treatment is likely to fall short of what it could have accomplished. Unfortunately, the couple will not have the faintest idea of what might have been had their therapist been different.

Some couples cannot live together without doing further damage to both themselves and their children. In those cases, and in couples too disoriented to accurately evaluate their real feelings, a carefully planned and executed therapeutic separation can be helpful. For many couples, a therapeutically designed separation represents the first time each has lived alone. Many such individuals lived at home or with a roommate after completing school and have avoided existential aloneness for years. The purpose of a therapeutic separation, in addition to getting the partners away from each other, is to help them come to grips with their dependency needs and feelings of aloneness. While separated, each should undergo individual treatment. In the same proportion that the partners experience their neediness and existential panic by being separated from each other, they will also recognize their own unreasonable, possibly idealized expectations in the relationship. For some, absence indeed makes the heart grow fonder.

However, absence may not make the heart grow fonder at all. For some individuals, absence is exactly what has been wanted for years. Often, the depressive partner (here, the wife) probably feels she has been involved in an abusive relationship and has wanted out for a long time, but has been too afraid or felt too guilty to try. Frequently, she has been emotionally castigated and psychologically abused for years by her manic-type husband. To the depressive, who prefers retreat and withdrawal, the absence of a castigating spouse is temporarily experienced as a feeling of well-being and peace. She is relatively contented staying at home, reading, listening to music, and being alone—for awhile. Not until she is ready to step out by herself does she begin to realize what is missing in her life. As she begins to know loneliness and the need for affection, it is time to examine in detail what was gained and what was lost in the marital relationship. At that time, the patient must come to grips with her tendency toward submission, compliance, passivity, and depression. During the therapeutic separation, she often fears that she will be pulled back into the critical, damaging, and overpowering relationship that she previously tolerated. Thus, her therapy is geared toward support, assertiveness training, and working through her guilt and dependency needs. She also needs assurance that she will be "heard" by the spouse and that there is no sense in returning to a destructive relationship. In many ways, her therapy is a coming-out process. The freedom of the separation allows her the safety and confidence to try new experiences, which can bolster badly damaged self-esteem. When she is feeling strong, relatively confident, and free to express herself, joint sessions may be considered.

Conversely, her manic-type husband needs not to come out more, but to be held down. To be genuinely effective, the therapist must attempt to keep him from scattering out to become invested in love affairs, projects, work, travel, or any of the numerous ways in which manic types ward off anxiety. As absurd as it may sound, the job of the therapist is to help the patient experience his underlying depression and dependency needs. If he can come to grips with these needs and then attempt to work through the underlying anger and depression, he will eventually become less needy and certainly less capable of blaming his unhappiness and feelings of being "unloved" on his partner. To the manic type, there is seldom enough love, but he is too impulsive and projective to realize his own contribution to feeling unloved. He is sure that it is because his partner does not love him enough. Thus, it is a difficult and therapeutically delicate maneuver to help the manic become aware of his anger and hurt from the first relationship.

If the manic can be "held down" and possibly be seen by the therapist twice each week while he is living alone, his depression, dependency, and panic will surface automatically. His deep dependency needs will be experienced almost immediately, and they can be delicately interpreted with little resistance. His biggest surprise usually comes when he realizes that his unhappiness had little to do with his spouse's inability to love him, and more to do with his high level of neediness. As the manic develops genuine strength by working through some of his basic dependency needs, the therapist must decide whether the couple can make optimal use of joint sessions or whether there is absolutely nothing there to salvage. The therapist must be careful not to fall into the trap of responding to the manic's impulsivity. When the manic begins to feel the pain of his depression, anger, and dependency, he either will want to get back with the partner immediately or will push to go ahead with a divorce. Despite the many logical reasons the manic will have for doing either one, the therapist must be sensitive and strong in order to prevent it. The therapist must also interpret the manic's impulsivity in terms of his inability to cope with anxiety and suspense. Possibly for the first time in the manic's adult life, he will feel helpless and controlled. His anger toward the therapist for creating such a state of impotence must also be interpreted. As soon as the patient settles down, feels less anxious, and can accept his contribution to the failing relationship, he might be able to see the spouse more clearly and appreciatively.

After the anxiety, depression, anger, and hostility settles, the couple may get together because they *want to* rather than because they are afraid to leave. When the blind eroticism of the initial pairing has been diluted by age, experience, and familiarity, and each partner has grown individually, the couple may be ready to begin a more mature relationship. After living alone for three to six months, each partner may begin to resolve conflicts and understand their individual needs, motives, and initial unconscious attraction for each other. Typically, each realizes that he can leave the relationship if he wants to. A most rewarding aspect for me occurs after the heat of the battle has disappeared: helping a couple resume their relationship at a higher level of intimacy, contentment, and maturity than they ever thought possible. After they have separated and realized that they could be reasonably contented alone, they become much less eager to take each other for granted again. Priorities such as spouse, marriage, "love," family, and work tend to fall into place as the couple becomes aware of what is important and what is not. As their relationship advances beyond what either had anticipated, each partner can once again see in the other what was seen long ago, this time without the distortions caused by erotic expectations. If the couple paired primarily for sex, there may be little to return to. However, if they once had something, they may, after they work their way out of the nemesis, be surprised at the treasure they overlooked.

The therapeutic separation naturally must include economic planning and resourcefulness for each partner for the duration of the separation. It is important that one partner move from the home to separate living quarters and that, if at all possible, the partners then take turns swapping quarters at no less than three-week intervals. "Separation" includes separating from house, family, children, and security. In a traditional marriage, when there are children involved, the wife should move out of the house for awhile to prevent her from investing her attachment energy directly onto the house and the children. Even though the mother often gets custody of the children when a couple divorces, during the separation she needs to experience a void in the network of security she

has created with her children, which may have mitigated her investment in the marriage relationship. The husband needs to feel some
of the demands of childrearing and homemaking, even if it is only
for a few hours each evening. Reversing roles for awhile can help
a couple appreciate each other's daily efforts. It's surprising how
much easier partners are to live with after they have walked a mile
in the other's shoes.

For either partner to return home to live with—and perhaps be
taken care of—by the parents will never do. If the reader cannot
understand why, the point of this entire book has been missed.
Living with a friend will also never do. Existential aloneness and
individual dependency needs must be experienced in full force,
analyzed, and hopefully understood. Experiencing one's real needs
is often not possible while living with others or by overinvesting
in one's children. If one makes no progress during the separation
in reducing his dependency needs (e.g., if one fails to gain the confidence that emerges from realizing that one could live reasonably
happy alone, that one does not need to be "in love" to be happy),
little will have been accomplished toward helping the couple enjoy a high quality of positive relatedness. Without ongoing individual psychotherapy, separation accomplishes little in terms
of genuine psychological change and growth. And, without genuine growth, the separated couple trying to resume their relationship will find that things may proceed fairly well at first, but they
will eventually return to exactly where they were before, and possibly become even worse.

Following a three-week therapeutic separation, Peg and Bert, a
couple in their late twenties met for their first joint session. As the session began, Bert was eager to share his experiences with his wife. He
got teary-eyed and said, "Do I ever miss you and the kids!" Peg attacked,
"Dammit, you haven't learned a thing from all this. The only reason
you miss home is because of the kids. You don't care two hoots about
me." I interrupted, "Will you please keep your mouth shut for a minute
and listen?"* She backed down and apologized for overreacting. He
understood and accepted her apology. Bert continued, "I'm sorry you
don't like what I'm saying, but I've had three lonely weeks to think

*The rapport established in individual sessions usually allows for such direct confrontation
in the joint sessions.

about it and that's the way it's coming out. I honestly cannot separate my feelings for you and for the children. After nine years of marriage, I think we have become an important part of each other." Three weeks later, after Peg had had time to be alone, she came to the session in full appreciation of her husband's earlier statement. She too could not parcel out her feelings of affection for their children and her husband. She had to admit that "pure love," whatever she thought that meant, included feelings for the children, family life, and all they had created together. She had missed him too.

Not all therapeutic separations help couples achieve new heights of relationship maturity. Many couples are critically mismatched, and it is surprising that they keep trying for as long as they do. Most people pay dearly for mistakes in pairing, even though such decisions are commonly made when they are young and immature. When couples pair for any of the aberrational reasons detailed in Chapter 4, they must pay the consequences. Psychologically, errors in human relationships, whether they be an inadequate first love or mismatched second love, never go unnoticed. Instead, they take their toll in destruction and misery. Sometimes, the therapeutically designed separation helps the couple to see that there were pathological needs in their decision to marry, or that they paired while one or both were in a severe emotional crisis. After the crisis was over, there may have been little left to sustain the relationship. One such couple provides ample illustration.

Herb was in his mid-forties, Joyce in her early thirties. Both were exceptionally attractive, and successful in their careers. Both were manic types. Each had been married before, Herb for 20 years and Joyce for 13 years. Both of the previous spouses had been depressives. Joyce and Herb reported that when they'd met, they'd felt like they had never felt before. There was instant attraction and uncontainable erotic arousal. Superficially, Herb was attracted to her beauty and sexual responsivity. Even though Herb was a manic type, he had begun to experience midlife doubt and a fear of aging; he had also been depressed for several years, but did not know it. Joyce's interest in his body and her sexual vitality rekindled his previous mania, which helped lift the pain of his depression. Joyce was attracted to Herb for his age, father image, and success. She also hoped that someone would take care of her so she could relax for awhile. Somewhat depressed because of her boredom and her responsibilities as a mother, she perked up when she saw hope for a "good life" with an older, successful man. Nevertheless, from the beginning, they fought over control, power, dominance, and dependency. They became aware that they essentially didn't like each other. They were incompatible and criticized each other relentlessly in order to gain the upper hand. Even so, as typical manics, they had an extremely vibrant and erotic love life. Nearly all their hurts could be temporarily forgotten in the bedroom, but they could never be resolved. Mutual hostilities kept mounting and came out in longer, more vicious battles. A six-month therapeutic separation helped them to uncover their pathological motives for pairing, their individual dynamics, and the ways they had destroyed each other. At the end of their separation, they decided to divorce.

Joyce and Herb profited from their separation. Their major problem was that they considered themselves to be miserable failures and an embarrassment to their family and friends, because it was the second marriage for both of them. After working through their guilt and resolving their hurts and conflicts, however, each reluctantly decided their marriage was a mistake. Even though they could have managed a relatively hectic coexistence if they had to, they wanted more. Each realized that if they became emotionally attached again they would be in trouble because of their similar character traits and their own needs. Rather than remain together in relative detachment just to preserve the marriage, they went ahead with the divorce. They would probably remain lovers, but they knew they could not be friends. As they left my office for the last time, they were both a little sad because their marriage could not work, but each wanted to go on with his own life. They will probably always remember the good times. Perhaps the bad times will be remembered should either decide to pair again.

Joyce and Herb were like two young lovers, home from college for summer vacation. Throughout the summer, they lived out a passionate, reckless romance with little regard for reality or responsibility. As they allowed their basic primitive instincts nearly full expression, they slowly discovered that being out of control is destructive. When the summer turned into autumn, both knew it was time to resume life with its efforts and responsibilities if they were ever to go on. Despite the heartache in their goodbyes, they acknowledged the end of their summer romance and were eager to rejoin the human race after a disastrous interlude.

In nearly all marital relationships, there is a strong need for stability, security, and familiarity. When that security has been accomplished, however, some couples manufacture a prohibition against new experiences that could facilitate growth, and so boredom and depression often result. In addition, it is not uncommon for manic types, while "maturing" and becoming older (typically between the ages of 35 and 45) to enter the depression they have been avoiding since early adolescence. In some cases, a couple become depressed together, even if they have been successfully paired for 20 years. Whether the maturity is real or superficial is not as important as the individual's tendency toward depression. As the pain and caution of depression become almost constant, it is likely that the characterological manic type experiencing a long depression will begin looking elsewhere for manic stimulation to subvert feelings of stagnation. Because manic-type individuals are excitable and can excite others, depressed middle-agers become extraordinarily attracted to much younger manics or to more disturbed manics of the same age to help lift their depression. Regardless of the duration of the new romance or the intensity of the eroticism, the underlying depression becomes an equally influential bed partner.

CHANGING THE CAPACITY FOR INTIMACY

As indicated throughout this volume, the amelioration of an individual's capacity for intimacy is extremely difficult. It is not possible to enhance such capacity by reading about it or by pretending to be more capable than one is. To alter an incapacity or limited capacity for intimacy requires a relatively long-term relationship with a therapist who is capable of intimacy and who has the clinical skills to experience the patient's unconscious needs in the relationship and to respond constructively to them. Typically, the therapist has been trained and supervised in detecting defense mechanisms, as well as the unconscious manipulations and unmet nuturing needs of the patient. Naturally, therapists need to be more than merely trained. They need to be able to show patients how to trust by being trustworthy and how to be open by being relatively vulnerable and nondefensive themselves.

Therapists need to have made substantial progress in resolving their own infantile dependency needs in order to allow patients to become temporarily dependent and to later let them go. They need to know about their own unconscious desires and conflicts to the extent that they neither foster overdependence in their patients nor prevent them from becoming dependent. A therapist's own life must be going well enough so that once a patient becomes somewhat dependent and begins to increase the level of trust, ego strength and confidence, the therapist does not unconsciously hang on to the patient because of his own needs. A therapist needs to be an astute observer of human feelings, able to calibrate genuine strength in those with whom he is working. Finally, the therapist must know when and how to begin gently pulling away so as to allow a patient's newly acquired strengths to facilitate a higher quality of confidence, strength, and, of course, capacity for intimacy.

The therapist needs to be especially sensitive to the nurturing needs of the patient and to the unique ways in which he tries to "get people to care more." With that insight, the therapist can help the patient understand his own nurturing deprivations from the first relationship and help him resolve these conflicts so that, eventually, should he desire to pair, he will know what is realistic and possible, and have the strength to derive satisfaction from his central relationship.

While I was teaching a graduate psychology class on defense mechanisms, a rather obese student offered to take a Rorschach test and to review it with the class. He needed to show his colleagues how "open" he was in order to get their approval, and so he tried to look calm despite his high anxiety. Detecting his anxiety, I slowly began to interpret his test to the class, but he became annoyed that I was being so careful. He urged me to hurry, and claimed I probably couldn't tell him anything new because he had been in therapy for five years. I replied, "I think I can tell you something new, but it might hurt." Arrogantly, he said, "I doubt it. I know myself better than anybody I know." I said, "I don't doubt that a bit, but what I want to tell you is that you probably wasted money on your therapy. You have good head knowledge, but your heart is as empty as it always was. Whether you know it or not, you are still paranoid and deeply mistrustful. It is obvious you have not had a close, open, trusting, dependent relationship with your parents or your therapist." His arrogance turned to humility, and he said, "You're right. But how can you tell from the inkblots?" He told the group that his therapist was an arrogant, brilliant, defensive, and distant individual who sat behind a large desk during his sessions. The young man may have gotten all that his therapist had to offer, and it showed: he was brilliant, arrogant, uptight, defensive, and distant. His "desk" was several layers of excess fat, and he carried that protection with him wherever he went.

Occasionally in the natural environment, a person develops a relationship with an adult that can significantly change his inadequate capacity for intimacy. Most often, such a relationship occurs between a child or an adolescent and an uncle, aunt, older sibling, grandparent, or neighbor. Seldom is the relationship a full one, however, in which the dyad appropriately deals with anger, hurt, and frustration. As a result of the one-sidedness of affect, these individuals can seldom express angry feelings toward someone they value and upon whom they might be emotionally dependent. The therapeutic relationship can often be managed in such a way that anger and hurt can be expressed directly and then analyzed. When a patient realizes he can become angry at someone he emotionally needs without being struck by a bolt of lightning, he can be helped to live a fuller life with his spouse. Witness the following case history:

Richard, was a graduate student who entered therapy with his wife, Natalie, because of severe marital disharmony. He was clearly the more needy of the two, so I began seeing him regularly. As he progressed through each session, the themes of what he wanted me to know about him so I would "like" him more became clear. Whenever Richard needed someone to admire him, he employed his quick wit and intellect, followed by pseudosincerity and then overcompliance. These were the exact patterns he used as a child to get his mother's attention and acceptance. Now as an adult he did the same things in order to get others to "love" and "admire" him. Carefully, I phrased questions in order to get Richard thinking about the purpose of his sharp wit and his high verbal intelligence. Rather than notice or compliment him for these attributes, which I'm sure nearly everyone else did, I pretended not to notice. In fact, each time he ran through his old nurturing pattern, trying to get me to compliment him, I deliberately looked a little bored. Finally, fed up with all his efforts for affection, he exploded. "God damn you! You sit there each hour and deliberately try to piss me off by looking dumb. I am tired of trying to please you, of kissing your ass by spilling my guts to get you to care more. I'm tired of this shit! I'll be damned if I'm going to keep trying to get you to care more. I am tired of trying to impress you! You're even doing it now! I know enough about this therapy bullshit to know you are trying to get me to have a tantrum, but God damn you! I wanted to impress you to get you to care more." Finally, his feelings of self-worth and anger, and his conviction that no one could care enough, were out in the open where they could be worked on and hopefully resolved. In much the same way, Richard had been angry at Natalie many times throughout their marriage because he believed she didn't care enough. Because she did not realize that whatever she did or said would not be enough, Natalie would try but only become more frustrated and angry. When she pulled back, he naturally became needier and more rejecting of her.

When the first relationship is inadequate in terms of intimacy and need fulfillment, the individual must proceed through a lifetime frustrated because he believes no one cares enough. In our therapy Richard eventually was able to work through some of his neediness. The caring he received from me—just because he was alive and human—helped to resolve some of the destructive things he would do to get others to care more. Eventually, he began to love himself because of the therapeutic caring and relationship. For the first time in his life, he didn't feel chronically anxious and on the run. He became important to himself and eventually to his wife just because he was. It was not necessary for him to do something to elicit admiration from others because he no longer needed *everyone's* love to feel contented. His neediness baseline was slowly raised until he could feel fairly comfortable being alone. With that level of comfort, he was better able to meet his wife's needs and she, his.

The therapeutic experience is by no means a magical route to peace and happiness. Nor is there one "key" that needs to be unlocked to help a patient become less needy and more self-reliant.

The power in the therapeutic endeavor comes from the personality of the therapist and his or her skills in facilitating deep levels of emotional growth. Many patients must use the therapeutic relationship to become a little "crazy," which to them means feeling those feelings and expressing those wishes that they are sure would be met with the therapist's rejection. In Richard's therapy, for example, his outburst toward me was not the end of anything but the beginning of greater honesty and personality integration. As he began to resolve and analyze the motives of his outburst and the accompanying feelings of desperation, he realized that his expectations and manipulations were not new, but were the same ones he had experienced with his mother and then later with his wife. He remembered becoming infuriated with both of them and with other people when they did not respond to him as he desired. When Richard discussed the session with his wife, she understood exactly what he was saying. She had felt his frustrations and experienced his anger for not caring about him for years. When he became aware of the duration and intensity of his early childhood nurturing patterns, he learned to control his impulses to do something to get recognition from others. For many years, he had been angry inside because he believed no one cared. Naturally, he blamed them and society for being cold and indifferent. He had no idea he was doing it to himself.

One advantage of working with couples jointly is that it does not take long to recognize what is actually occurring in their lives. That is, a clear picture of social facades, defense mechanisms, emotional neediness, and personal values tend to show more readily. People can easily delude themselves into being what they are not while in public, but it is more difficult to pull off such a show in the presence of the spouse. In that single relationship, many of an individual's unconscious needs and psychodynamics are brought to the surface. Using that relationship as a therapeutic springboard, it is possible to help an individual grow and mature more readily than if he had not paired, or if only one spouse had been seen.

If a couple decides to seek professional assistance, there is no guarantee that the therapist will be able to help because clinicians vary greatly in training, maturity, philosophy, level of adjustment, area of specialty, and their own capacity for intimacy. Moreover, the fields of psychology, psychiatry, social work, and marriage counseling tend to attract an overabundance of severely disturbed people who enter the field in an unconscious attempt to find "answers" for their own psychopathology. It takes many years for them to realize that "knowledge" has little to do with working through their own unmet nurturing needs. This is not to suggest that therapists with severe disturbances will be ineffective in helping patients. On the contrary, some are excellent; because of their own disturbance, they are adept at helping people with similar difficulties. Whether a patient can raise his capacity for positive relatedness, however, is dependent upon the relationship with the therapist. Since all severe disturbance carries an inability for sustained intimacy, it is possible for someone to be in individual psychotherapy with a distant, detached therapist for years and not make significant progress in areas where it really matters. The therapist might become an excellent ego ideal for the patient, but if the therapist is empty, detached, and distant, the patient will be too.

Psychotherapy, whether sought individually or for family and marriage work, should be entered cautiously. The training, philosophy, and personality of the therapist are most important—unlike many other walks of life where the service rendered is paramount and the personality of the renderer irrelevant. Unfortunately, there are few if any ways for a lay person to locate a competent therapist. Even though most states require clinicians to pass stringent tests to obtain a license to practice, the tests are primarily academic and intellectual. They insure the general public that the therapist is a knowledgeable graduate of an accredited university. However, they cannot insure that the therapist is qualified to heighten one's capacity for intimacy. Fortunately, most responsible clinicians are somewhat aware of their limitations and so select only the areas of expertise in which they feel qualified. Those not caring to involve themselves with marriage work or in-depth work usually limit their practice to other areas of psychology. Before an individual or couple enters treatment, they should make sure the therapist is interested and qualified in the areas where they need help. Many responsible clinicians, when they understand what brought the patient to their office, will make a judgment about whether or not they are qualified to help; if not, they will usually refer the patient(s) elsewhere.

During the first session with a therapist, it is always appropriate to inquire about the therapist's training, state licensing requirements, formal education, supervision, and personal therapy. In addition, the patient should evaluate the therapist's openness, defensiveness, guardedness, empathy, and spontaneity. Because psychotherapy is a substantial investment in time, money, emotion, and the quality of life in the future, it is important to work with the best therapist available. Those seeking help specifically for their marriage should ask about the therapist's own marital relationship. If the therapist cannot discuss what is personal, it may not be possible for the patient to make much progress in emotional closeness and openness. It is also fair to ask about a "major issue" from the therapist's own previous therapy and how it still affects his or her life. If the therapist has been divorced, inquire about his or her contribution to the failure of the relationship. A therapist who makes it sound as though it was entirely the spouse's fault or decision might be a blaming and defensive individual. Finally, it would be foolish to enter marriage counseling with a therapist who views sustained intimacy, commitment, marriage, or family life as symptoms of severe disturbance.

A couple seeking marriage counseling or a partner wishing to ameliorate the capacity for intimacy should be aware of the "ax to grind" righteousness seen in some therapists. A therapist who seems too rigid and too righteous may not be able to genuinely understand and empathize with the uniqueness of a patient's situation. Because righteousness can make others feel inadequate, wrong, bad, or stupid, a righteous therapist might appeal to those who feel guilty, because they unconsciously detect the therapist's desire to make them feel bad about their "wrongdoings"; such "therapy" however, will not have long-term benefits. One must also beware of the angry therapist who condemns other types of therapy, other schools of thought, other professionals, or the social system. Although some individuals are attracted to angry therapists, eventually they will find it defeating.

Finally, having read this far, it should be obvious to the reader that intimate relationships are extremely complex. Thus, couples who wish help should beware of claims made by adherents of weekend growth groups, marriage and intimacy workshops, and communications-building workshops. Although they can be helpful at getting a couple started in recognizing problem areas that need work, all too frequently they are run by inexperienced or naive individuals who offer immediate growth. Obviously, it is not possible for a weekend seminar to heal a destructive relationship or change one's level of psychological adjustment.

7 / Change

In increasing numbers, people who have been "successfully" married for many years are choosing to leave their partners and children behind to attempt the alternate life-style of the single adult. Many of them have had relatively satisfying relationships with their spouses, and some have been excellent parents.

Friends and relatives sometimes have difficulty understanding why anyone could leave a partner of long duration. They erroneously conclude that the couple must have had "severe marital problems" for many years, but had remained together for the sake of the children. In many cases, of course, this may be accurate. In others, however, the couple may have had an excellent relationship, yet one or both partners nevertheless decided to try living alone.

Because of the devotion and commitment required for successful parenting, family life can become totally consuming for some couples. The time and emotional energy required to meet children's needs almost always force parents to sacrifice their own interests, needs, desires, and creative potential. As children mature and move through the natural separational milestones, however, they need a different type of emotional investment from their parents; the result is that many parents discover that they now have more time and greater energy available. With the increased energy, a significant increase in self-interest occurs. It is at this time that some individuals decide to live alone, try a new career, or attempt a different life-style, which may not necessarily include continuation of the marital relationship.

Regardless of whether people want to change, alteration in the quality of inner life is inevitable. Early childhood experiences, which initially shape one's feelings about oneself and one's interpretation of the world, in conjunction with day-to-day frustrations, joys, and hardships, force significant changes in one's values, beliefs, basic psychodynamics, and a vitality for living. The result, called *psychological change*, is a human certainty. Change in no way, however, implies growth or mastery, for many individuals experience a decline in happiness with increased years and adult responsibility.

Many people are unable to achieve a satisfactory balance between adult responsibility and emotional comfort, and they begin to deteriorate from early adulthood onward. Such people view life as a nearly insurmountable hardship. Over the years, the agony of daily living for these overburdened people takes a conspicuous toll, and psychologically they die a little each day. On the other hand, some people adapt well to the accrued responsibilities and become more resolved, confident, and naturally serene. Often, these people look happier and healthier at 40 than they did at 20.

No one can identify the exact cause or direction of significant, inner life changes. In short, change is nearly always unpredictable, unexpected, and uncontrolled. It just happens from living and adapting. When people change, however, so does the intensity of their unconscious needs. No longer needing one's spouse in the same way one did when first paired is one of the side effects of change. If partners haven't developed individually and if the relationship has not matured according to the process described in Chapter 5, both partners might indeed feel that they are getting few if any emotional needs met in the relationship. If the couple cannot communicate their needs to each other and come to a mutual agreement about how the needs will be met, there is little choice but for them to feel that there is little or nothing left in the marriage.

Another factor influencing psychological change and, for some, greater levels of emotional maturity, is the gradual working-through of childhood conflicts and nurturing-dependency issues from the first love. In close relationships, individuals are nearly always playing and replaying early childhood relationship roles, conflicts, and feelings, which while either helps them to temporarily feel "better" by reducing unconscious tension or forces them into greater feelings of hopelessness. Similar to the role the "best friend" plays during latency and adolescence, that of attempting to work through parent-child hurts and conflicts, is the adult experience of marriage and parenting. Through marriage, the individual has the opportunity, in a very idiosyncratic way, to select a partner who fulfills the individual's basic dependency needs and who simultaneously offers several of the missing or underdeveloped aspects of the self. It usually does not take long before those aspects of one's spouse that were most desirable prior to marriage also become the most threatening or conflictual. Over the years, each partner must come to grips with those conflicts, and, if they are successfully resolved, significant personality development and change may result. Similarly, parenting and the relationship between oneself and one's children can also facilitate partial resolution of one's childhood conflicts, which may lead to greater emotional maturity. Because children are continuously changing and developing, involved parents have little choice but to almost continuously relate to their children on such important issues as nurturing, dependency, affection, anger, discipline, control, and separation. Throughout this process, reflective parents will notice that they react in a manner very similar to the way they were treated as children. In fact, some parents, in dealing with their children, use the very same reprisals and verbal indictments that annoyed them most when they were children. In short, it is the *emotional relationship* and fluid psychological changes of the children that help facilitate resolution of the parents' childhood conflicts, thus leading to further emotional growth and maturity.

Further resolution of childhood conflicts is also accomplished when an individual can honestly forgive his own parents for their "mistakes" in the way he was raised. It is only in raising one's own children that one comes to grips with how difficult parenting is. If parents can remain emotionally involved with and attached to their children from birth to adulthood, the diligent parent can be said to have "grown up with the child." It is life's natural way of facilitating emotional maturity. Psychologically, it is not accidental that many people become more creative, energetic, and psychologically comfortable after age 40. Helping their children resolve adolescent conflicts almost automatically frees some parents from their own "unresolved psychological adolescence" and propels them into psychological adulthood. From this final resolution, there is no turning back.

An accidental but sometimes disquieting side effect of genuine personal growth is that psychological needs change. When deep psychological needs become altered and a couple has not made adaptive adjustments to each other through the years in accordance with the emerging maturational changes, one or both partners may conclude that neither "does anything for the other." Specifically, one or both may have changed so much that they are no longer capable of meeting each other's adjusted emotional needs. When this happens, the relationship slowly disintegrates, and each realizes that they are no longer "in love" and that there is little that is satisfactory between them.

In view of the unconscious dynamics involved, genuine growth essentially implies *less* neediness and a greater feeling of completeness and self-sufficiency. The depressive spouse, for example, may have sufficiently developed the incomplete parts of the self so that he does not need the same degree of the partner's mania to "feel right," as he once did. In couples who relate to each other well, the manic individual may become less manic, and the two of them can balance out, thereby continuing to meet some of the deeper psychological needs. In a couple unable to make progressive adjustments to each other over the years, reduction of needs and emotional maturity for one or both individuals forces them not to need each other as much as they did when they felt as though they loved each other.

FLIGHT FROM ADULTHOOD

From age 30 through the early forties, a rather unique but fairly widespread phenomenon occurs, which plays havoc with the stability of some marriages. I am referring to the alleged "midlife crisis" that nearly all manic-type males must sooner or later experience. Before I attempt to relate the dynamics of this crisis, I must make it clear that not everyone goes through it. Depressive-type individuals, for example, seldom go through the conspicuous emotional turmoil experienced by manic-type males in their thirties and early forties. And few women go through this type of crisis, especially not those who have had the primary nurturing responsibility for their children.

In order to understand the subtleties of the crisis, the reader might wish to reread Chapter 3, which describes the manic-depressive character opposites. It is important to recall several specific character features of the manic-type individual. Those manifested during the crisis are idealism, dependency needs, guilt, and exhibitionism. Manic types usually employ expressive channels to ward off anxiety and their underlying depression. Consequently, they present an image of confidence and flippancy, which the reader will recall is one feature that unconsciously attracts the depressive-type spouse. But, to appear confident, vivacious, and relatively carefree, one has to employ the denial of essential features of reality as a major psychological defense. The major question is: how long can a person successfully deny certain aspects of reality before the denial overloads the psychological system and he becomes severely depressed? Part of the psychological purpose of denial is that the individual also tends to overlook responsibility—usually by unloading it upon a depressive-type spouse, or, if an executive, by delegating responsibility to subordinates. But reality eventually has a devastating impact, leaving the manic type almost unable to cope with the underlying depression and feelings of responsibility, isolation, alienation, and despair. The accumulation of these feelings and the individual's frantic attempt to deal with them is called a *midlife crisis*.

The most predictable crisis occurs with manic-type males in their thirties or early forties who have accelerated professional ranks and progressed from a staff position to a managerial position. Others may make a similar move toward a position that carries the connotation of "success." Within that framework, the additional responsibility incurred begins to stimulate the final break from adolescent-level asceticism and idealism toward what might be called adult maturity. Unconsciously, the individual is frustrated at the most basic level of his dependency needs and comes to the rather frightening realization that there is no one to take care of him. Whether the manic-type male arrives at the point of the "final disillusionment" gradually, through the burdens of living, or whether it is thrown upon him by a promotion that requires additional responsibility, the effects are the same. The pervasive feeling that there is no one to take care of him causes accompanying feelings of high agitation, anxiety, aloneness, and severe depression, which has heretofore been avoided by jocularity, denial, and a firm adherence to idealism.

In many respects, the harsh reality of the underlying depression represents the letting go of what some psychoanalysts refer to as the "last vestige of adolescence." Toward the end of typical adolescent development, many youngsters come to grips with the final separation from parents and attempt to resolve the depression that emerges from letting go their infantile belief that parents (or someone) will forever take care of them. Most manic-type males, however, have managed to avoid the final stage of adolescent resolve because they handled some of their earlier separation anxiety by using their talents and leadership ability to get "love" from others, and by placing their basic dependency needs onto their peers. Even if they weren't really receiving bona fide peer support, they twisted reality enough in order to believe that they were important to their peers. During the thirties, however, these same peers have their own families and responsibilities and tend not to be especially interested in recognizing and supporting an outsider," thereby stimulating feelings of loss in the manic. Whatever he accomplishes, no one really cares very much. Nearly all of the previous externalizing functions used to acquire symbolic parental love from peers slowly becomes irrelevant.

Glenn had always been adept at eliciting support and recognition from others and was highly dependent upon their approval and "love" in order to feel worthwhile. As his midlife crisis surfaced, so did his need for nurturance. Feelings of depression were a constant companion until he began to fight against them. He joined various civic organizations in order to "feel right." Eventually, his life was consumed by long, hard hours at the office, civic projects, and involvements with several women. Only when he was getting plenty of support from others could Glenn avoid feeling deprived and temporarily escape his underlying depression. Because of his early childhood deprivations, however, he still could not "feel right" for very long. His wife began to emotionally pull away because Glenn was not home enough to receive what she had to offer. In essence, his need for dependence was in perpetual motion, as he tried to get what he knew he needed in order to be happy. A heart attack forced him to slow down and evaluate priorities. Fortunately for Glenn, he hadn't driven his wife and chldren totally away. When he recovered, both he and his wife entered treatment, and they eventually built a satisfactory relationship.

When the final disillusionment hits and the individual becomes severely depressed, an unconscious shift of one pleasure modality also occurs, which is multipurposive. Almost unexpectedly, the genitals become more eroticized and important than ever before. The genitals are emphasized partially because they are the most sensitive organs and partially because the severe depression can be temporarily alleviated by sexual-emotional arousal. The depth of the individual's unmet dependency needs also sensitizes the genitals because they are the body's "connecting organs" for the transmission of pleasure and intimacy. As the depression surfaces, so does doubt, insecurity, and, as one individual expressed it, "the most god-awful feelings of loneliness I have ever experienced." Another reported, "I need my wife or some woman so much that I wish I could crawl inside of her and stay there until the tension goes away." With the genitals becoming more eroticized and the depth of denied dependence coming more into full force—along with the accompanying depression—even the most diligent spouses can seldom meet the individual's needs. The spouse usually resents what appears to be childish, selfish demands of the partner to "care more" and so pulls back. To the manic who suddenly becomes more consciously needy than ever before, the unwillingness of the spouse to respond so he will feel "better, less depressed, and more loved" is the final blow. With the dynamics set in place, the automatic response is to seek out an affair. It is in the affair that the individual attempts to heal the bruises of wounded self-esteem by regressing to the "safety" of adolescence. The irresponsibility of the affair serves as a temporary relief from the depression and responsibility of adult living, and provides the pseudoassurance that almost anyone can "love" him more than his partner.

Recall that *love* is defined, in essence, as the attachment to an individual who is capable of meeting one's unconscious needs and conscious desires. As the individual is thrown into crisis, the most basic of all human needs—those related to dependency—surface, thus convincing the individual that the spouse no longer cares. Whether the manic's spouse cares is irrelevant; as his needs heighten, the manic *feels* that there is not enough caring, love, or sex in the relationship. The energy of the unmet needs forces the couple apart, and the manic-type spouse goes toward others who together might offer the illusion of being able to take care of him and to sexually arouse him.

During the crisis, the individual frequently shows signs of poor judgment because the emerging needs force him to seek one or more people who might compositely offer the feeling that he is cared for and not alone. It is not uncommon for the male to buy a new car (reminiscent of youth), or to leave the partner and family for a younger, sexually aggressive woman. Some theorists interpret this return-to-youth syndrome as a fear of aging. However, it is more accurate to interpret it as a flight from the responsibilities that people consider a heavy burden and from the very destructive underlying depression toward the regressive "irresponsibility and safety" of adolescence. Going with a younger woman (or several women) does not necessarily represent a fear of aging. Instead, these people are attracted to the eroticism, enthusiasm, and vibrancy of youth, which vicariously helps them to want to live rather than die.

Tom, a professional in his early forties, revealed the powerful destructive powers of his unmet dependency needs when he said, "Probably in ten years it will be all over anyway." "What do you mean?" I asked. "Well," he replied, "I cannot go on this way. I'm so goddamn miserable and depressed I almost look forward to the day when I can let go and the turmoil and hurt will be over." Realizing what he was saying, I asked, "On what date do you plan to have your heart attack?" Astonished, Tom said, "How did you know I was planning to have a heart attack?" I replied, "Even though some doctors might doubt it, I see many heart attacks in people who are severely depressed and feel abandoned."*

---

*The author does not mean to imply that all heart attacks are caused by depression and loss, but that there are many heart-attack victims who die literally "from a broken heart" (which means letting go of the will to live following the loss of a partner, parent, or child).

It is not uncommon for those suppressing the desire to act out to act in, thus becoming chronically and severely depressed for several years. More often than not, their depression is interspersed with myriad physical symptoms and illnesses. Those who act out could be said to be fighting for their lives, while those who internalize their conflicts are beginning to succumb to the pull of death. The manic's push against death reveals itself in the identification with youth, irresponsibility, love affairs, and self-centeredness.

Relatively well-adjusted individuals who are fortunate enough to have maintained a powerful, emotional support system of friends, relatives, and religious-moral values can usually derive sufficient support from the system to "pick up the dependency slack" while in their crisis. More often than not, the crisis for these individuals stimulates their love life and they find renewed pleasure and intimacy in the sexual relationship. To be able to remain with spouse and family during the depression and dependency conflict and not to regress into adolescence usually helps an individual matriculate into psychological adulthood. Typically, these individuals become more family-oriented and feel a significant increase in self-confidence, energy, vitality, and peace of mind. The months—or, in most cases, years—of depression, with the accompanying feelings of wanting to run away or give up, frequently have a side effect of significantly increasing genuine ego strength by elevating the individual's ability to cope with subsequent stress and depression. Often, they begin to experience genuine feelings of appreciation for life and toward their children and spouse. A notably higher level of living is enjoyed by those who resolve the "last vestige" of adolescent conflict and accept responsible adulthood.

For example, toward the end of his crisis, Tom spontaneously said, "Gee, am I ever a young man! A few years ago, I couldn't imagine life beyond 50; now I think I'll live to be 80. In fact, the cliche, 'life begins at 40,' has more and more relevance each time I realize I'm over 40 and happier than I've ever been. Hundreds of times over the past 10 years I wished I could be strong, and I often pretended I was. Now I don't have to pretend. I feel it happening inside."

Some people are not as fortunate as Tom. While in the throes of panic, some employ poor judgment and let their feelings control rational functions. They abandon what frequently is the only genuine source of support and caring they have and regress to adolescence. Even though they may temporarily feel more "alive," most often they have merely substituted the pain of their depression for the more inconspicuous pain of anxiety and hyperactivity. For a short period, it might seem that they have located an alternative to the painful, slow, working-through process of leaving behind the idealism of adolescence and moving into the enjoyment of adulthood. When one examines their lives closely, however, the quality of their living has not increased at all, and they are continuously on the move in a desperate attempt to run from themselves.

Not long ago, I overheard two colleagues discussing the fate of the Western family. One was certain that monogamous marriage and the family (two parents and children) would soon be extinct. The other was convinced that there is a trend toward stronger family unity and a greater commitment to marriage and child-rearing. Overinvolved with their own ideas, they failed to see that they were both partially correct.

The relative permissiveness in contemporary society, which some view as a sign of declining civilization, may, in fact, be the most significant factor affecting the quality of individual experience. The so-called permissiveness and societal leniency regarding variations in life-styles and sexual practices at best offer a choice in and alternatives to pairing, marriage, and parenting. Although there is still pressure for couples to marry and have children, there are "pockets" of society where marriage and family life are disdained and seen as symptoms of rigidity, naivete, guilt, and emotional stagnation. Regardless of extremes in attitudes concerning sexuality, marriage, and parent-child relationships, the most insidious consequence is that people now have an almost unlimited arena in which to either act out their pathological impulses or to utilize their experiences to increase their emotional maturity and personal fulfillment.

As divorce, extramarital affairs, sexual freedom, personal growth, seeing a therapist, and individual awareness become common, even the most naive and rigidly defended couple is faced with wondering why they remain together, especially if each is unhappy. When couples become aware of their individual unhappiness, few alternatives remain open that are free of emotional consequence. The couple can attempt to "try harder," which usually means greater submission of the self and of personal development, which inevitably makes matters worse. They can get professional help, which few couples do for any number of reasons. They can live with it and attempt to make the best of their situation, by getting their needs met elsewhere, or they can decide to divorce. Even though divorce may seem to be the simplest and most effective solution to marital disharmony or individual unhappiness, the consequences are not without ill effect, at least not when children are involved.

Children need healthy, happy, devoted parents in order to develop into psychologically strong and healthy adults. At one time, people were slighted by the label "neurotic" because they believed themselves to be "normal." As shown in an earlier section, individuals in the neurotic range of adjustment have reason to rejoice. Should the divorce rate continue in its epidemic proportions, leaving a wake of boys and girls with one full-time and one part-time parent, and many children without devoted, secure, reliable adult attachments, the aggregate of human suffering is sure to increase. Neurotic levels of psychological and emotional adjustment will be supplanted by the more severe and agonizing of personality disorders. Historically, men and boys have showed a high incidence of personality disorders; more recently, women and girls have also shown a higher incidence of the more severe personality disorders. As families dissolve, the parent with custody often must be both breadwinner and homemaker. Thus, there is less emotional energy available to attend to the emotional needs of dependent, demanding children. When a child's needs for dependence, security, nurturance, support, and an intimate adult attachment are thwarted, he is forced into premature self-dependence. Some overworked or weak mothers or inadequate parents tend to unconsciously foster a premature self-dependence in their children because the youngsters will then require less fuss, less emotional involvement, less physical effort, and less parental affection. Unknown to many parents, forcing the child to become a little adult merely produces irreversible character defects, which will later attenuate the quality of his experience. Oversimplified, if children cannot be dependent, carefree, and valued when they are children, their unmet needs will surface in pathological proportions when they become adults.

Presently, there are several societal epidemics between which few theorists see a correlation. As the number of marriages and families dissolve, leaving behind more children without significant and reliable emotional attachments, signs of anger, depression, loneliness, despair, and hostility will become more evident. Children are needy. If their basic psychological and nurturing needs are not met by a caring, strong, reliable parent, they are unlikely to be met by fate, chance, God, the family pet, or anyone or anything else. If parents are unable to provide their children with a genuine sense of intrinsic worth (i.e., to love them simply because they exist), it is unlikely that anyone else will have the interest, desire, or energy to complete their emotional void. When parents cannot care, the child concludes that he is not worthy and does not matter. Unconsciously, the child wonders what he did to deserve the loss of the only two people who have the potential to care.

Intellectually, it would be ideal if children could derive relief from the understanding that their parents have problems or want to care but cannot. But it does not work that way. Perhaps it is reasoned that as long as the children see their father (or mother) on Saturdays, they will get all the caring they need. Perhaps . . . but not only is that unlikely, it leaves much to chance. But to wait until Saturday to tell mother or father about a broken heart, a disappointment, or about the bully at school might be too long a delay. To have to wait days to have a parent respond to their needs, provides children an unmistakingly clear message about their lack of worth to their parents.

The most conspicuous sign that all is not well is the high incidence of divorce. Because personality-disordered individuals *cannot* maintain a sustained intimate relationship, seeking a divorce and subsequently adopting a life-style of flippant, superficial, detached affairs will seem the natural choice. Of course, not everyone who divorces should believe he is personality-disordered, but everyone divorcing after diligent effort to preserve the relationship might wish to examine their own and their ex-partner's capacity for intimacy. If they discover that one or the other is not capable, it is likely the relationship could have never worked. In addition to the epidemic of divorce, there is a disquieting epidemic of adolescent suicide. In fact, statistically, suicide is recorded as the second most frequent cause of death among adolescents. In addition, many adolescent deaths recorded as "accidents," which are thought to be the most prevalent cause of death among adolescents, are actually intentional. Even more alarming is the number of children who commit suicide. Suicide can stop the incessant anguish caused by chronic anxiety, agitation, hostility, despair, loneliness, and depression, which the child believes has always been there. Suicidal youngsters always realize their suffering has something to do with feeling unloved by their parents, but they seldom understand that their parents might not have much to give. because of their own deprived childhoods. Even if they did understand, the hurt and despair from the unmet nurturing needs would remain. It should be obvious to the reader that happiness, high ego strength, and intrinsic mattering, generated from a healthy first relationship with caring and responsible adults, are inconsistent with suicide.

The high incidence of homicide, rape, child abuse, and other acts of sexual violence are additional manifestations of angry, hostile, and unloved adults. In their own way, these disturbed individuals discover ways to matter to somebody's parents because they could not matter to their own. Those who prefer not to act out their chronic anxiety and agitation, act in. Experts looking for the causes of severe hypertension so common in Western culture, for example, may well be looking in the wrong place. Some blame society, the age of anxiety, and the rapid pace of technological advancement for increased hypertension and psychosomatic disorders. In order to more accurately understand chronic tension, however, one needs to look inside at the high levels of anxiety caused by insufficient nurturance in childhood and the subsequent incapacity for positive relatedness. It is also necessary to examine the erroneous values personality-disordered individuals have adopted. How can one expect to be comfortable and at peace with oneself while chasing after artificially acquired values and goals that have nothing to do with satisfying deep unmet emotional needs? As mentioned previously, when an individual's character is defective, he is unconsciously forced to shut out stimuli or jump an express train to nowhere to search for what they believe is missing. Physiologically, they are sprinting nearly all of the time in order to get more of what is missing. There is no doubt that something is missing; the conflict within will be over exactly what that is.

Correlates of the personality-disordered culture will also be seen in other more insidious types of symptoms. Heart attacks, various forms of cancer, and obesity persist despite efforts to educate people in preventive medicine. When people are chronically anxious, the pain must be displaced somewhere. Such relaxation methods as meditation and biofeedback may temporarily neutralize chronic anxiety, but eventually some people relinquish these because they take too much time. And time is what people race against in their search. The more diligent students of relaxation techniques must become fanatical in order to derive release from anxiety. Even then, it is not long before their unmet psychological needs push forward, causing further agitation and painful anxiety. It seldom occurs to them that the anxiety is not coming from outside pressures, but pressures from within. In keeping aligned with their own tendency toward self-dependency, drugs and alcohol remain favorites for those who need relief from the internal turmoil.

One positive influence of a permissive society is that some people, especially those in the neurotic range of adjustment, have the freedom to act out and experience life in a way that was not possible before. To engage in various sexual encounters is considered an integral part of adolescence and young adulthood; it provides individuals with a diverse range of experience and intimate relationships that they then must attempt to integrate into their own values and self-guidance operations. The freedom of today's younger generation, especially in terms of sexuality and intimacy, carries with it a responsibility not known to their elders who had little choice but to suppress sexual impulses. Sexual freedom has forced many young people to raise the quality of their priorities to the point where the importance of, and commitment to, genuine intimacy, marriage, and effective child-rearing far surpasses the empty conformity and obligatory rituals previously seen in many families.

Almost in the same proportion that some people are becoming more disturbed, others are becoming relatively free of their neurotic conflicts. Frequently, in workshops and seminars on marriage and families, members of the audience ask me about the types of problems for which people seek professional help. They are often surprised when I tell them that a high percentage of people come mainly to iron out rough spots in their marriage, to work out some unresolved conflicts because they are not as happy as they think they should be, or to have a diagnostic assessment done on their children and themselves in order to detect unmet needs that will enable them to change their responses to their children. It's almost paradoxical that those couples who are doing exceptionally well sometimes seek help in order to live more enjoyably with each other and to be more effective parents.

An elderly psychologist once exclaimed to me, "You know, David, I have been a clinician for a long time, and there is greater confusion in the area of diagnosis than ever before. With the higher incidence of pathology these days, people can no longer distinguish between who's crazy and who is well. It's come to a point where those who are crazy believe they are well, and those who are well, and more sensitive to their conflicts and anxieties, are convinced they are crazy."

It should be obvious by this juncture that the first relationship is what determines one's fulfillment in subsequent relationships and the overall quality of human life. As a clinical psychologist, I wish it were not so, but my wishes and those wishing before me have not been able to change the harshness of that reality.

Works Cited

Erikson, E. H. 1964. *Childhood and Society*. New York: W. W. Norton.

Haley, Jay. 1967. *Advanced Techniques of Hypnosis and Therapy: Selected Papers of Milton H. Erickson, M.D.* New York: Grune & Stratton.

Pratt, C. L. and Sackett, G. P. 1967. Selection of social partners as a function of peer contact during rearing. *Science* 155: 1133–35.

Spitz, R. A. and Cobliner, W. G. 1966. *First Year of Life: A Psychoanalytic Study of Normal and Deviant Development of Object Relations*. New York: International Universities Press.

Suomi, S. J., Harlow, H. F., and Lewis, J. K. 1970. Effect of bilateral frontal lobectomy on social preferences of rhesus monkeys. *Journal of Comparative and Physiological Psychology* 70: 448–53.

The Way. 1972. Wheaton, Illinois: Tyndale House Publishers.

Westermarck, E. A. 1921. *The History of Human Marriage*, vols. I–III. New York: Allerton Press.

Index

307